THE CHAN'S GREAT CONTINENT

Also by Jonathan D. Spence

*The Chinese Century: A Photographic
History of the Last Hundred Years*
(coauthor with Annping Chin)

*God's Chinese Son: The Taiping Heavenly
Kingdom of Hong Xiuquan*

*Chinese Roundabout: Essays in
History and Culture*

The Search for Modern China

The Question of Hu

The Memory Palace of Matteo Ricci

*The Gate of Heavenly Peace: The Chinese
and Their Revolution, 1895–1980*

The Death of Woman Wang

Emperor of China: Self-Portrait of K'ang-hsi

*To Change China: Western Advisers in
China, 1620–1960*

*Ts'ao Yin and the K'ang-hsi Emperor:
Bondservant and Master*

THE CHAN'S GREAT CONTINENT

China in Western Minds

Jonathan D. Spence

W. W. Norton & Company

New York   London

The text of this book is composed in
ITC Legacy Serif with the display set in Papyrus
Composition by A.W. Bennett, Inc.
Manufacturing by the Haddon Craftsmen, Inc.
Book design by Charlotte Staub

Library of Congress Cataloging-in-Publication Data
Spence, Jonathan D.
    The Chan's great continent : China in western minds / Jonathan D.
  Spence.
       p.   cm.
    Includes bibliographical references and index.
    ISBN 0-393-02747-3
    1. China.   2. China—Civilization.   I. Title.
  DS706.S62   1998
  951—DC21   98-10823
                                                                CIP

W. W. Norton & Company, Inc.
500 Fifth Avenue, New York, N.Y. 10110
http://www.wwnorton.com

W. W. Norton & Company Ltd.
10 Coptic Street, London WC1A 1PU

1 2 3 4 5 6 7 8 9 0

For HAROLD BLOOM

—biding the moon
Till dawn should clear that dim frontier, first seen
—The Chan's great continent . . .

—Hart Crane, "The Bridge"

Contents

Preface

THE SHAPE AND CONTENT OF THIS BOOK REFLECT THE form in which the material was first presented—as the William Clyde DeVane lectures at Yale University in the spring of 1996. These lectures, named in memory of one of Yale's great teachers who also served as dean of the college from 1939 to 1963, are customarily delivered to an audience composed jointly of Yale students and members of the general public. They are thus expected to be scholarly enough to meet some basic academic requirements, but accessible to anyone who cares to attend.

Since I delivered them, these lectures have undergone various modifications. Partly these are the inevitable changes that accompany the shift from an informal oral presentation based on notes to a finished written version. Partly they involve the inclusion of quotations—sometimes fairly lengthy—from the original works cited, since in the lectures themselves each oral presentation was supplemented by assigned readings from the relevant texts. In some cases I have made cuts in the interests of concision, and at other times additions for the sake of clarity. In keeping with the original lecture format, notation is held to a minimum. Notes are used mainly to identify quotations, and occasionally to highlight a useful supplementary source. There is no attempt to give a comprehensive bibliography for each person discussed, or of works about them. Indeed, for most of the close to fifty people included here, discussions of China formed only a fraction—albeit to me a significant one—of a given writer's complete work.

Before I was invited to give the DeVane lectures, I had for some years at Yale led a small seminar in which the students and I read and discussed numerous examples of the ways that China had been refracted over time in Western minds. I would like to thank those students collectively for the range of figures they came up with, and the adventurous ways in which they explored them. Several of the sources included in the lectures came from their suggestions, including the unlikely trio of Mary Fraser, Steinbeck's "Johnny Bear," and Richard Nixon. The current selection of forty-eight figures is culled from a number perhaps three times as large whom we read or discussed in one way or another; many of the figures omitted had striking or subtle things to say about China and their reactions to it, and their inclusion would have greatly broadened the panorama subsequently offered in the lectures and in this book. At the same time, however, they would have threatened to compress an involved story into a catalogue, and I wished to avoid that at all costs.

Each of the twelve DeVane lectures was followed by an hour of usually lively and sometimes excitable questions and discussion, and a certain amount of thoughts derived from those sessions has undoubtedly filtered in here. The same is true of audience comments at Princeton, Peking University, and the Chinese University of Hong Kong, where I explored some of these topics. I also owe thanks to my editor at Norton, Steven Forman, whose consistent skill in asking innocent-sounding questions that are almost impossible to answer, has, I trust, smoothed many rough edges and brought more clarity to the presentation. Mei Chin, acting as roving researcher, explored the worlds of eighteenth-century British taste and French late nineteenth-century exoticism with her customary imagination and aplomb, for which I am sincerely grateful. She, along with Annping, Yar, and Maddux, ensured that bringing this book to completion was more of a joy than a travail.

West Haven
August 22, 1997

Introduction

ONE ASPECT OF A COUNTRY'S GREATNESS IS SURELY its capacity to attract and retain the attention of others. This capacity has been evident from the very beginnings of the West's encounter with China; the passing centuries have never managed to obliterate it altogether, even though vagaries of fashion and shifting political stances have at times dulled the sheen. The sharpness of the feelings aroused by China in the West, the reiterated attempts to describe and analyze the country and its people, the apparently unending receptivity of Westerners to news from China, all testify to the levels of fascination the country has generated.

This book seeks to give a sense of the multiplicity of intellectual and emotional attitudes that Westerners have brought to their attempts to deal with the phenomenon of China. So as not to give too formalized or deliberate an air to this process, I borrow the title from Hart Crane's idea of China as imagined by Columbus, sensed rather than seen in the pre-dawn dimness. The Chan (or Khan) had ruled China at the time of Marco Polo's thirteenth century account of the fabled land. In Columbus's mind he ruled it still. Drawing the term from the history of navigation and exploration, we would call such a moment a "sighting." A sighting in those contexts was fleeting or intermittent: one seized on whatever chance one had to get one's bearings; one found oneself by the often random viewing of the anticipated destination. By extension of this idea, in gunnery the act of sighting was the act of finding the range, of getting a balance or a bracketing effect so that one's own shots would hit the tar-

get. In earlier times, for example in the 1750s when Oliver Goldsmith, Commodore Anson, and Montesquieu were all writing in
their very different ways about China, "sighting" was also used
as a gaming term, specifically in the sense of cheating at dice. In
the thirteenth century, at the time William of Rubruck and
Marco Polo were first sharing their thoughts on the Chinese
with a select few Western readers and listeners, "sighting" served
as an alternate form for "sighing," and "weeping and sighting"
were not uncommonly found in conjunction.[1]

The sightings of China that we will be considering were
passed on to others in many forms, as diplomatic reports or as
poems, as stage plays or as letters home, as philosophical tracts
or novels. In the course of this book we look at forty-eight such
sightings in some detail, spread across a period of over seven
hundred years, from 1253 down to 1985. The first of these dates
marks the year that Friar William of Rubruck set off on an ecclesiastical and diplomatic mission to the Great Khan in Karakorum, and his experience feeds inevitably into that of Marco Polo,
at once the most celebrated and the most problematical of all
the sightings we will be considering.

The legacy of Polo lay to some extent in the data that he provided, but even more in the curiosity that he aroused. The development of printing in the West in the fifteenth century brought
published versions of his earlier manuscripts into readers' hands
by the 1480s, and it was one of these early editions that was read
and annotated by Christopher Columbus. By the 1540s, the
spillover from Columbus's discoveries had brought the Portuguese to Macao and the Spaniards to the Philippines, inaugu-
rating what can be fittingly called the "Catholic century" of
China sightings. The reports, polemical tracts, and the novels
that were written at this time—we look at five such examples—
rooted China with a totally new level of specificity into Western
minds, and introduced strong currents of emotion into what
was becoming a heated European debate over the nature of

China and its people, and over the uses to which one might put the new information.

As the seventeenth century waned, and with it the peak of the Catholic nations' program of overseas conquest and expansion, the naval powers of the emerging Protestant states were ready to seize the opportunities this offered. Diplomats and soldiers from the Netherlands and Great Britain became the next group to explore China. These men saw themselves as realists, with certain tasks to perform; they viewed with a new kind of hostility China's attempts to force them to accept traditional forms of ritualized subservience, especially the kowtow, involving a series of nine prostrations before the figure of the emperor or even before the symbols of his authority in his absence. The British, who saw in such ritual observances an abandonment of national dignity rather than a convention of international relations, were inevitably headed for confrontation: such a passage can be traced through three of the sightings left to us across the century by Bell, Anson, and Lord Macartney.

It is an assumption of mine that the impact of China need have little or anything to do with the literalness or precision of an actual experience. Thus I follow the diplomats—who would have claimed to be realists—with their contemporaries who stayed away from China, content to transpose it into fiction. There was now more than enough material around for them to do so, and the creativity and stylistic force of a Defoe or a Goldsmith, along with the irony of a Walpole, spread thoughts about China to a far wider audience than ever before. This popularization of China, along with the fashion of imitating aspects of Chinese culture, was given the name of "Chinoiserie" in the French circles where it received its greatest welcome. In yet a third reprise over the course of the eighteenth century, we can see how powerful synthetic minds were also drawn to the China they had never seen. Goldsmith had his fictional Chinese narrator wondrously observe that the English were trying to reason him out of his own country. Leibniz, Montesquieu, Voltaire, and Herder can perhaps be charged with doing that, as each of them made his own cut into the available historical records in an attempt to create a system into which the totality of China as they understood it could be inserted—though at least the first three writers corresponded or conferred with those who did know China at firsthand.

The poets of the Romantic movement clearly offer one convenient bridge for moving from the revolutionary epoch that climaxed the period of the Enlightenment into the different world of the nineteenth century. But Jane Austen forms another kind of bridge, by marking the emergence of women as the makers of China sightings. Though it is only a premonitory flash, her use of Lord Macartney's journal in her novel *Mansfield Park*, and the lived experiences of her brother Frank in Canton, prepare us for the new generations of Western women who made more personal and protracted China sightings in the nineteenth century. Many of these women were Americans, who thus brought twin new perspectives of gender and nation to the China scene: as we move from Eliza Bridgman at the century's beginning, to Jane Edkins in its middle, and on to Sarah Conger and Eva Price at the end, through their eyes we see the charm of China tinged with deeper dangers, with the Boxer Uprising of 1900 serving as the fitting coda to their experiences.

In the mid-nineteenth century, for the first time Chinese laborers began to travel to the United States in search of work, and to construct around themselves their own frail simulacra of their native land in the form of American Chinatowns. For a generation of Americans, China had now come home, and the experience was unnerving to them. The sightings of China by Mark Twain and Bret Harte were compounded of bemusement, affection, and irritation; it was hard for them to see these new settlers in the context of an existing Chinese culture, and accordingly they tried to humanize their misapprehensions, blending their own experiences into fictional forms in which they both absorbed and opposed the implicit rules of racial discrimination. Other writers who came after took the process a step further, and a specific new series of hostile stereotypes was the result: the Chinatown fictions of the later nineteenth century blended insensibly into the world of Fu-Manchu.

The French, at the same time, had been distilling the experiences and collective China sightings of two centuries into a fairly coherent type of vision which I term a "new exotic," one compounded of violence, allure, and nostalgia. The three writers Loti, Claudel, and Segalen all lived in China for periods of time between 1895 and 1915, and believed they had caught its true sights, sounds, and smells. As writers of considerable power, they enlarged Western literary vocabulary even as they restricted the full play of Chinese personality in their own imaginative renderings.

Having identified—perhaps overconfidently—what seems to be a French exotic, I move to the question of whether some kind of American China exotic was also in formation, replacing the crudities of Chinatown characterizations with something at least partly rooted within China and Chinese culture. A film like D. W. Griffith's *Broken Blossoms* perpetuated a view of China that blended threat with vulnerability, but at the same time sought for some universal values at the culture's heart. Ezra Pound's protracted explorations into Chinese poetics and history, or Pearl Buck's detailed attempt at a reconstruction of the values of Chinese rural life, in almost inconceivably different ways pursued similar themes. Harsher were the views of Eugene O'Neill in his retelling of Polo's relationship with Kublai Khan as an anti-capitalist parable, or John Steinbeck's tale of the destruction wrought by Chinese passions in a small western American town. But still, one could argue, they gave a universal dimension to what they depicted as a localized Chinese reality.

Polemics find a natural home in politics, and there was certainly a residue of Western rhetoric that could be applied to what were seen as new political forces emanating from China after the

Bolshevik Revolution of 1917. The Chinese Communist Party was formed in 1921, the first great purges of the party by the Nationalist forces took place in 1927, to be followed by the period of rural guerrilla socialism, and the anti-Japanese war. The radicalization of China sightings crossed many national and perceptual boundaries. André Malraux moved from a stance steeped in the French exotic perception of China to a passionate fictional involvement with China's revolution as representative of man's fate. Bertolt Brecht saw within Chinese experience a way to grasp the levels of revolutionary ruthlessness and the paradoxes of compassion in such a context. American anti-authoritarians like Edgar Snow could find in China's guerrilla socialism and Mao's rustic ways a potential promise of salvation for the people as a whole. Graham Peck could fasten on the enigmatic smile of Chinese as the flickering point of focus for his own experiences.

The mystique of the rulers' power in China had dominated many Western sightings, ever since Polo's depiction of the mighty Kublai in the 1270s. During the late nineteenth-century period of China's weakness, and the forty years that followed the collapse of China's last dynasty in 1911, such a vision of centralized power had yielded place to one of localized violence and implicit threat. The re-establishment of Chinese central power under the Communists, and especially the nature of that regime and the violence of the Korean War, drew some observers' minds back to the earlier mystiques. But these views were tinged now with other dark experiences, those of Stalinism and Nazism, which between them seemed to have fostered new levels of totalitarian organization that could be blended into new forms of total tyranny and total power. Such a dark vision was spelled out by Karl Wittfogel in an analysis that deliberately recalled the great system-building attempts of the past two centuries, but also drew on historical records of China's emperors' past excesses. Though softer, the view of Mao's presence as in some ways close to imperial was shared by both Richard Nixon and Henry Kissinger when they made their celebrated 1972 visits to China in a bid to reopen relations between China and the United States. The mystique of the abuse and inner hollowness of allegedly absolute power was restated in fictional form by the French novelist Jean Lévi, whose own depictions of the imperial character circled back into the French exotic of a century before.

The book ends with the China sightings made by three twentieth-century writers of acknowledged genius, even though they never set foot in the country at all. But to close with them is to reemphasize a thought that runs through this book, that one of the proofs of China's strength is its capacity to stimulate and to focus creative energies at specific moments in time. In these three cases, we see how China for Franz Kafka served to channel his ideas on authority and individual endeavor, how for Borges it drew together the flow of time and the apparently endless permutations of human consciousness, and how for Calvino it allowed the intersecting of cross-cultural contact with the varying layers of memory and experience.

One can see that this is a book about cultural stimulus and response as much as it is in any way a book about China. As such, it is not in the business of assigning blame or praise to those who made the sightings. Often the stimulus was viewed as a negative one, and the response was correspondingly harsh. But at other times the stimulus was sweet, and those making the sightings remained in a state of blissful self-denial, regardless of other levels of reality that swirled around them. More often, as one might expect, the responses were mixed, and overlapped in space and time in ways that make tight categorizations virtually impossible.[2]

It can be objected that many of these sightings reified or in other ways denigrated China, and that is certainly true. Assessments of China and the Chinese people were often coarse-grained or inaccurate; they drew on imagination and stereotype as much as on any kind of informed application of intellect. By using the terms "Western" and "the West," I am similarly reifying the culture in which I was born and raised, and one could argue—as so many have—that there is simply no such thing as the West. So be it. But those making the sightings we examine here felt that they shared in certain traditions that were different from those they encountered in China, or thought that they encountered, or imagined that they might have encountered.

Throughout this book we are dealing with individuals reaching out in their various ways toward another world, which each of them saw differently, but which they gave the same name, that of China. They did not necessarily understand it, or seek to do so. Most of them knew, as most of us know, that bigotry, gullibility, and ignorance are closely entwined. Most of them knew, too, that words can be violent and wound deeply. Certainly amongst them we find many examples of a language of dominance or dismissal; at the same time, we find many examples of a language of respect, affection, and awe. One can find cultural and historical roots for both sets of reactions.

As a historian, I am interested in the ways that levels of reality intersect and overlap. It is my implicit belief that bold generalizations are usually wide of the mark, and that the individual experience rarely matches the allegedly universal trend. It is in that spirit that I offer these sightings of a great but distant culture. We must imagine our pilots and navigators—and perhaps also our cheats, and those with broken hearts—holding rather simple instruments in their hands as they make those sightings. Furthermore, the hands that hold the instruments are often chapped with cold or sleek with sweat. Our guides are standing on sloping decks that shift angle without warning, and are often blinded by a burst of spray or dazzled by an unexpected dart from the previously beclouded sun. And the target of their curiosity remains distant and often somber—"the color of mourning," as Loti wrote. And then, too, they cannot even be sure that they have come to the right place. But that, after all, is a risk that all of us must take.

THE CHAN'S GREAT CONTINENT

CHAPTER 1

The Worlds of Marco Polo

IT IS ENTIRELY APPROPRIATE TO THE COURSE OF OUR own exploration that the first Western work devoted mainly to China should be evasive and problematic. As far as we know, Marco Polo's book *The Description of the World,* usually known as the *Travels,* was dictated to a man named Rusticello in the year 1298, while Polo was in jail or under house arrest. Purporting to describe the travels that Marco Polo took through Asia between 1271 and 1295, and concentrating especially on the period from 1275 to 1292 when Polo lived and worked in China as an agent for the Mongol ruler of China, Kublai Khan, the book is a combination of verifiable fact, random information posing as statistics, exaggeration, make-believe, gullible acceptance of un-substantiated stories, and a certain amount of outright fabri-cation. The same is true of other works written before and afterwards, but what matters to us about Polo's text is that it was the first such work by a Westerner to claim to look at China from the inside, and the force of the narrative description was strong enough to imprint itself in Western minds down to our own time.

Polo's is not the first account in a European language to dis-cuss Chinese people with some specificity. That distinction goes to the Franciscan friar William of Rubruck, who in 1253 was dispatched to the Mongol capital of Karakorum, northwest of the Chinese border, by King Louis IX of France, in an attempt to win the Khan Möngke to the Christian cause against Islam. Though William did not get to China itself, while he was in Karakorum he noted down whatever information he obtained

1

from the Chinese living there. Rubruck realized that the "Cata-ians" he was meeting in the Mongol base area were the same people who had been known to the Romans as "Seres" or "Silk People" because the finest silk came from their domains. After noting that he was "reliably informed" that in Cataia could be found a city with "walls of silver and battlements of gold," Rubruck gave a thumbnail sketch of the Chinese:

> The Cataians are a small race, who when speaking breathe heavily through the nose; and it is a general rule that all orientals have a small opening for the eyes. They are excellent craftsmen in whatever skill, and their physicians are very well versed in the effi-cacy of herbs and can diagnose very shrewdly from the pulse. But they do not employ urine samples [*urinalibus non utuntur*], not knowing anything about urine: this I saw [for myself], since there are a number of them at Caracorum. Their custom has always been that whatever the father's craft all his sons are obliged to follow it.[1]

Rubruck followed this observation with two equally precise sen-tences on Chinese calligraphy and paper money: "The everyday currency of Cataia is of paper, the breadth and length of a palm, on which lines are stamped as on Mangu's seal. They write with a brush of the sort painters use, and in a single character make several letters that comprise one word."[2]

In other parts of his narrative, Rubruck showed a blunt skep-ticism about some of the Chinese information he was given. After recounting a story of how in eastern Cataia, among "soar-ing crags" there were little hairy creatures whose legs would not bend, and who were hunted down by means of traps baited with wine so that they could be pricked for the drops of blood that yielded a rare purple dye, Rubruck twice mentions that he was "told this" by a priest of Cataia but had not seen it himself. And as to the country bordering Cataia where people remain forever the same age once they enter, Rubruck comments that though this was "told for a fact," he himself "[did] not believe it."[3] Despite its many values, Rubruck's report on Asia in which these remarks were embedded remained a private report for the eyes of King Louis. Only three manuscripts of it from the thirteenth or fourteenth century have ever been located, all of them in England, presumably because Rubruck's English contemporary, the scholar-philosopher Roger Bacon, was impressed by it. But even if Roger Bacon drew on a manuscript version of Rubruck for his own studies, there is surely no way that Polo could have seen it.[4]

The China that Polo gave to the world in his own extended account was a benevolently ruled dictatorship, colossal in scale, decorous in customs, rich in trade, highly urbanized, inventive in commercial dealings, weak in the ways of war. Whether all that is true or not is only the beginning of the conundrum. Equally intriguing are two other aspects of the problem. Was Polo there at all? And was he writing about China or about something else? The difficulty of grappling with these questions is compounded by two other factors. First, we have less corroborative evidence about the life and upbringing of Marco Polo than about almost any other celebrated writer in history. Second, despite the intricate trail of the various manuscript versions of his book—over eighty have survived from the Middle Ages in a range of libraries and collections, and there is always the chance of more being discovered—we do not have the original manuscript, but only copies of a lost original, amended copies of those copies, and translations or abbreviations of copies. Nor do we even know with certainty the language of the "first" version. Most probably it was in Venetian or "Lombard" dialect, subsequently translated into Italianate French, and thence into Latin.

The difficulty of finding out anything precise about Marco Polo intensifies the mysteries about the text itself. The only iron-clad evidence we have of the existence of the man Marco Polo is from his last will and testament, dictated as he lay at home in Venice, seriously ill, on January 9, 1323, in the presence of a priest and notary. This document also shows that as of this date, Marco's wife Donata was still alive, along with three of their daughters, Fantina, Bellela, and Moreta, the last alone still unmarried. The will shows Marco to be comfortably off, though not especially wealthy, as can be seen by his bequests to family and Venetian religious institutions. His social status is further indicated by a clause in the middle of the will: "Also I release Peter the Tartar, my servant, from all bondage, as completely as I pray God to release mine own soul from all sin and guilt. And I also remit him whatever he may have gained by work at his own house; and over and above I bequeath him 100 *lire* of Venice denari."[5] Five years later the city of Venice gave to this same Peter all the rights of a Venetian citizen, due to his long residence in the city and his good deportment.

But the depiction of Peter as a "Tartar" does not mean that Marco Polo bought Peter in the Far East, or that Peter was of partial Chinese stock. Virtually all slaves used in Venice, whether brought in from the Black Sea or elsewhere, were described as Tartars. There are brief references to Marco Polo in two other legal documents, one the will made by his younger brother, Maffeo (who seems to have been rather wealthier than Marco, whom he named one of his trustees), and one a complaint lodged by Marco against a fellow merchant who cheated him out of the profit on a half pound of musk. Marco won the case, with costs. These and a handful of other legal documents establish Marco as the son of Niccolo Polo (deceased by 1300) and the nephew of another Maffeo, deceased by 1318.[6] None of these documents, despite prodigious research by many scholars, has yielded up a specific China connection of any kind.

Thus the weight of evidence concerning the life of Marco Polo is thrown back onto his own book. Lacking any other evidence concerning the lost original, we have to accept the statement in the earliest surviving prologue that what we have now was dictated by Marco Polo to a certain Rusticello of Pisa, who claims in his prologue to the work that Marco dictated it to him while the two were in prison together in Genoa during the year

1298. That makes sense, for Pisa and Marco's native Venice were both at war with Genoa in the late thirteenth century, and prisoners captured by the Genoese were often held for some time in Genoa, while awaiting a ransom payment or a prisoner trade arranged through diplomatic channels. A Rusticello of Pisa had been quite a celebrated narrator of Arthurian romances some twenty years earlier, and since Marco Polo's book has much of the form and content of a typical romance-adventure of the time, the supposition is that the author of the Arthurian romances and Marco Polo's travels was the same man.

Marco Polo himself probably could write fairly well, and dealt with correspondence in the course of his business, but would have had no experience composing any form of general narrative or travelogue. Nor was literacy among even the well-born assumed late in the thirteenth century. Several versions of the manuscript prologue to Marco Polo's *Travels* start with the words: "Great Princes, Emperors, and Kings, Dukes and Marquises, Counts, Knights, and Burgesses! and People of all degrees who desire to get knowledge of the various races of mankind and of the diversities of the sundry regions of the world, take this Book and cause it to be read to you." Such an opening sentence echoed directly the beginnings of many courtly romances, and would have been comfortingly familiar to readers and listeners alike.[7] Stylistically, too, Rusticello as transcriber often followed the conventions of courtly romance rather than what we assume would have been the words of a seasoned traveler like Marco. For instance, Marco Polo's narrative contains quite lengthy accounts of seven of the greatest Far Eastern conflicts of his age, but all of them are stilted, formulaic, and repetitive, as they deal with vaguely defined massed armies and mounds of severed heads and limbs. As one of the great nineteenth-century scholars of Marco Polo expressed himself on this particular point: "One finds it impossible to conceive of our sober and reticent Messer Marco pacing the floor of his Genoese dungeon, and seven times over rolling out this magniloquent bombast, with sufficient deliberation to be overtaken by the pen of the faithful amanuensis."[8]

The one specific example in the book of Marco Polo's successful activities at a field of battle is at first sight far more convincing than these other seven. Every detail seems to be in place. The mighty Mongol Khan is asking his assembled advisers how he should subdue the Chinese city of "Saianfu," which is stubbornly resisting his armies. The Khan's generals admit they are baffled, for the walls of Saianfu are so strong they resist direct assault, and the city also continues to receive regular relief supplies by river. But among the listeners are Marco Polo, his father, and his uncle. Polo's narrative continues:

> Then spoke up the two brothers and Messer Marco the son, and said: "Great Prince, we have with us among our followers men who are able to construct mangonels [catapults] which shall cast such great stones that the garrison will never be able to stand them, but will surrender incontinently, as soon as the mangonels or trebuchets shall have shot into the town."
>
> The Kaan bade them with all his heart have such mangonels made as speedily as possible. Now Messer Nicolo and his brother and his son immediately caused timber to be brought, as much as they desired, and fit for the work in hand. And they had two men among their followers, a German and a Nestorian Christian, who were masters of that business, and these they directed to construct two or three mangonels capable of casting stones of 300 lbs. weight. . . .
>
> And when the engines were got to the camp they were forthwith set up, to the great admiration of the Tartars. And what shall I tell you? When the engines were set up and put in gear, a stone was shot from each of them into the town. These took effect among the buildings, crashing and smashing through everything with huge din and commotion. And when the townspeople witnessed this new and strange visitation they were so astonished and dismayed that they wist not what to do or say. . . .
>
> So the men of the city surrendered, and were received to terms;

and this all came about through the exertions of Messer Nicolo, and Messer Maffeo, and Messer Marco; and it was no small matter. For this city and province is one of the best that the Great Kaan possesses, and brings him in great revenues.[9]

There appears to be great documentary precision to this passage. Saianfu—an earlier variant of the name of the present Xiangyang, in northwest Hebei on the south bank of the Han River—is described in fourteenth-century Chinese sources as being the site of a protracted siege by the armies of the Mongol ruler of China, Kublai. The city held out from 1268 to 1273, and its fall marked the first stage of the collapse of the southern Song dynasty. The city was forced to surrender, according to these Chinese sources, because Kublai "sent to the West for engineers expert at the construction and working of machines casting stones of 150 pounds weight."[10]

Unfortunately for our acceptance of Polo's story, the siege was over by 1273, and from every item of evidence that we have there is no way that Marco Polo could have reached China before 1274. And also according to the narrative prologue to Marco Polo's book, his father and uncle must have left Kublai's capital of Karakorum on the way back to Venice after their first journey to the East by 1266 at the latest, well before the siege began. One of the earliest surviving manuscripts, as if aware of half this problem, mentions only the two brothers Niccolo and Maffeo as making these recommendations to the Khan three years into the siege, supervising the manufacture and deployment of the mangonels, and causing the surrender of the city.[11] This version also does not include the statement that there were two Western technicians who helped in the manufacture and design. But we cannot be precisely sure if this manuscript chose to drop Marco because the copyist or editor knew for some reason that Marco Polo could not have been there, or whether this is in fact a copy very close to the original, and that though Marco Polo never said he was there, later editors wrote him into the story to make the narrative more vivid.

These technicians, however, cannot be wished away along with Marco Polo, for Asian sources place them firmly at the siege site; but though agreeing that the technicians were from the west of China, these sources place the technicians' origins as being in what Europeans would call the Muslim Middle East: the Chinese sources even name the two men, Ala'uddin of Miafarakain and Ismael of Herat. Persian sources state that the experts came from Damascus (or Balbek) and mention there were three of them.[12] To confuse the issue further, both Chinese and Persian sources agree that the Mongol armies had used such catapults to considerable effect since the time of Genghis Khan, around 1230. Yet, even if Polo cannot have been there, and might have been spuriously aggrandizing himself and his family, his account is astonishingly accurate about the general situation of the siege; and if he had an "outside source," written or personal, we do not know what it was.

A different aspect of the authenticity problem arises in relation to Polo's career in China, those seventeen years between 1274 and 1291 in which he allegedly labored in Kublai Khan's service. Rusticello's prologue states that during his service with the Khan, Marco Polo learned the Mongol language (both spoken and written) and was familiar with the "written characters" of four other languages. As Polo grew in experience and knowledge, the Khan sent him on ever longer official journeys. At a certain point in his career, according to Rusticello, Polo made a key conceptual leap:

> Now [Polo] had taken note on several occasions that when the Prince's ambassadors returned from different parts of the world, they were able to tell him about nothing except the business on which they had gone, and that the Prince in consequence held them for no better than fools and dolts, and would say: "I had far liever hearken about the strange things, and the manners of the different countries you have seen, than merely be told of the business you went upon;"—for he took great delight in hearing of the affairs of strange countries. Marco therefore, as he went and

returned, took great pains to learn about all kinds of different matters in the countries which he visited, in order to be able to tell about them to the Great Kaan....

When Marco returned from his ambassage he presented himself before the Emperor, and after making his report of the business with which he was charged, and its successful accomplishment, he went on to give an account in a pleasant and intelligent manner of all the novelties and strange things that he had seen and heard; insomuch that the Emperor and all such as heard his story were surprised, and said: "If this young man live, he will assuredly come to be a person of great worth and ability." And so from that time forward he was always entitled Messer Marco Polo, and thus we shall style him henceforth in this Book of ours, as is but right.[13]

But these superficially precise references are never clarified in the long, descriptive body of the text that follows, and Marco Polo himself tells the reader neither the exact details of the business he conducted nor what "novelties and strange things" he had encountered that would have absorbed a man as experienced in the ways of the world and war as his master Kublai Khan.

There is only one passage in the *Travels* that more precisely delineates Marco Polo's bureaucratic tasks. With reference to the city of "Yanju," which all scholars agree refers to the modern Yangzhou, a commercial hub on the west bank of the Grand Canal, just north of the Yangzi River, there is this passage: "And Messer Marco Polo himself, of whom this book speaks, did govern this city for three full years, by the order of the Great Kaan. The people live by trade and manufactures, for a great amount of harness for knights and men-at-arms is made there. And in this city and its neighbourhood a large number of troops are stationed by the Kaan's orders. There is no more to say about it."[14] Quite apart from the problematic reference to "knights" and their "harness"—which sounds more like an extrapolation from the chivalric warfare of the European Middle Ages than anything we know about Chinese warfare and society—is the fact that after generations of diligent searching of Chinese and Mongol records by scores of scholars, no reference to any Westerner or member of the Polo family has ever been found in the extant lists of officials posted to the city.

But if one might have been tempted by this to go further, and say the whole notion of Europeans being in the middle of Yangzhou in the late thirteenth century is inherently absurd, one would be brought up short by a discovery made by construction workers of the People's Liberation Army working to dismantle the walls of Yangzhou City in 1951, two years after the Communist victory in China. For embedded in the wall they found a marble slab, decorated with incised scenes from the life of St. Catherine, on which was the following inscription: "In the Name of God the Father, Amen. Here lies Katerina, daughter of the noble Dominico Yllionis, who died in the year of Our Lord 1342, in the month of July." The early transcriptions of this discovery rendered the woman's name as "Vilionis," but the great medievalist Robert Lopez was able to correct the reading and trace this family to a certain Domenico Ilioni, who was listed in a Genoese legal record of 1348 as having been the executor at some unspecified earlier time of the merchant Jacopo de Oliverio. This Jacopo had lived, says the document, "in partibus Catagii" (in the realm of China), where he had quintupled the stock of capital he brought out with him.[15]

A few years later another smaller tablet was found in Yangzhou, again with Christian sculpture above a brief Latin inscription, recording the death of a son of the same Domenico named Antonio in November 1344. [16] What we seem to have here, therefore, admittedly thirty to forty years after Marco Polo's alleged tour of duty in Yangzhou, is a small but apparently flourishing commercial community of Italians in Yangzhou, making a good profit. Might not such a cluster have called for an administrator appointed by the Khan now ruling China to watch over their affairs? Such a community in the Middle Ages would also have needed some kind of religious support system if possible, and evidence for exactly this is provided by the Franciscan friar Odoric of Pordenone, who traveled to China on papal business in the 1320s. Odoric reported that he visited Yangzhou in 1322, and while there stayed at a house of the Franciscan Order, which was inside the city along with three Nestorian churches.[17] The feasibility of Polo's service in Yangzhou is thus reborn just as it seemed easiest to reject it.

Polo's text is full of countless such conundrums. This is not surprising, for he writes as a man of his time, and this generalization seems sustainable whatever manuscript is being discussed, or whatever role one ascribes to Rusticello as author or amanuensis. This means that the format of each description follows certain rhythms which can be found in medieval writings and in the diplomatic reports of the ambassadors from Venice serving overseas: in sequence the rulers, the ruled, the social rankings, the provinces, the clans, the customs, the products.[18] Polo's book may seem an odd merchant's handbook to us, but there were others rather like it for other areas of the world; pioneering traders and roving missionary diplomats all mingled what we now call "marvels" with their sober detail, for marvels were what their readers expected to hear, and if they had heard them before, so much the better, and so much more trustworthy the source became. "Any medieval traveler was the bearer of news," as John Critchley observes. The ideal landscape was always a cultivated one, in such accounts, and mountains were full of strangeness and danger.[19]

Polo seems to have known no Chinese, and his transcriptions of Chinese names are invariably similar to or related to those in Arab travelers' texts. But even contemporary Italian merchants in London garbled English names so totally that many are almost unrecognizable. Polo never mentioned tea, or Chinese calligraphy, which seems extraordinary if he lived in China for seventeen years; nor did he record cormorant fishing, or comment on the bound feet of Chinese women, or mention or visit the Great

Wall. But he did record the use of coal for fuel, the size of Peking's brothel quarter and its position—outside the main city walls; he did see paper money and try to describe its manufacture and function. He did describe the massed boats on China's eastern rivers, and note the importance of salt and its bulk shipment in China's economy. He also noticed price stabilization techniques and stockpiling of grain in state storehouses, and public baths.

This combination in Polo of ignorance and precision has led centuries of readers down to the present day to wonder about his sources of information. Later versions of Polo's manuscript, say those made after 1340, had many new sources to draw from, and hence copyists and editors could have added their own embellishments, rather than go back to other (now lost) original drafts of Polo's own words. Odoric of Pordenone traveled extensively in China during the 1320s, and the report that he submitted to the papacy on his return circulated in at least seventy-three manuscript copies. The pioneering "world history" of the Persian scholar Rashid ad-Din, which gives many details on China he gleaned from Chinese texts and perhaps Mongol respondents, was completed by 1310, and the elaborate and immensely popular fictions of Sir John Mandeville—which were believed to be accurate by many fourteenth-century readers—were already widely circulated in the 1350s.[20] There were houses of Franciscan friars in several Chinese cities, and so many Italian merchants were traveling to China that Balducci Pegolotti in his famous handbook of 1340 spent two chapters delineating the route.[21]

Most intriguingly, one Nestorian Christian from North China named Rabban Sauma, of Turkic-Mongol descent, was dispatched to the West by Kublai Khan around the year 1276, just as Polo is believed to have reached China. After many adventures, Rabban Sauma reached Naples in 1287, and France later that same year. But there is no evidence that his original narrative, written in Persian, was known in Europe at the time; indeed, no Persian version has ever been found, and the account has survived only in a Syriac translation that came to light in the nineteenth century.[22] Thus for any Polo manuscripts that were circulating before 1330 or so, there is no clearly authenticated rival text from which he or his copyists might have borrowed.

One obvious source of information that Marco Polo might have naturally drawn upon was the two people who are described as having accompanied him on his travels, his father Niccolo and his uncle Maffeo. It was they who pioneered the commercial route to Karakorum in the 1260s to which they returned with the seventeen-year-old Marco in 1273–75. Deeply experienced and courageous travelers that they were, and skillful traders, what were they doing for the long period between 1275 and the year 1291, at which time (both Western and Mongol sources agree) they began the dangerous route back to Europe by sea, as escorts to a Mongol princess sent as bride to the Mongol Khan in Persia? The prologue to Marco Polo's *Description of the World* is rich in details on their activities on their first journey, but silent about them on the second—except for the incident of the siege and the mangonels. It is feasible that they were traveling and trading in Mongol China and Central Asia in the 1270s and 1280s, and that Marco was only with them some of the time if at all. Maffeo Polo, a well-off merchant, had a house on the north shore of the Black Sea, in the town of Sudak, as attested by various sources. Could Marco have been based there, gathering potentially relevant commercial and travel information from a range of European and Arab traders, which he then fused with information supplied by his father and uncle when they at last returned?[23]

Such speculations may or may not have weight, but in an important sense they are irrelevant to the story. For as the British medievalist John Critchley puts it, what makes Polo extraordinary is not the route he took on his travels, or his specific experiences, or his own character and person. It is quite simply his book, and the fact that it got written at all.[24] Thus the salient question is not so much how as *why* it got written.

On this, we have no evidence at all. But we can be pretty sure it was not to make money—one could not make money from a manuscript copy painstakingly written by someone else and recopied to be deposited in a monastery or royal or aristocratic library. Was it just dictated to pass the time in jail? Yule, in the passage I quoted above, wrote of Marco Polo "pacing his dungeon floor" in Genoa, but that may be wide of the mark. If Polo was a well-connected Venetian prisoner of war being held for ransom, then he might have been held under some form of quite comfortable house arrest, pledged not to leave Genoa but otherwise fairly free to roam. His book could have grown discursively, through question and answer applied to some fundamental outline of the kind supplied in the existing prologue.

One early manuscript, known as the "Z" manuscript, discovered in Toledo only in the 1930s, seems to suggest this. In it there are a number of comments that are found in few or no other manuscripts, and appear to be answers directed to an unknown interlocutor, perhaps skeptical or merely curious about certain details of Polo's experience. It may or may not be significant that this Z manuscript does not include any mention either of Marco Polo's three-year appointment in Yangzhou or the activity by him or his family with siege equipment in the battle for Xiangyang.[25] Could Polo have withdrawn such claims after insistent questioning? Or could later copyists have inserted the details in their own manuscripts after reading some other source to give what they thought was extra circumstantial weight to Polo's account? Did Polo himself modify different versions of his story to different copyists at different times? Apart from the later will that indicates his marriage to Donata, we know nothing of his life in Venice after his release from prison, probably in 1298 or 1299. The Venetian records show no ransom agreements, no civic responsibilities, no real estate purchases or commercial ventures. No Venetian men of letters mention reading his accounts; none of their great libraries record early acquisition of a copy. But in some circles he had acquired the nickname of "Il Milione" by around 1310, probably because of the millions of fables he recounted rather than the millions of ducats he had accumulated.

One ingenious explanation of the book's existence is that Polo wrote it to gain preferment, perhaps in the suite of some ambassador to or from Venice. Thus the long descriptions of Mongol court politics and Polo's bureaucratic and traveling experience were designed to present him as an able and experienced man of the world, who could undertake any assignment requiring tact, calmness, courage. In this view, we might see his book as a kind of résumé or vita—rambling indeed according to our current procedures, but not without vigor and effectiveness in the context of the times. This speculation, like so many others, has some evidence to support it. Two of the earliest known Polo manuscripts, preserved in France, have a passage written on the front stating that they were presented by Polo himself to the French ambassador Thibaut of Cepoy in Venice in 1307. As a commoner, Polo would have had little chance of preferment in the Venetian world, where in the 1290s social hierarchies were congealing and the elite protecting and reinforcing its own privileges. But France may have seemed more open, and certainly the Travels contain many passages on the Mongol-Chinese flexibility in hiring the more lowly born and on their generous rewards to those who served them loyally.[26]

If much of Polo's account was thus designed as a mixture of self-promotion and oblique criticism of Western meanness as contrasted with Eastern opulence and openness, then other aspects of his description may have had similar polemical or moralistic intent. His book might have been designed in part as a commentary on his own native city, as much as an accurate representation of life in China. Polo was the father of three daughters, as stated clearly in his will, and we may hypothesize that he sought to bring them up as well as he could. Did this perhaps give him an added inducement to portray a China of moral certainties that would contrast favorably with the notoriously free and easy sexual attitudes of many Venetians? According to one of the manuscripts that can be dated to around 1315, Polo—who never noticed that Chinese women had bound feet—nevertheless chose to describe the character and deportment of Chinese women at some length:

> You ought to learn too that the girls of the province of Catai are beyond others pure and keep the virtue of modesty. They do not indeed skip and dance, they do not frolic, they do not fly into a passion, they do not stick at the windows looking at the faces or passers nor showing their own faces to them, they give no ready hearing to unseemly talk, they do not frequent feasts and merrymakings. And if it happens that they go to some proper place, as perhaps the idol temples [or] to visit the houses of kinsfolk and relations, they would go in the company of their mothers, not staring improperly at people but wearing on the head certain pretty bonnets of theirs which prevent an upward look, so that in walking they always direct the eyes on the road before the feet. Before their elders they are modest; they never speak foolish words, nor indeed any in their presence, except when they have been asked. In their rooms they keep at their tasks and rarely show themselves to fathers and brothers and the elders of the house. And they pay no attention to suitors.[27]

Is this really China? Or is it a reverse image of Venice, as Critchley has suggested, one that shows us not so much Polo the traveler as Polo the "ageing father of teenage daughters"?[28]

However, if chastity and decorum were two of the aspects of his China—whether real or imagined—that Marco Polo hoped to pass on to his readers as well as to his daughters, it was not the aspect that caught the attention of later medieval or Renaissance readers. From the start, readers were searching in Polo for support of their own fancies, rather than for moralistic musings, and he did not disappoint them. The most significant of the fourteenth-century works that can be shown to contain material drawn from Marco Polo—Chaucer and Dante have been combed in vain by dedicated Polo scholars—is the *Romance of Bauduin de Sebourc, Third King of Jerusalem.* Much of this romance's background incident is drawn directly from Polo, and the lady of the story, Ivorine, who is wooed and won by the future King Bauduin, comes entirely from an early chapter of Polo's history on an evil caliph who brought up his band of assassins in a carefully constructed Paradise, complete not only with "wine and milk and honey" but also with "ladies and damsels, who dallied with them to their hearts' content, so that they had what young men will have."[29] Even the description of Ivorine's eyes—black and lustrous—comes from Polo's description of the black and lustrous eyes of his master Kublai. Polo fed many later dreams with his depiction of the Khan's host of concubines attending their lord in groups of six at a time, in revolving three night shifts, "both in the room and in the bed and for all that he needs; and the great Kaan does with them what he pleases."[30]

Marco Polo's most famous early reader, Christopher Columbus, was impressed by the sensual elements in Polo's discussion, as well as by the commercial possibilities he opened up. The first printed version of Polo's work (from a Latin manuscript of the 1300s) was published in 1485, and Columbus clearly had a good knowledge of its contents before his voyage of 1492. In 1496, after his return, he ordered his own copy, and either then or later made close to a hundred notations in the margins.[31] These marginal notes—written mainly in Latin, with some Spanish words interspersed—show the passages that most sharply caught Columbus's attention. He was struck by the practice of burning retainers and womenfolk to accompany their lord after his death, mentioned on one occasion by Polo; and next to a passage on the marriage practices of Tibet, Columbus jots down the words, "They do not want wives save from among the women who have already had intercourse." Reading Polo's discussion of the people of "Cayndu," Columbus is caught up sharply by another custom, and notes that "the men offer their wives and their daughters to passing travellers."[32] He also notes the assassins with their garden of sensual delights, discussions of miracles and unicorns, and the location of the home of Prester John.[33]

But despite these expressions of interest in the sensual and the arcane, most of the time, as we would expect, Columbus is tracking Polo's text for items of trade and clues to its dangers and successes. Thus he highlights Polo's references to gold and silver, bulk sales of fine silk, spices, porcelain, and precious and semiprecious stones, from rubies and sapphires to topaz and lapis lazuli, along with fine wine, and pearl divers.[34] Equally significant to Columbus are the direction and seasonal time of monsoon-fleet sailings, the prevalence of pirates or cannibals, and the locations of likely sources of food and other supplies.[35] Columbus highlighted several promising-sounding cities in China, including Yangzhou and Hangzhou,[36] and commented on their trade possibilities, but next to only one city did he write the phrase *mercaçciones innumeras*—an "incalculable amount of trade." This he wrote opposite the name of "Cambalu" (or Kambaluk), Polo's name for the city of Peking, Kublai Khan's new capital in China. And to highlight his sense of excitement, Columbus added a new motif to his marginal words. It was a drawing of a hand resting on what could be a bank of clouds or a rolling sea. The fingers of the hand were all closed tight, except for the topmost index finger, which pointed straight out, dramatically, at the news that had aroused it.[37]

CHAPTER 2

The Catholic Century

IT WAS THE THIRTEENTH-CENTURY PERIOD OF MONGOL dominance in Central Asia and China, combined with the European zeal for trade and the religious impetus of the Crusades, that had made possible the initial flowering of contacts between the two regions. With the spread of the Black Death in Europe in the 1340s, the collapse of the Mongols' Chinese dynasty in 1368, and the concurrent consolidation of Ottoman Muslim power over much of the Near East, these preliminary contacts came to a halt. A burst of Chinese maritime explorations of the Indian Ocean and East African coast marked the reign of Ming emperor Yong Luo (reigned 1402–24) and might have brought a reopening of economic relations, but the great voyages were discontinued for economic reasons in the 1440s. Thereafter, European commercial and Christian expansion, though still having "the Indies" as its focus, was diverted for a time by the accidents of geographical miscalculation to the Americas, and the casual contacts with China ceased.

By early in the sixteenth century, however, the voyages of Magellan and Vasco da Gama had brought the Portuguese to the edges of the Chinese empire at Macao, while the Spaniards, leapfrogging from their new American possessions, had made a Far Eastern base in the Philippines at Manila. Here, as the two expansive nations debated about how the mid-Atlantic lines of demarcation of the world (originally drawn by the papacy at the Treaty of Tordesillas in 1492) should be applied to the Pacific and the Spice Islands of Southeast Asia, missions and traders from both nations began to probe China's coastline. The unintended result was the first new flow of information on the nature of Chinese society and government to reach Europe for two hundred years.

This new information era did not get off to an encouraging start. Though Portuguese had been trading peaceably and profitably with the Chinese earlier in the century, and had even received permission to send an embassy to Peking to discuss further commercial prospects, their work had been ruined by one of their own captains, Simão de Andrade, who verbally and physically attacked Chinese officials on the coast. When news of his depredations reached the Chinese emperor, the members of the Portuguese embassy were sent back as prisoners to Canton, where they were imprisoned and tortured, and forbidden to trade further. The result was a clandestine period of smuggler-trading off the coast of Fujian, which led to further Chinese government reprisals in 1549, including the capture of two Portuguese-owned junks, the slaughter of most of their crew members, and the imprisonment of the remainder in the Fujian capital of Fuzhou.

After protracted judicial hearings—and some further executions—the remaining Portuguese were separated and sent to live in exile in various areas of South China. Among these was Galeote Pereira, a Portuguese soldier and trader. By 1553, Galeote Pereira had managed to bribe his way to freedom through Portuguese and Chinese intermediaries, and sometime in the next few years he wrote down an account of his experiences and a sketch of Chinese customs and government that reached the Jesuit college of Goa in 1561. Transcribed by the children in the seminary there, this account was sent to Europe as the appendix to the annual Jesuit report on the Indian mission, and was soon translated into both Italian and English.[1]

Given the nature of Pereira's harrowing experiences, and his complete ignorance of Chinese language, his account was naturally fragmented and sometimes inconsistent. But as the first detailed report by a non-clerical Western visitor to China since that of Marco Polo, it was an important and illuminating document. Galeote Pereira often gave signposts as to when he was relating his personal experiences or when he was reporting hearsay. Thus he made it clear in describing Peking and Nanking that he did not visit Central or North China and was relying on books or earlier travelers' tales for information on those areas; similarly, his lengthy analysis of the duties and organizational structure of the Chinese provincial bureaucracy was presented schematically and at a distance. But when he talked of the prison experience and the techniques of judicial torture—whether the sleeping conditions in jail jammed side by side with other prisoners in a kind of heavy wooden cage or frame that made all movement impossible, or the effects of a heavy split bamboo on naked human flesh—his words were so terrifyingly immediate that they became a fundamental source for later depictions of the Chinese capacity for cruelty, introducing a permanent new element into the Western view of China. As Pereira described the beatings:

> Their whips be bamboos, cleft in the middle, in such sort that they seem rather plain than sharp. He that is to be whipped lieth groveling on the ground. Upon his thighs the hangman layeth on blows mightily with these bamboos, that the standers-by tremble at their cruelty. Ten stripes draw a great deal of blood, twenty or thirty spoil the flesh altogether, fifty or threescore will require a long time to be healed, and if they come to the number of one hundred, then are they incurable—and they are given to whosoever hath nothing wherewith to bribe these executioners who administer them.[2]

But Pereira's account does not only focus on these harsh aspects of China: he looks around with open eyes, and speaks with many voices that still reach us with a rare directness. Thus it is as an experienced military man that he notices the absence of artillery on city walls, and the probability that China would be easy for well-trained European troops to conquer. It is as an engineer that he carefully gauges the size of the stone slabs used in bridge and road building and the exact nature of the construction. It is as a trader that he notes the rivers and fish farms, and the comparative costs of a whole range of foodstuffs from goose and beef to dogs and snakes, along with the bridges of barges and the modes of transit tax collection, the Chinese merchants' preference for living outside the main cities in the suburbs to avoid the strict urban curfews, and the huge amount of wares and services that are hawked by peddlers and craftsmen door-to-door.[3] As a religious man, he approves what he has learned about the existence of government-supported rest homes and hospitals for the blind, sick, and lame, and the absence of beggars in the streets, and reflects how lightly the Chinese seem to wear their religious beliefs. He concludes that the spread of Christianity would proceed much more successfully than that of Islam if only the Western missionaries would allow their Chinese converts to continue eating pork and drinking wine.[4] And, most surprisingly, it is as a victim of the Chinese judicial system (albeit one later granted clemency) that he extols Chinese justice, despite the severity of its punishments.

By comparing Chinese legal flexibility favorably both to Roman law and to what one might expect at home in current Europe, Pereira was introducing a comparativist approach to Chinese culture that was to become a central part of Western thought. His introduction of this concept is forceful:

> And as for questioning the witnesses in public, besides not confiding the life and honour of one man to the bare oath of another, this is productive of another good, which is that as these audience chambers are always full of people who can hear what the witnesses are saying, only the truth can be written down. In this way the judicial processes cannot be falsified, as sometimes happens with us, where what the witnesses say is known only to the examiner and notary, so great is the power of money, etc. But in this country, besides this order observed of them in examinations, they do fear so much their king, and he where he maketh his abode keepeth them so low, that they dare not once stir; in

sort that these men are unique in the doing of their justice, more than were the Romans or any other kind of people.[5]

Pereira reinforces this idea by speaking specifically to his own experiences, and wondering aloud how a Chinese would have fared in comparable Western circumstances:

> For wheresoever in any town of Christendom should be accused unknown men as we were, I know not what end the very Innocents' cause would have; but we in a heathen country, having for our great enemies two of the chiefest men in a whole town, wanting an interpreter, ignorant of that country's language, did in the end see our great adversaries cast into prison for our sake, and deprived of their offices and honour for not doing justice, yea not to escape death, for as the rumour goeth, they shall be beheaded,—now see if they do justice or no?[6]

Among other facets of the society that especially strike Pereira are the meticulous practice of night-soil collection—whether human or animal—in Chinese cities, the use of two small sticks for hygienic eating, the practice of fishing using tethered birds that yield up their catch to their masters, and the extraordinary density of the population, which he describes in a striking image: "For the multitude of them [is] everywhere so great, that out of a tree you shall see many times swarm a number of children, where a man would not have thought to have found any one at all."[7] But just as one side of Chinese social order is daunting—for "no suspicion, no not one traitorous word is long borne withal"—so do the crowds of the curious have their menacing side, leaving Pereira and his friends feeling "loathsomely oppressed by the multitude of people that came to see us."[8] Either because of his prison experiences, or because of rumors that have reached him, Pereira adds one further element to his description of Chinese social life: "The greatest fault we do find in them is sodomy, a vice very common in the meaner sort, and nothing strange amongst the best."[9]

Thus did Galeote Pereira bring a host of new topics to the dis-

cussions of China, though like Marco Polo he also left unre-
marked several subjects that he might be expected to have
noticed: Pereira follows Polo precisely in having no references to
tea, for example, none to printing or the Chinese writing system,
and none to the bound feet of Chinese women, even though
Pereira mentions that when he and his captured companions
were in Fuzhou, they were taken "many times abroad, and were
brought to the palaces of noblemen, to be seen of them and
their wives", and he had also heard or seen enough of Chinese
prostitutes to know that they were often proficient players on
the lute.[10]

Among those who read Galeote Pereira's account with care
and interest was the Dominican friar Gaspar da Cruz. After
spending a year in Cambodia as a missionary, da Cruz had
visited Canton for a few weeks during December 1556, and
decided to write down his experiences and impressions. But
some time before completing his manuscript, da Cruz read
Pereira's account, and generously wrote that he believed Pereira
to be "a gentleman of good credit," one who "did not lie," so that
it was from Pereira that he "took a great deal of that which is
here spoken of."[11] Da Cruz died in his native Lisbon in February
1570, while trying to help plague victims there, and his China
memoir was published the same month, assuring him at least a
posthumous kind of fame. For it is to "this humble Dominican
friar," Charles Boxer feels, that "must be given the honour (if
that is the right word) of writing the first book on China which
was published in Europe."[12]

The goal that da Cruz set himself, as he wrote in the prologue
to the work he called his *Treatise,* was to give as careful a description of China as possible, using his own and Pereira's experiences, so that China might be included among the other
countries where his fellow Dominicans—along with Franciscans
and Jesuits—had recently been making so many converts. As da
Cruz observed, the Chinese offered awesome new opportunities
to those seeking to spread the Christian faith:

> Because among all these peoples whom I have mentioned, the Chinas exceed all the others in populousness, in greatness of the realm, in excellence of polity and government, and in abundance of possessions and wealth (not in precious things such as gold and jewels but in wealth, dispositions and goods which chiefly minister to bodily needs), and because these peoples have many very memorable things.[13]

Da Cruz felt that his own eyewitness stance had real value here, because of the tendency of many in his own day to dismiss travelers' tales—especially those about China—as gross exaggerations.

> I also hereby give readers a necessary warning by which they can conjecture the greatness of the things of China, viz.—that whereas distant things often sound greater than they really are, this is clean contrary, because China is much more than it sounds and the sight thereof make a very different impression from what is heard or read about it, as has been verified by myself and others after we have seen the things of China. This must be seen and not heard, because hearing it is nothing in comparison with seeing it.[14]

The acuteness of da Cruz's personal observations on his short stay in China is indeed astonishing, and even on the topics already noted by Galeote Pereira, da Cruz has a host of new information to give to European readers. Thus he notices that the night-soil collectors carry off their burden in tubs scrubbed spotlessly clean outside, to lessen the odor, and often barter some of the vegetables they have grown with the fertilizer for the next batch they collect. Chinese women prostitutes are often blind and are forced to live outside the city walls (Marco Polo too had commented on this); they are housed in special streets and have to be registered by those who manage them, have usually been sold by their mothers into prostitution, and taught to play music and sing.[15] Da Cruz notes the exact way the necks of cormorants are ringed while they fish and the way they are made to disgorge their catch. He describes the pincerlike motion of chopstick usage in detail, and parallels their use to that of the long fingernails—"which they keep very clean"—favored by some of the wealthy.[16]

Da Cruz also reports on many facets of Chinese life not previously considered in the West: the clothes and lifestyles of the strong and independent boatwomen who ply the waterfront of Canton; the artificial egg hatcheries and duck-farming practices of the locals; the joy of owning caged nightingales, which "melt themselves in music" if kept in separated but nearby cages; the stuffing of chickens with water or sand to get them to sell for more by weight; the use of hair-pulling in private quarrels; the existence of printing in China for over nine hundred years.[17] Da Cruz also has the aesthetic flexibility to be interested in Chinese music, something most Westerners never appreciated. He finds the sung chants even of China's idolatrous priests to be "very tunable," while Chinese music generally was of "very good harmony . . . very good consonancy," and Chinese plays on the public stage "very well acted and to the life."[18]

Da Cruz fills in with accuracy and clarity each of the three significant areas of Chinese life that Polo and Pereira had failed to mention: footbinding, the nature of the language, and the drinking of tea. Footbinding, he sees, has a mainly aesthetic justification: "The women commonly, excepting those of the sea coast and of the mountains, are very white and gentlewomen, some having their noses and eyes well proportioned. From their childhood they squeeze their feet in cloths, so that they may remain small, and they do it because the Chinas do hold them for finer gentlewomen that have small noses and feet. This withal is the custom among the well-bred people, and not among the basest."[19]

As to language, da Cruz describes how he came to realize that the nature of Chinese characters was not alphabetic or "athwart" as in the West, but from top to bottom in columns, each word being represented by a character (of which there were some five thousand in all), each readable by other people regardless of the local pronunciations. "What had previously puzzled me," added da Cruz, "became clear," and the Chinese language turned out not to be "outlandish" after all.[20]

He had this to say on tea:

> Whatsoever person or persons come to any man of quality's house, it is customary to offer him on a fair tray in a porcelain cup (as or many cups as there are persons) a kind of warm water which they call *cha*, which is somewhat red and very medicinal, which they use to drink, made from a concoction of somewhat bitter herbs; with this they commonly welcome all manner of persons that they do respect, be they acquaintances or be they not, and to me they offered it many times.[21]

Da Cruz was aware of dark sides to China, and these too received his commentary. His descriptions of Chinese beatings of prisoners with bamboo poles "thick as a man's leg" soaked in water "for to beat them more cruelly" were as vivid as Pereira's. The aftermath of the beatings was equally terrible to da Cruz, leaving the courtyards of the official's residence "full of blood." Da Cruz noted how the "beadles" who gave the beatings subsequently dragged the prisoners "like sheep by one leg to the prison," while one could see the watching mandarins "altogether void of compassion, talking one with another, eating and drinking, and picking their teeth."[22] Like Pereira, he too felt that "unnatural vice" was "common among them" and in "no wise reproved"; but to da Cruz, that was simply because the Chinese "had never had any who told them that it was a sin, nor an evil thing done."[23]

Pereira and da Cruz between them added many new notes to the China story, even though they clearly shared many of the same commercial and religious drives as Marco Polo and Friar Odoric some two hundred and fifty years before. And just as then the romancer John Mandeville had woven a tapestry of Chinese fictions out of the stories reaching him, so in the mid-sixteenth century did the Portuguese adventurer-novelist Mendes

Pinto embroider the stories he had been hearing and reading. Unlike Mandeville, Pinto had traveled in the Far East: there is considerable evidence to place him in Siam and Burma, as well as Japan, at various times between 1537 and 1558, though he probably never visited China. He began work on the huge manuscript he called his *Peregrinations* in the 1560s and finished it around 1578, though the book was not published until 1614, thirty years after the author's death.[24] It is possible that not just the memoir but also the persona of his fellow Portuguese adventurer Galeote Pereira was a specific source and model for Pinto, for it would have been well known at the time that as well as attempting to trade on China's coast, Pereira had fought with other mercenary Portuguese soldiers on the side of Siam against Pegu (in the region of Burma) during the 1540s, and had witnessed the exhumation and the later ceremonies of beatification of the Jesuit missionary Francis Xavier. Many of the most powerful and detailed passages in Pinto's book are dedicated to just such episodes as the Siam-Pegu wars and Xavier's last years and death.[25]

Pinto's descriptions of his travels in China occupy around 120 pages of his 520-page volume and are an amalgam of documentary material drawn from Pereira and da Cruz with Pinto's own unembarrassedly fabricated material. His description of the prison treatment of his party after their capture by the Chinese authorities echoes Pereira's in virtually every detail, and many other depictions of local Chinese life—such as Pinto's meticulous descriptions of the battery raising of ducks and the shipping of them along the rivers to their feeding grounds, and the Chinese thoroughness in collecting every scrap of human waste to be used as fertilizer—are lifted without apology or comment straight from the similar passages in da Cruz.[26] Pinto's deadpan attack on the practice and "depravity of the unspeakable sin" in China, however, though it initially seems to be a simple amalgam of da Cruz and Pereira, is clearly also designed to be a critique of church practice in general, being "not only allowed among them publicly, but according to the doctrine of their priests, it is regarded as a great virtue."[27]

On such subjects as food and the wonders of China, Pinto also draws on both Pereira and da Cruz, but it is a distinguishing mark of his style that he often abandons his sober predecessors and dances into his own world of lighthearted parody. For instance, when Pinto begins a descriptive passage on China's food warehouses and the butchers slicing, salting, curing, and smoking every delicious kind of food, he seems the very soul of documentary veracity. But the reader's suspicions are slowly aroused by the growing oddity of the meat on the Chinese butchers' blocks, as we watch the butchers first prepare "ham, pork, bacon, ducks, [and] geese," and then proceed to "cranes, bustard, ostrich, venison, beef, buffalo, tapir, yak, horse, tiger, dog, fox, and the meat of every other kind of animal on earth."[28] Such devices are common in Pinto, though he keeps the reader off balance by often slipping back into a more logical mode, which almost convinces us that he has seen everything he is talking about after all. On the subject of dog meat, for example, he notes that "we also saw many vessels loaded with dried orange peel, which is used in the low-priced taverns for boiling with dog meat in order to eliminate its characteristic bad odor, improve its soggy texture, and make the flesh firmer."[29]

In her recent meticulously edited version of Pinto's *Peregrinations*, Rebecca Catz has pointed out that Pinto's style consists of four separate narrative voices which yield to each other at different points of his book: one voice is that of a decent and reliable observer; one of the ingenue, "slightly dim-witted," presenting the reader with ironies the author professes not to understand; one is a hero, patriot and defender of the Catholic faith, always ready to lay about him in the name of a higher truth; and one is a picaresque hero who participates in dissembling fashion in the most hateful acts of his protagonists. The overall scheme of Pinto's book, Catz believes, is that of "corrosive satire," designed to belittle the institutions of his native Portugal, and to discredit the lingering ideology of the crusading mentality still so prevalent among Portuguese expansionists. Read in this light, the book is in Catz's words neither simple adventure nor tall tale, but "a subversive book," and one that "deceived his countrymen and threatened the very foundation of his society." The passages on China, in particular, are presented in the "form of a utopian satire," which "depends for its effects on the stratagem of the innocent observer who travels the world over and discovers civilizations superior to his own." Though the Chinese are pagans, they are nevertheless far ahead of their Western contemporaries in the matter of practical morality.[30]

Perhaps the most subtle, historiographically complex, and morally intriguing of such passages is that in which Pinto discusses the various forms of social protection provided by the Chinese state—something first noticed by Marco Polo almost three centuries earlier. Pinto here slides the reader inexorably along a scale of human suffering, so that it is impossible to tell exactly where compassion ends and parody begins: First come the orphans, abandoned by their parents, fed by wetnurses, and placed in special city schools where they are taught to read and write, and to practice one of the "mechanical trades." Then come the blind children, employed by the owners of hand-operated flour mills to work the machines for which no sight is needed. Those who are too crippled to work the mill equipment are employed by rope- or basketmakers, in hoisting the cordage and weaving the rushes. Those without use of their hands travel from market to market with produce on their backs. Those crippled in both hands and feet are placed in special buildings—"like monasteries"—where they join in prayers for the dead and share the resulting fees with the priests. Then, as the satirical edge becomes unavoidable, we learn how the deaf and dumb are paid for with funds gathered from "loud-mouthed and shameless women who dishonor themselves in public." Elderly prostitutes with incurable diseases, on the other hand, are nourished by a special tax on the younger, healthier prostitutes; orphaned girls are fed with fines levied on women caught committing adultery; and those "penniless men addicted to a free and easy life" are supported with funds collected from "lawyers who persist in bringing unjust claims before the court," as well as by "judges, who, swayed either by influence or bribes, do not uphold the lawful process of justice."[31]

At one point in his narrative, Pinto introduces a character named Vasco Calvo, whom he says was living in exile outside Peking, where Pinto ran into him on his travels. This Calvo had been in China for twenty-seven years, ever since the disastrous early embassy of Tomé Pires in 1517. Loosely basing his story on that of a real-life Vasco Calvo, a Portuguese merchant imprisoned in China who wrote the first letter about China to be seen in the West, Pinto gives his own Calvo a new life, as a man married to a Chinese woman and raising their four children—two boys and two girls—in a house in the town near his wife's "respected kinsmen." This Sino-Portuguese household is presented as a model of domestic harmony, order, and religious devotion, where nightly prayers are offered up to the Christian God in the family's tiny private chapel, kept locked but beautifully appointed in a wing of the house. The sight was such that "the tears came rushing to our eyes," says Pinto of himself and his companions, and left the party "amazed by what we had seen as one would expect, in view of the circumstances."[32]

Such a small and secretive mixed-marriage Christian household did not—as far as we know—exist in the China of 1544, where Pinto set the scene with apparent documentary specificity, nor even in the 1570s when he wrote the passage. But by the year 1583, when Pinto died, such a ménage was becoming at least a possibility. For in that same year the Jesuit Matteo Ricci and a companion opened the first Catholic mission on Chinese soil since those of the Franciscans just over two and a half centuries before, and slowly began to make a number of Chinese Christian converts, both men and women.

Ricci's account of his labors in China was to give European
readers a new level of insight into the realities of Chinese society, even if one tinged with exaggeration and nostalgia. Born in
the Italian city of Macerata in 1552, Matteo Ricci was educated
in the Jesuit College of Rome, which at the time was probably
the best school in Europe for science and mathematics. There he
also received a broad training in Latin and theology, in geography, and in the then important field of mnemonic training—one
of Ricci's memory teachers, Panigarola, could allegedly recall as
many as a hundred thousand mental images by using the memory placement and storage theories then in vogue. After formally joining the Society of Jesus, Ricci was posted to Goa, on
the West Indian coast, where a Catholic enclave was ensconced
in the recently established Portuguese base. By 1582 he was
transferred to Macao, on the tip of southern China, and after
intensive Chinese language training in Macao, he entered China
in 1583 and established a small residence near Canton.[33]

Ricci was to live the remainder of his life in China, first in the
south, then in Nanjing on the Yangzi River, and finally in Peking,
where he died in 1610. No Westerner had ever come near to
attaining his levels of knowledge of Chinese culture, language,
and society. Within a year of settling in China, Ricci realized that
if he was to convert the Chinese to Christianity, he must do it by
proving the advanced level of Western culture to the Chinese
elite. In pursuit of this goal, as soon as his language was good
enough he produced a global map, with commentary, to show
the advanced levels of Western geography and astronomy; a
book on friendship, to demonstrate the high levels of intra-
personal morality in the West; a manual on memory theory, to
show the Chinese how the Westerners organized their knowledge; and a translation—completed with the aid of a highly educated Chinese collaborator—of the opening chapters of Euclid's
Geometry. He also carefully crafted a complex series of religious
dialogues between a Catholic priest and a Chinese scholar,
designed to show the superiority of the Western spiritual tradition and the balance of logic and faith that lay at its heart.

Ricci's early views on China are known only through his letters home and to his superiors in the order, but after his death
his colleagues found that he had left two lengthy manuscripts,
one analyzing and describing Chinese culture and society, and
one summarizing the history of the Jesuit mission in China, and
his own role in the conversion process. (He destroyed a third
manuscript, his own spiritual diary, on his deathbed.) When
edited by his fellow Jesuits, translated into Latin, and published
in Europe in 1616, the two surviving manuscripts at once established a new benchmark for the study and description of China.

Like those that had come before, Ricci's portrait of China was
strongly favorable. In contrast to the fragmented states of post-
Reformation Europe—the murderous Thirty Years War erupted
in 1618, following hard on the heels of the bitter religious wars
in France and the Netherlands—China offered a picture of a vast,
unified, well-ordered country, held together by a central con-
trolling orthodoxy, that of Confucianism. Of Confucius himself, Ricci wrote that "if we critically examine his actions and
sayings as they are recorded in history, we shall be forced to
admit that he was the equal of the pagan philosophers and superior to most of them."[34] Ricci wrote that though directed at a distance by reclusive emperors, the daily administration of the
country was in the hands of a professional bureaucracy selected
by a complex hierarchical examination based on merit. Social life
was regulated by complex laws of ritual and deportment that
induced social harmony. The working classes knew their place,
marriages were harmoniously arranged by the young people's
parents, and the practice of footbinding kept the women
chastely at home. The classical Chinese language itself was so
difficult that the years spent in mastering it curbed the "youthful licentiousness" to which China's young men might otherwise have been prone. China's patent distrust of foreigners could
be easily explained by their worries over national security and the
unsettling effect of newcomers and merchants on their long-
established ways. Even the Chinese mode of drinking alcohol
was so well controlled that hangovers were virtually unknown.[35]

Given this generally favorable depiction of Chinese moral and social life, Ricci was at some pains to point out why the Chinese were resistant to the appeals of Christianity. He explained this by a number of factors: one was the dominant role of Buddhism in China, which Ricci described harshly as a mass of primitive superstitions, fostered by uneducated and often immoral monks and priests. Another was the deeply entrenched belief in astrology, which had replaced scientific astronomy as the primal mode for studying the heavens, and had come to dominate many levels of Chinese decisions over private and public life. Overlapping in some ways with both these aspects, but also raising new elements and problems, was the system of Chinese ancestor worship. Ricci spent many years pondering these ceremonies, and their relationship to the conversion procedure. Since it became clear that most Chinese could not be persuaded to embrace Christianity if they were also told to give up the homage they paid to their ancestors, Ricci redefined ancestral worship. He concluded that the Chinese rites to ancestors were acts of homage to the departed rather than religious invocations designed to obtain favors or benefit. The same in essence was true of Chinese ritual ceremonies in the name of Confucius. Accordingly, Chinese might continue to observe such ceremonies even after they had been converted to Christianity. (They should, however, be persuaded to give up their concubines before conversion.)

In choosing the Chinese characters that should be used to translate the Christian monotheistic concept of God, Ricci took another characteristically ingenious yet compromising stance. He decided that the two Chinese characters *Shang-di*, connoting something approximating the "Lord-of-all" or "Highest Ruler," could be retained for use in the new context. This was partly because current Chinese use of *Shang-di* was not religious in the Christian spiritual sense. Ricci also argued that in the far recesses of the Chinese past such a concept of the one true God had existed, although the knowledge of that God had subsequently faded from Chinese consciousness with the reediting of the cultural past by the Buddhist-influenced neo-Confucians of the twelfth century. Yet to balance these interpretations, Ricci suggested that a new coinage—*Tian-zhu* or "Heaven's Lord"—might also be used by missionaries and their Chinese converts to avoid the confusing cultural overlays of *Shang-di*.[36]

Ricci made few criticisms of the Chinese in his lengthy manuscript. He did suggest—and this was later to become a fateful argument—that Chinese science had somehow fallen behind that of the West by failing to develop its full potentials, once so strongly part of Chinese culture. The Chinese, wrote Ricci, "have no conception of the rules of logic," and consequently "the science of ethics with them is a series of confused maxims and deductions." Similarly, though "at one time they were quite proficient in arithmetic and geometry, in the study and teaching of these branches of learning they labored with more or less confusion."[37] The implication was clearly that with a more rigorous system of logic, and a renewed concentration on mathematics and science, which the West was in a position to offer, China would become a better place. The only harsh charge Ricci's manuscripts included against the Chinese was one that Pereira and da Cruz had both raised, and Pinto had elaborated and mocked: the Chinese men were too much drawn to homosexual practices, evidence for which Ricci had observed in the elaborately dressed male prostitutes visible in the streets of Peking. Ricci also estimated that there were forty thousand female prostitutes in Peking—Polo in his *Description* had guessed the number to be twenty thousand. Like that of da Cruz, Ricci's view of such weakness was benign: "This people is really to be pitied rather than censured, and the deeper one finds them involved in the darkness of ignorance, the more earnest one should be in praying for their salvation."[38]

This generally favorable Western Catholic view of Chinese civilization survived the collapse of the Ming dynasty in 1644, and was continued by a number of other talented Jesuits who traveled to China and settled there under the new Qing dynasty in the later seventeenth century. Qing rulers appointed Jesuits to senior positions in the state astronomy bureau, used them as imperial confidants, and welcomed their new concepts—whether these were in medicine (including quinine), warfare (casting of cannon), astronomy (Copernican), or painting (both perspective and chiaroscuro). In 1692, the Jesuits even won toleration for the Christian religion throughout China and permission to erect churches in the capital and the provinces. But the puzzling fact of the Ming dynasty's fall to the Manchu Qing—if the Ming were so strong and virtuous, how had they been conquered so easily by a comparatively tiny force of untutored hunter/horsemen from the north?—left lingering questions in European minds. So did the Jesuit practices of proselytizing among the Chinese elite, living in style, studying classical Chinese with such thoroughness, using what could be seen as a pagan word for the one true God, and continuing to insist that Chinese ancestral and Confucian rites were not religious in goal, when much evidence seemed to be surfacing to the contrary.[39]

One of the toughest assaults on the Jesuits came from the fiery Spanish Dominican, Domingo Navarrete. Born in 1618, Navarrete reached China in 1659, after a long spell of service in Mexico and the Philippines. Navarrete lived and worked in China from 1659 to 1664, and learned Chinese, until he was arrested and questioned along with other Catholic missionaries in a Qing roundup of foreign missionaries. For the rest of his life he was convinced these hardships had been brought on by Jesuit scheming and political meddling. After a lengthy period of incarceration with other missionaries in Canton between 1666 and 1669, Navarrete set off home to Europe, which he reached, after a nightmare voyage of storms and adventures, in 1672. Yet the hard experiences had no wit diminished his affection for China. According to his own account, when he went ashore in Lisbon he was wearing Chinese dress.[40]

After a period of intensive lobbying in Rome against the elitist and accommodationist practices followed by the Jesuits in China, Navarrete settled for a time in Madrid. Here, between 1674 and 1677, he wrote the two massive volumes through which Europe received his views on China, the *Tratados* and the *Controversias*, which had a combined length of close to one million words. On Jesuit urgings the Inquisition ordered an examination of the *Tratados;* true to his character, on hearing this, Navarrete took a copy of his book in person to the office of the Inquisition and suggested they burn both him and his book in the public square. Navarrete also claimed Jesuits blocked the proofs of the *Controversias* at the printers. He never did get the full text cleared by the censors, and the *Controversias* was finally printed with many polemical passages omitted.[41]

In his books, Navarrete's harshest comments were reserved for the Jesuits, who—he insisted—had lacked all charity and concern for him in the various predicaments he encountered. The Manchu soldiers—"Tartars" as Navarrete called them, following contemporary usage—were by contrast "very civil" and showed constant "courtesy, calmness and good behaviour," as did the Chinese he encountered. Their good practices, indeed, put not only the Jesuits to shame but even those in Navarrete's own homeland of Spain. "The Pagans and Gentiles," Navarrete wrote, echoing St. Augustine, "are become the teachers of the Christian faithful."[42] Navarrete was fully aware of the comparative dimensions of what he was saying, and spelled out his thoughts in detail for his readers in the opening section of the *Tratados:*

> Here we might discuss whether we must call the Chineses, the Tartars that govern them, the Japoneses and other Nations in those Parts, Barbarians or not. St Thomas says those are properly Barbarians who are "Strangers to human Conversation", and who "are strong in Body, and deficient in Reason, and are neither govern'd by Reason, nor Laws". Whence it follows that the Blacks [Negritos] who live in the Mountains of the Philippine Islands,

the Chichumecos of Mexico, those of the Islands Nicobar, Mada-
gascar, Pulicondor, and the like, the others near the Strait of
Dryan, are Barbarians in the strictest Sense; and that the Chineses, Tartars, Japoneses, and other People of Asia are not so, for
all these latter live politickly and orderly, and are govern'd by
Laws agreeable to Reason.

Even the most civilized people have their own peculiarities,
wrote Navarrete: Japanese slash themselves with their swords,
Chinese cut their hair short and mock those who do not, while
the Spaniards love "to fight, Body to Body, a fierce, mad Bull."
Sexual practice was no different: "Some in Europe thought
simple Fornication no Crime, and others believ'd the same of
Sodomy, in which the Chineses, Japoneses, and others are
included."[43]

Navarrete praised China as "the noblest Part of the Universe
[and] the Seat of that, the most Glorious Empire in all natural
respects, that the Sun ever shines upon."[44] Almost everything
Chinese seems to have met with Friar Navarrete's approbation:
the ingenuity of China's artisans, who "have their contrivances
for everything"; the fact that Chinese schoolchildren had only
eight "play-days" a year and "no vacations at all"; even the benevolent nature of Chinese "piss," which helped Chinese crops to
grow whereas European urine "burns and destroys all plants."[45]
The fact that Chinese men never "hoot" at women unlike the
vulgar crowds of Europe with their "scoffings" and "insolent
and shameless expressions" pleased Navarrete, as did the tasti-
ness of bean curd—especially when lightly fried in sesame seed
oil. He was also pleased by the "good government, quietness and
ease and cleanliness of the Jail," the convenience of chopsticks,
the simple place settings that obviated the need for washing
tablecloths and napkins with soap and lye, the cleanliness of the
ice used in summer drinks, and what Navarrete saw as the
admirable habit of footbinding: "The custom of swaithing
women's Feet is very good for keeping females at home. It were

no small benefit to them and their menfolk if it were also prac-
tised everywhere else too, not only in China."[46]

Sometimes Navarrete seems to tumble into self-parody, and
reads more like a descendant of Pinto than of Pereira and da
Cruz. Thus a seventy-year-old senior Chinese official Navarrete
encounters—"as active as if he had been but 30"—did "eat for his
Breakfast every morning 30 eggs, and a Dogs leg, and drank two
Quartillos of hot wine."[47] And on a few occasions, the horror of
what he has seen is unbearable. Even Navarrete himself seems
shaken by the memory of watching a man dying from being
beaten on his exposed testicles, or of an unwanted baby girl left
to die of suffocation and starvation in her own parents' presence, "her little feet and arms drawn up, her back upon hard
stones in wet and mud," while "she that had pierced my heart
with her cries could make no slightest dent in the bowels of those
tigers."[48] These few negative examples did not deflect Navarrete
from the overall judgment that "It is God's special Providence
that the Chineses don't know what is done in Christendom, for
if they did there would be never a man among them but would
spit in our faces."[49]

In his general discussion of China, Navarrete reintroduced
the economic themes that had been emphasized by Polo and
Pereira in their own ways, but he gave them a curious new twist.
For Navarrete was struck by the possibilities of China's bulk
trade in novelty items, rather than in a small-volume trade in
high-value goods:

> A great deal might be said of the Handy-craft rank of People,
> for in China there are Handicraft Workmen of all sorts that can
> be imagined, and such numbers of them that it is prodigious.
> The Curiosities they make and sell in the Shops amaze all Euro-
> peans. If four large Galeons were sent to the city of Nan King, to
> that of Cu Cheu [Su-chou], to Hang Cheu, or any other like
> them, they might be loaded with a thousand varieties of Curiosi-
> ties and Toys such as all the World would admire, and a great

Profit be made of them, tho sold at reasonable Rates. All things
necessary to furnish a Princely House, may be had ready made in
several parts of any of the aforesaid Citys, without any further
trouble than the buying, and all at low Rates in comparison of
what is sold among us.[50]

Navarrete had also noted that the Chinese were the most art-
ful of copyers, and he raised the disturbing thought that the
Chinese might use these skills to coopt the Western export trade.
"The Chineses are very ingenious at imitation," he wrote, "they
have imitated to perfection whatsoever they have seen brought
out of Europe. In the Province of Canton they have counter-
feited several things so exactly, that they sell them Inland for
Goods brought out from Europe."[51] Though the context of
these remarks was nominally economic, the churchman Navarrete was raising questions concerning the separation of the true
from the false, and genuine creativity from its lesser variants,
that were central to the nature of religious faith. To apply these
questions now to China was to change the dimensions of what
had hitherto been a mutually reinforcing relationship.

CHAPTER 3

The Realist Voyages

JUST OVER A CENTURY SEPARATED THE PUBLICATION OF the accounts of China written by the two Dominican friars Gaspar da Cruz and Domingo Navarrete, and though the two men shared various preoccupations, the level of detailed knowledge had grown prodigiously in that period. The most important sources were Matteo Ricci's lengthy description and analysis of China, along with the numerous letters and annual reports sent from China by Jesuits to the superior of their order, which were speedily published as a means to increase the order's prestige and assure them wider support. There were also a number of Church-sponsored histories of China, of which Juan Mendoza's history of 1587 was an early example. Pinto's work circulated widely, though readers were—correctly—not sure how much to trust his reliability. Marco Polo was still in wide circulation, though he too had now sunk somewhat in the scales of believability. In a revealing passage of his *Tratados*, Navarrete mentioned that at a dinner party he attended in 1665 at which China was under discussion, the question was raised, "Who was most misinform'd concerning the Chinese, Marco Polo the Venetian, or Father Martini?" Martini was a Jesuit in China, author of a just-printed book that had been found to contain many errors—some of which, curiously enough, came from Father Martini's direct use of passages from Polo rather than his own observations. The group's conclusion was that "both of them writ many mere chimera's."[1]

Within a few years of that conversation, information on China began to emerge from a new type of source, the accounts of the official embassies that were—after the collapse of the Ming in 1644—now allowed to visit Peking by the Qing government. Seizing this opportunity, and hoping to exploit those very openings for trade that Navarrete discussed in his own *Tratados*, four embassies appeared in less than a decade: two from the Dutch, in 1668 and 1687, and two from the Portuguese, in 1670 and 1678. These were followed by two embassies sent by the Russians. The papacy also sent two legations early in the eighteenth century, in an attempt to clarify the theological arguments over Chinese ancestral and Confucian ceremonies that had remained unresolved since the time of Matteo Ricci.

These various embassies and legations, though from proudly independent sovereign states in the West, all adhered to the cumbersome Chinese rituals of deference to the emperor—including the nine prostrations of the kowtow, and the use of self-demeaning language—that the Chinese considered an essential part of a tributary system of foreign relations. By ignoring their own recently acquired codes of correct diplomatic contact between sovereign nations, in order to achieve their short-term goals, the Westerners were unwittingly shoring up the Qing court's views of China's superiority.[2]

Despite that unfortunate result, the overall effect of the embassies was to bring so much new information on China into the West that the lines of debate underwent a major shift: they moved away from the confines of the missionaries, and into a fresh domain of realistic reportage, some of it exceedingly frank.

The first full account of a foreign embassy's experiences in Peking was that published by the Dutchman Olfert Dapper after the visit of Van Hoorn in 1667 to the Qing court. It contained good details on the ritual procedures, and also some observant remarks on the young emperor Kangxi.[3] But in fact it was a Portuguese Jesuit, Father Francisco Pimentel, attached to the retinue of the Portuguese embassy of 1670, who should get the credit for being the first to introduce a new note of realism in his report. Pimentel's opening remarks were in no way out of line with his priestly predecessors, as he praised the emperor of China for "the vastness of his territories, the greatness of his cities, the richness of its commerce, the infinite number of its revenues, the teeming world of his court and the magnificence of his palace"—which would make any European ruler "feel very small."[4] But when he discussed such apparently mundane details as the extraordinary difficulty of keeping one's hat on one's head while performing the ritual protestations of the kow-tow, he was starting to puncture both Chinese and Western pre-tensions with the cleansing gift of laughter.[5] And when it came to one of the most central and solemn moments of the rituals of Chinese diplomatic intercourse, the great official banquet, he gave his prose full flight:

> At the first two banquets, they put before me the head of a sheep, with two horns so large that they frightened me. I don't know how they found me, or by what sign they knew me, in order not to mistake me and to present me with these points two days in a row, for I did not sit in the same place. The head was so little cleaned that by its wool I knew that the sheep had been black. One should not be astonished that I refer to such a base matter in such clear words, for I believe it behooves me to oppose the zeal and attention with which some people so exaggerate the civility of the Chinese that they prefer it to our Europe, and want to place it above our heads. . . . I acknowledge in the Chinese much politeness, grandeur, and richness, but in all these things there are intolerable basenesses.[6]

Pimentel applied his barbs also to the vaunted city of Peking, which ever since Polo's day—when it was known as Kambaluc—had been conventionally praised for its geometrically precise layout, its grand scale, and the vibrancy of its commerce. Pimen-tel, however, found other things to notice:

> In summer the heat is excessive, and a greater torment is the dust, of which there is so much and fine that, when we went out on the street, our hair and beards looked like those of millers covered with flour. Bad water; innumerable bugs that get in one's cloth-

ing at night, and while we were there they bit many of us. The flies
are infinite and importunate, and the mosquitoes worse. Everything is very expensive. The streets are not paved, as it is said they
were in the past, for the Tartar ordered the removal of the paving
stones, because of the horses, for in China they don't know what
horseshoes are, and this is the reason why there is so much dust,
and when it rains unbearable mud.

When they were thinking of Peking, Pimentel warned, readers
should beware of false comparisons drawn from their own cultures:

> One who hears of the grandeur of this capital will conceive of
> something like Lisbon, Rome, or Paris, but, so that he will not be
> deceived, I warn him that, if he entered it, he would think he was
> entering one of the poorest villages of Portugal, for the houses
> are all built very low, for they may not exceed the height of the
> wall of the Palace, and so badly made, that the walls for the most
> part are of mud, or plastered wattle, and very few with any bricks
> or any view outside, and all China is like this.[7]

As these words perhaps indicate, the Portuguese embassy
that Pimentel attended was no more successful than the Dutch
had been in gaining the trade protections, lowered tariffs, or
rights of residence in Peking that they had been seeking. But
early in the eighteenth century a Russian embassy from Peter
the Great under Leon Vasilievitch Izmailov had better luck. Two
of the requests that Izmailov brought to China in 1720—for permission to establish a Russian Orthodox church in Peking, and
for an increase in the number of trade caravans allowed into
China—were granted by the now elderly emperor Kangxi. The
emperor also did not entirely dismiss a third Russian request,
for the permanent stationing of a Russian consul in Peking,
though his own bureaucracy put such massive obstructions in
the way that the idea was eventually abandoned.[8]

The Izmailov embassy also had its role to play in the widen-
ing of Western knowledge of China, thanks to the presence in

the ambassador's staff of a young Scottish doctor, John Bell. Restless and high-spirited, Bell had set off for Russia in 1714 after receiving his medical degree from the University of Edinburgh, to try his fortunes in the court of Tsar Peter. Almost immediately, he had been given an assignment to accompany a Russian embassy on an extended journey to Persia; after his return, learning that Izmailov was about to leave for Peking, he applied for the post of attendant physician on that embassy as well, and again was successful.[9] Bell's writings about China marked a decisive shift away from the once-dominant tradition of writing about China from a Catholic standpoint—whether explicit or implicit. Gone now is the fascination with the inner significance of Chinese religious beliefs, or the exact institutional weight of the components of government. In its place we find an informal, probing, humane, and somewhat skeptical view, fully in accord with the prevailing attitudes of the new age of reason.

In describing the court banquet he attended, Father Pimentel had been both judgmental and amusing, but he had not tried to understand the experience at any deeper level. To John Bell, when confronted with the same experience, there was not just something disgusting to be described, there was something to be explained. Bell wrote:

> I cannot but take notice of the uncommon manner the people here have of killing their sheep. They make a slit with a knife between two ribs, through which they put their hand, and squeeze the heart till the creature expire; by this method all the blood remains in the carcass. When the sheep is dead, and hungry people cannot wait till the flesh is regularly dressed, they generally cut out the brisket and rump, wool and all, and broil them on the coals; then scrape off the singed wool, and eat them. This I have found, by experience, to be no disagreeable morsel, even without any kind of sauce.[10]

Since Bell was traveling with a Russian embassy, he had taken the overland route from St. Petersburg to Peking, as opposed to the sea route that brought most Westerners into China either through Canton or Fuzhou. Thus it was that his first view of his destination was "the famous wall, running along the tops of the mountains, towards the northeast. One of our people cried out 'Land,' as if we had been all this while at sea. . . . The appearance of it, running from one high rock to another, with square towers at certain intervals, even at this distance, is most magnificent." The favorable image was reinforced once he saw China at first hand. "Every thing now appeared to us as if we had arrived in another world," wrote Bell:

> Our route now lay along the south side of a rivulet, full of great stones, which had fallen from the rocks in rainy weather. In the cliffs of the rocks you see little scattered cottages, with spots of cultivated ground, much resembling those romantick figures of landskips which are painted on the China-ware and other manufactures of this country. These are accounted fanciful by most Europeans, but are really natural.[11]

In line with the new fashion for meticulous observation, nothing was too trivial for Bell's attention. The details of daily life, the small ingenuities by which people plied their trades and solved their problems, genuinely intrigued him:

> My lodgings, in this village, happened to be at a cook's house; which gave me an opportunity of observing the ingenuity of these people, even on trifling occasions. My landlord being in his shop, I paid him a visit; where I found six kettles, placed in a row on furnaces, having a separate opening under each of them, for receiving the fewel, which consisted of a few small sticks and straw. On his pulling a thong, he blew a pair of bellows, which made all his kettles boil in a very short time. They are indeed very thin, and made of cast iron, being extremely smooth both within and without. The scarcity of fewel, near such a populous city, prompts people to contrive the easiest methods of dressing their victuals, and keeping themselves warm during the winter, which is severe for two months.[12]

In terms of tight description, a cook deserved the same consideration as an emperor:

> The Emperor sat cross-legged on his throne. He was dressed in a short loose coat of sable, having the fur outward, lined with lamb-skin; under which he wore a long tunic of yellow silk, interwoven with figures of golden dragons with five claws; which device no person is allowed to bear except the imperial family. On his head was a little round cap, faced with black fox-skin; on the top of which I observed a large beautiful pearl in the shape of a pear, which, together with a tassel of red-silk tied below the pearl, was all the ornament I saw about this mighty monarch. The throne also was very simple, being made of wood; but of neat workmanship. It is raised five easy steps from the floor, is open towards the company; but has a large japanned screen on each side to defend it from the wind.[13]

Izmailov had maneuvered strenuously to avoid having to kowtow to Kangxi, but had been compelled to yield by the intransigence of the Chinese bureaucrats in charge of rituals. Bell described the event without rancor, and without embellishment:

> The master of ceremonies brought back the ambassador; and then ordered all the company to kneel, and make obeisance nine times to the Emperor. At every third time we stood up, and kneeled again. Great pains were taken to avoid this piece of homage, but without success. The master of ceremonies stood by, and delivered his orders in the Tartar language, by pronouncing the words *morgu* and *boss;* the first meaning to bow, and the other to stand; two words which I cannot soon forget.[14]

The experience in no way diminished Bell's ability to admire the ruler Kangxi, of whom he wrote, "I cannot omit taking notice of the good nature and affability of this ancient monarch, on all occasions. Though he was near the seventieth year of his age, and sixtieth of his reign, he still retained a sound judgment, and senses intire; and, to me, seemed more sprightly than many of the Princes his sons."[15] Bell's ability not to be humiliated by his experience is matched by the curious new element he introduces into his description, one that is almost intimate and is certainly self-confident. For "good nature and affability" were not the words that earlier visitors to China would have normally applied to emperors; yet coming from Bell's mouth, they sound perfectly natural.

Shortly after the court audience and the ritual prostrations, Bell was invited—along with other members of the embassy staff—to a banquet presented by the emperor's ninth son. The feasting was accompanied by a series of plays, acrobatic performances, and tableaux with dramatic sound and lighting effects. Once again, Bell attended closely, and it is to his careful eye that we owe our first realization that the Chinese were themselves becoming interested in representing Westerners, that the watchers were now being watched. Near the end of the party, the prince had arranged for

> several comical farces, which, to me, seemed very diverting, though in a language I did not understand. The last character that appeared on the stage, was a European gentleman, completely dressed, having all his cloaths dedawbed with gold and silver lace. He pulled off his hat, and made a profound reverence to all that passed him. I shall leave it to any one to imagine, what an aukward figure a Chinese must make in this ridiculous habit.[16]

The Chinese, of course, had conveyed all too effectively how ridiculous the foreigners themselves appeared, and the prince, realizing that his guests "might take offence," dismissed the actor with a wave of his hand. With this sole exception of a joke at his expense, Bell was fascinated by both Chinese clowning and the amazing dexterity of their acrobats and jugglers: "I am fully persuaded, that, in tricks and feats of dexterity, few nations can equal, and none excel, the Chinese."[17]

While watching the actors in the prince's home, Bell had wondered to himself whether the attractive actresses were women, or boys and youths playing women's roles. He did not discover which they were. But in the streets, Bell, whose own first extended tour of duty had been in Muslim Persia, had remarked at once that the women of Peking were unself-consciously "unveiled" as they watched the embassy's progress.[18] As he got to explore Peking more thoroughly, he wrote that "In most of the shops I found both men, and women, unveiled. They were extremely complaisant, and gave me a dish of tea in every shop."[19]

In one episode discussed by Bell, this complaisant attitude led to a potential complication. After a lavish dinner in Peking with a hospitable "Chinese friend" who "put about his cups very freely," says Bell, "at last, he took me by the hand, and desired I would let the ambassador return and remain with him; and he would give me my choice of which of his wives or daughters I liked best. I could not but return my friend hearty thanks for his obliging offer; which, however, I thought it not proper to accept."[20] Bell was, in fact, unmarried (many years later, he would marry a Russian woman with whom he returned home to Scotland). Nevertheless, despite declining this particular offer, Bell was attracted to Chinese women, whom he found to "have many good qualities besides their beauty. They are very cleanly, and modest in their dress. Their eyes are black, and so little, that, when they laugh, you can scarce see them. Their hair is black as jet, and neatly tied up, in a knot, on the crown of the head, adorned with artificial flowers of their own making; which are very becoming. The better sort, who are seldom exposed to the air, have good complexions."[21]

Like many others before him, Bell noted that "as soon as a girl comes into the world, they bind her tender feet with tight bandages, which are renewed as occasion requires, to prevent their growing," but his reflections on footbinding gave that much-commented-on practice a new twist: "The women of all ranks stay pretty much at home. The smallness of their feet, which renders them unable to walk to any considerable distance, makes their confinement less disagreeable."[22]

If the women of the "better sort"—including perhaps the one allegedly offered to him as a bride—were pale of complexion, that left, for Bell, the world of the other women, "those who are inclined to the olive." Such women "take care to add a touch of white and red paint, which they apply very nicely."[23] Though Bell is at pains to point out that at this point he is speaking only from hearsay, he certainly seems to have a detailed knowledge of the netherworld of Peking:

> It may easily be imagined, that, in so populous a city, there must be many idle persons of both sexes; though, I believe, fewer than in most other cities of the world, even in those of much less extent than that of Pekin. In order to prevent all disorderly practices, as much as possible, the government have thought fit to permit, or connive at, certain places, in the suburbs, for the reception and entertainment of prostitutes, who are maintained by the landlords of the houses in which they dwell; but not allowed to straggle abroad. I have been informed, that these ladies of pleasure have all separate apartments; with the price of each lady, describing, at the same time, her beauties and qualities, written, over the door of her apartment, in fair legible characters; which price is paid directly by the gallant; by which means, these affairs are conducted without noise in the houses, or disturbances in the neighbourhood.[24]

Bell made no comment at all on the phenomenon of male prostitution in Peking, which had been discussed by some sixteenth-century observers like Matteo Ricci. It may well be that after their conquest of China in 1644, the somewhat more puritan Manchus had effectively banned such activities, or at least driven them off the streets. But a more subtle change of attitude might also have taken place in Western thinking, one in which Chinese men as a whole were beginning to be marked by "idleness and effeminacy," to cite the phrase Bell himself used.[25]

Bell's overall judgments on the Chinese were positive, and seemed to promise good prospects for the future of trade and diplomacy. In business, the Chinese were "honest, and observe the strictest honour and justice in their dealings." If it were true that "not a few of them are much addicted to knavery, and well skilled in the arts of cheating," that would be because they had "found many Europeans as great proficients in that art as themselves." A basic knowledge of Chinese, due to the monosyllabic nature of the language, seemed to Bell "easily acquired" as far as ordinary conversation were concerned, though he admitted it would require "much labour, and considerable abilities, to acquire the character of a learned man in China." Trade opportunities were excellent in tea, silk, damask, porcelain, and cotton, since the Chinese "deserve great praise for their patience in finishing, completely, every thing they undertake." Militarily, China should be left alone: "I know but one nation who could attempt the conquest of China, with any probability of success," concluded Bell, "and that is Russia." Despite its isolation, China could perhaps be attacked by sea, from the southeast, thought Bell, but why should any European monarch "think it proper to disturb his own repose, and that of such a powerful people, inclined to peace with all their neighbors; and satisfied, as they seem, with their dominions?"[26]

Given the general aura of Bell's comments, it is perhaps not as surprising to us as it seemed to Bell's Scottish neighbors that years after his return to his native land, he could be seen riding over the rain-drenched moors wrapped in the Chinese robes he had acquired while on his embassy. The publication of his memoirs had long been anticipated. And when they were published in final form in 1763, their success was assured by the long and distinguished list of eminent figures who had subscribed for the book in advance.

Commodore George Anson, who visited China in 1743, left the country with a view of its government and people diametrically different from Bell's in almost every conceivable way.

Admittedly, the context of Anson's visit was also immeasurably different from Bell's. Bell was an ambitious Scotsman from modest background, in the retinue of a grandee at China's capital, and free from all personal responsibility for whatever might happen on the wider stage. Whereas Anson was from a powerful and well-connected family—one of his uncles was Lord Chief Justice of England—responsible for the lives of the crew of his ships and the safekeeping of the Spanish galleon he had just captured, his share of which would total half a million pounds sterling. Anson, furthermore, was an unwelcome visitor to China's shores, whereas Bell's presence was authorized.

George Anson personified the newly assertive side of an expansionist Great Britain, self-confident, bellicose, swift to condemn the weak, impatient with delays. His current command aboard HMS *Centurion,* a man-of-war of sixty guns, had not begun auspiciously. He had lost three out of his six ships rounding the Cape of Good Hope, and of the complement of 961 men with whom he set sail from England, only 335 remained alive when he sought shelter in Canton's harbor, upriver from Hong Kong and Macao. The capture by Anson, on June 20, 1743, of the annual Manila galleon homeward bound from Acapulco had been a brilliant feat of daring and seamanship, but had left the *Centurion* badly battered and totally unseaworthy. Thus, when he approached Canton with his prize in tow on July 14, he seems to have thought his troubles were over. Instead, they had just begun.

It was Anson's opinion that a man-of-war, by definition not engaged in trade, should pay no dues and be furnished all necessary pilotage and supplies, and that he himself should be received at a meeting with the viceroy. Informed by the Chinese officials that no ships were exempt from dues, that his passage would be prevented, and that the viceroy was too busy (and the weather too hot) to receive him, he forced his way upriver regardless, guided by a Chinese pilot whom he had threatened to hang at the yardarm unless he did his bidding. Not surprisingly, the Chinese authorities did nothing to help Anson, and stalled at his every request. By late September, with no supplies yet furnished, no interview with the viceroy yet granted, one of his officers robbed and beaten when strolling on shore, and a spare topmast stolen from the deck of the *Centurion,* the commodore's temper was at a snapping point.[27]

Anson's account is full of the continued travails that followed from this impasse, and clearly reflects his personal conviction that only a mixture of fortitude and intransigence on his part allowed him to achieve his goals and get his ships once more underway. But it was the conclusions he reached about the Chinese that had more impact than the particulars, especially his abandonment of those elements of comparative thinking about European and Chinese cultures that had appeared a staple of Western accounts from Pereira through to Navarrete. Though he claimed to be aware that "it may perhaps be impossible for an *European,* ignorant of the customs and manners" of China, to analyze Chinese motivations, that sense of limitation did not impede his own judgments:

> Indeed, thus much may undoubtedly be asserted, that in artifice, falshood, and an attachment to all kinds of lucre, many of the Chinese are difficult to be paralleled by any other people; but then the combination of these talents, and the manner in which they are applied in particular emergencies, are often beyond the reach of a Foreigner's penetration: So that though it may be safely concluded, that the Chinese had some interest in thus amusing the Commodore, yet it may not be easy to assign the individual views by which they were influenced.[28]

To reinforce these general statements, Anson listed a whole roster of dishonest Chinese procurement practices that he encountered, from cramming ducks and chickens with stones and gravel to bloating hogs with water, and drew the conclusion that "these instances may serve as a specimen of the manners of this celebrated nation, which is often recommended to the rest of the world as a pattern of all kinds of laudable qualities." As if to underline this distance, Anson described how the linguist he had hired to negotiate on his behalf—who also turned out to be willing to cheat both the Chinese and his temporary employer—admitted that there was nothing the Chinese could do about their dishonesty, it was simply innate. And to sharpen the distance further, Anson records the Chinese linguist's answer as it was delivered in the new hybrid mixture of English words with Chinese sentence structure (later known as "pidgin" English) that was becoming common wherever Western traders congregated in China. Hitherto, the convention followed by all Westerners writing about China had been to convey the words of their Chinese respondents in fluent and colloquial English, echoing the natural flow of the original Chinese speech. When Anson recorded his "linguist's" words to him as being "Chinese man very great rogue truly, but have fashion, no can help," he might indeed have been recording accurately, but he had also turned a representational corner.[29]

Anson was brief and dismissive about the Chinese military defenses that he observed around Canton, and noted sardonically that even the "armor" the Chinese wore with such display was not of steel but made from "a particular kind of glittering paper." As a result of the "cowardice of the inhabitants, and the want of proper military regulations," China was doomed "not only to the attempts of any potent State but to the ravages of every petty Invader."[30] But it was the nature of their industry and their lack of basic creative skills to which he paid more attention:

> That the *Chinese* are a very ingenious and industrious people, is sufficiently evinced, from the great number of curious manufactures which are established amongst them, and which are eagerly sought for by the most distant nations; but though skill in the handicraft arts seems to be the most important qualification of this people, yet their talents therein are but of a second rate kind; for they are much outdone by the Japanese in those

manufactures, which are common to both countries; and they are in numerous instances incapable of rivalling the mechanic dexterity of the *Europeans*. Indeed, their principal excellency seems to be imitation; and they accordingly labour under the poverty of genius, which constantly attends all servile imitators.[31]

In fine arts, Anson found the Chinese no better: "it may perhaps be asserted with great truth, that these defects in their arts are entirely owing to the peculiar turn of the people, amongst whom nothing great or spirited is to be met with."[32] And even China's vaunted written language, far from being at the high level to which it had been elevated, was the fruit of "obstinacy and absurdity." As Anson explained, while all the rest of the world had been busy learning sensible alphabets, the Chinese had shown their typical stubbornness:

> the *Chinese* alone, have hitherto neglected to avail themselves of that almost divine invention, and have continued to adhere to the rude and inartificial method of representing words by arbitrary marks; a method, which necessarily renders the number of their characters too great for human memory to manage, makes writing to be an art that requires prodigious application, and in which no man can be otherwise than partially skilled; whilst all reading, and understanding of what is written, is attended with infinite obscurity and confusion; for the connexion between these marks, and the words they represent, cannot be retained in books, but must be delivered down from age to age by oral tradition.

Instead of reflecting on China's literary and cultural traditions, Anson made it clear he was basing this opinion on the way that his arguments with the Qing officials had been handled by the various linguists and intermediaries at his disposal:

> How uncertain this must prove in such a complicated subject, is sufficiently obvious to those who have attended to the variation which all verbal relations undergo, when they are transmitted through three or four hands only. Hence it is easy to conclude, that the history and inventions of past ages, recorded by these

perplexed symbols, must frequently prove unintelligible; and consequently the learning and boasted antiquity of the Nation must, in numerous instances, be extremely problematical.[33]

No one before Anson had advanced an argument quite as odd as this one: that the Chinese language was itself a giant form of confidence game, that had ended up bewildering the Chinese themselves as much as those they had sought to hoodwink. Such an argument would be the merest historical curiosity, were it not for the fact that Anson's account of his voyage was immensely popular after it was published in 1748, circulated widely in Europe, and influenced several influential thinkers, amongst them both Montesquieu and Herder.

One of those who had Anson's book in his own personal library was Lord George Macartney, who traveled to China on behalf of the East India Company and King George III in the year 1793. Macartney's intellectual credentials were impeccable, and if anyone could be expected to make a sensible synthesis of the contrasting views of Bell and Anson it was he: educated at Trinity College in Dublin, a friend to Edmund Burke, Voltaire, Samuel Johnson, and Joshua Reynolds, he had served on delicate diplomatic missions to the St. Petersburg of Catherine the Great, been governor of Grenada—where he experienced the humiliation of being captured by the French in 1779—and served as governor of Madras from 1780 to 1786. As well as reading Anson, and perhaps Bell (though his name does not appear on the original subscription list), Macartney had read the detailed four-volume history of China written by the scholarly French Jesuit Jean du Halde, published in 1735, and the philosophical reflections on China by Leibniz and Voltaire. Catherine the Great, at whose court he had served, was also a fanatical admirer of Chinese culture, and had herself created an entire imitation Chinese township which Macartney visited.[34]

After this exposure to a wide range of information and views, both negative and positive, Macartney was disposed to favor

China, as he showed in remarks jotted in his journal shortly after reaching the country in early August 1793. Standing on shipboard and watching the way the Chinese unloaded the presents and baggage that he had brought with him, he found that "the Chinese sailors are very strong and work well, singing and roaring all the while, but very orderly and well regulated, intelligent and ingenious in contrivance and resource, each of them seeming to understand and exercise his proper share of the business and labour going forward." Chinese women also seemed healthy and energetic:

> they tripped along with such agility as induced us to imagine their feet had not been crippled in the usual manner of the Chinese. It is said, indeed, that this practice, especially among the lower sort, is now less frequent in the northern provinces than in the others. These women are much weather-beaten, but not ill-featured, and wear their hair, which is universally black and coarse, neatly braided, and fastened on the top of their heads with a bodkin. The children are very numerous and almost stark naked.

Drawing these various impressions together, Macartney noted:

> I was so much struck with their appearance that I could scarce refrain from crying out with Shakespeare's Miranda in the "Tempest":
>
>
>
> Oh, wonder!
> How many goodly creatures are there here!
> How beauteous mankind is! Oh, brave new world
> That has such people in it![35]
>
>

Macartney had brought a fine array of presents from George III for the Qing emperor Qianlong—including telescopes, a planetarium, celestial and terrestrial globes, a great lens, barometers, lustres, clocks, airguns, fine swords, Derbyshire vases and porcelain figures, and a carriage, and he sought important concessions from the emperor: an end to the limitation of trade to Canton and the small group of licensed Chinese merchants there, the opening of several new ports to British residence, long-range tariff agreements, and right to station a permanent British embassy in Peking.[36] These goals were not dissimilar to those sought by the Izmailov embassy that John Bell accompanied seventy-three years before, but Macartney was the representative of the British Crown, and saw himself as the upholder of Britain's national pride. Thus in some important ways, particularly in his refusal to submit to what he considered humiliations, of which the kowtow was a prime example, he was closer to Anson than to Izmailov.

Suitably reflecting his own priorities, much of Macartney's account is occupied with a meticulous explanation of the elaborate ballet he danced with the Chinese and Manchu officials over the kowtow question until an acceptable arrangement could be reached. It was on August 15, 1793, according to Macartney, that the Qing officials first raised this issue, with a combination of "art, address, and insinuation" that he "could not avoid admiring":

> They began by turning the conversation upon the different modes of dress that prevailed among different nations, and, after pretending to examine ours particularly, seemed to prefer their own, on account of its being loose and free from ligatures, and of its not impeding or obstructing the genuflexions and prostrations which were, they said, customary to be made by all persons whenever the Emperor appeared in public. They therefore apprehended much inconvenience to us from our knee-buckles and garters, and hinted to us that it would be better to disencumber ourselves of them before we should go to Court.[37]

But the tussle quickly grew wearisome to Macartney and his staff, despite the kowtow demonstrations offered them by some "wonderfully supple" senior mandarins.[38] The issue was only settled after weeks of wrangling, when Macartney agreed to go down on one knee and bow his head at the same time—the officials wanted him to go down on both knees—and both parties decided the added detail of kissing the emperor's hand could be dispensed with.[39]

When Macartney was finally received by the eighty-three-year-old emperor Qianlong, offered up his presents, and made his formal requests for changes in the conditions of trade, the responses were polite but vague. This did not initially discourage Macartney, who wrote of the emperor in his journal: "His manner is dignified, but affable, and condescending, and his reception of us has been very gracious and satisfactory. He is a very fine old gentleman, still healthy and vigorous, not having the appearance of a man of more than sixty."[40] "Affable" had also been the word chosen by Bell to describe Qianlong's grandfather, Kangxi. Macartney seems to have been drawn in part to this word by the emperor's treatment of the ambassador's twelve-year-old pageboy George Staunton, who had spent his long months on shipboard learning Chinese language with a tutor, and was able to make a short speech in Chinese to the emperor at the formal audience. Impressed, Qianlong had taken an embroidered pouch from his own belt and handed it to the boy.

Despite this and scores of other flattering remarks about China that can be found scattered through the journal, the dominant feelings Macartney had acquired by the end of his visit were wariness and a kind of exhaustion that teetered on the edge of raw dislike. He had discovered that his genuine curiosity about Chinese life and social customs, far from being appreciated, had led the Chinese to suspect him of "dangerous designs."[41] He was conscious at all times of being "very narrowly watched, and all our customs, habits and proceedings, even of the most trivial nature, observed with an inquisitiveness and jealousy which surpassed all that we had read of in the history of China."[42] When Macartney showed a senior Qing minister that he had a genuine knowledge of certain aspects of Chinese history, he found that the minister "rather wonders at our curiosity than esteems us for our knowledge," and that the

Chinese declared the British search for knowledge to be "impertinent towards them and useless to ourselves."[43] In a phrase that later became celebrated, Macartney likened Qing China to "an old crazy first rate man-of-war," which had long overwhelmed her neighbors "by her bulk and appearance," but was doomed under inept leaders to be "dashed to pieces on the shore."[44]

But Macartney remained fair-minded enough to realize that in the few places where there was contact between the races, as in Canton, England was doing everything wrong in trying to heal the breaches:

> We keep aloof from them as much as possible. We wear a dress as different from theirs as can be fashioned. We are quite ignorant of their language (which, I suppose, cannot be a very difficult one, for little George Staunton has long since learned to speak it and write it with great readiness, and from that circumstance has been of infinite use to us on many occasions). We therefore almost entirely depend on the good faith and good-nature of the few Chinese whom we employ, and by whom we can be but imperfectly understood in the broken gibberish we talk to them. I fancy that Pan-ke-qua or Mahomet Soulem would attempt doing business on the Royal Exchange to very little purpose if they appeared there in long petticoat clothes, with bonnets and turbans, and could speak nothing but Chinese or Arabic.[45]

Thinking back over his meetings with Qianlong and his ministers, and over the long negotiations and colossal expense of the embassy that in the end had achieved nothing at all, Macartney added this comment on China's long-lived emperor: "Thus, then, have I seen 'King Solomon in all his glory.' I use this expression, as the scene recalled perfectly to my memory a puppet show of that name which I recollect to have seen in my childhood, and which made so strong an impression on my mind that I then thought it a true representation of the highest pitch of human greatness and felicity."[46]

By linking the imposing image of Solomon to the belittling one of a puppet, Macartney suggested an air of charade about this meeting of the West and the East, parallel to that observed by Bell. Elsewhere in his account, Macartney gave a fuller example. In the early days of his mission, he recalled, he was shown a broadsheet printed in the northern city of Tianjin that gave a *Chinese* version of the list of presents that he was bringing with him to the emperor. This bizarre listing had circulated in the city after his vessel had docked there. The British presents were said to include:

> Several dwarfs or little men not twelve inches high, but in form and intellect as perfect as grenadiers; an elephant not larger than a cat, and a horse the size of a mouse; a singing-bird as big as a hen, that feeds upon charcoal, and devours usually fifty pounds per day; and, lastly, an enchanted pillow, on which whoever lays his head immediately falls asleep, and if he dreams of any distant place, such as Canton, Formosa, or Europe, is instantly transported thither without the fatigue of travelling.[47]

From such an account we can see that an abyss had opened up between China and the visitors that made a genuine meeting of the minds problematic. In this new context, though the great issues of international trade and diplomacy remained, their deeper meanings were being reduced, apparently by mutual agreement, to the inconsequential nonsense of cloud-cuckoo-land.

CHAPTER 4

Deliberate Fictions

IN PUSHING HIS DIPLOMATIC MISSION TO THE VERY edges of fantasy, Lord Macartney was refracting one of the central aspects of the eighteenth-century European view of China. The cult of "Chinoiserie," a dreamy parody of aspects of Chinese art and culture as expressed through the decorative Rococo style, had found its way into many aspects of Western life: wallpaper and willow-pattern plates, mantelpieces, wooden cornices, lattice and furniture, pavilions and pagodas (like the one at Kew Gardens in London), and above all in the art of the garden. The rigorous geometricality of the classical designs that one could see in palaces such as Versailles, or even in Christopher Wren's designs for the naval hospital at Greenwich, with their rightangles and precise linear vistas, had yielded to what were seen as Chinese perceptions of meandering informality, where intimacy grew from the enclosed space and the sense of surprise. Macartney sized up this aspect well in a passage inserted into his journal near the end of his China visit:

> A Chinese gardener is the painter of nature, and though totally ignorant of perspective as a science, produces the happiest effects by the management of or rather pencilling of distances, if I may use the expression, by relieving or keeping down the features of the scene, by contrasting trees of a bright, with those of a dusky foliage, by bringing them forward, or throwing them back according to their bulk and their figure, and by introducing buildings of different dimensions, either heightened by strong colouring, or softened by simplicity and omissions of ornament.[1]

What Macartney was recording here was in fact the end of a cycle, as modes and tastes changed, and the revolutionary sentiments that helped to fuel the French and the American revolutions led, rather surprisingly, either to a revival of classical concepts, or to the total abandonment of the classical and the Chinese in the new cult of the Gothic.

One of the earlier seventeenth-century witnesses to the initial cult for things Chinese was the British diarist John Evelyn. It was on June 22, 1664, Evelyn noted, that "one Tomson, a Jesuite" showed him a collection of "rarities, sent from the Jesuites of Japan and China," that were on the way to Paris, but were temporarily in London since they had been transported on a British East India Company vessel. In all his life he had never seen the like, observed Evelyn, as he laid out his lustrous list:

> The chiefe things were very large Rhinoceros's hornes, Glorious Vests, wrought & embrodered on cloth of Gold, but with such lively colours, as for splendor & vividnesse we have nothing in Europe approches: A Girdill studdied with achats, & balast rubies of greate value & size, also knives of so keene edge as one could not touch them, nor was the mettal of our Couler but more pale & livid: *Fanns* like those our Ladys use, but much larger, & with long handles curiously carved, & filled with Chineze Characters.

Some of these objects, Evelyn wrote, particularly the sheening yellow parchment papers, could have come straight out of Francis Bacon's utopian novel, *New Atlantis*. But the elegance of this one group of curios was balanced by the other, which contained mysteries and more than a touch of menace:

> prints of Landskips, of their Idols, Saints, Pagoods, of most ougly Serpentine, monstrous & hideous shapes to which they paie devotion: Pictures of Men, & Countries, rarely painted on a sort of gumm'd *Calico* transparant as glasse: also Flowers, Trees, Beasts, birds &c: excellently wrought in a kind of sleve-silk very naturall. Divers Drougs that our Drougists & physitians could make noth-

ing of: Especialy, one which the Jesuite called Lac *Tygridis,* it look'd
like a fungus, but was weighty like metall: yet was a Concretion
or coagulation of some other matter: Also severall booke MSS.[2]

Other returned Western travelers, at least one of whom liked to
dress in "Eastern habite" to receive his visitors, regaled Evelyn
with tales of China or showed him their newly acquired "Land-
skips of the Skreenes, representing the manner of Living, &
Country of the Chinezes."[3]

The kind of products listed by Evelyn, the affectation of Englishmen wearing Eastern robes, the intrusion of Chinese land-
scapes into sturdy British country houses, were exactly the kind
of thing that exasperated other Englishmen, especially those
who regarded themselves as guardians of the traditional middle-class virtues of simplicity and thrift that were under threat
in the loose moral atmosphere of the Stuart court.

In the course of the seventeenth century, China had been
slowly inserting itself into British life. Shakespeare had ignored
it, apart from two brief references to the "Cataians"—both of
which were dismissive.[4] Francis Godwin, in his social satire *The
Man in the Moone* of 1628, arranged for his courageous space
traveler to return to earth in China, where he was well cared for,
finding the "mandarins" to be kind, curious, and intelligent.
Milton, writing at midcentury, was still in something of a mud-
dle about China's exact location and past history. In *Paradise
Lost,* for instance, Adam gazes out from the highest hill of Paradise and sees:

> The seat
> Of mightiest empire, from the destined walls
> Of Cambalu, seat of Cathaian Can . . .
> To Paquin, of Sinean Kings.[5]

Since "Cambalu" was clearly merely a variant spelling of the
Kambalik lovingly described by Marco Polo, and "Paquin" a
variant of Peking, if the lines were taken literally, Adam would
simply have been letting his gaze wander across the same city.

John Evelyn had drawn up his list of Chinese curios in 1664; only five years later, the British scholar John Webb had completed his life's greatest labor, in which he endeavored to prove that Chinese was the first basic world language. Shortly after that, in 1685, the first recorded Chinese person to set foot on English soil—Shen Fu-tsung—was brought to the Catholic court of King James II by French Jesuits who were escorting their young convert to France. Shen was made much of: the king ordered his portrait painted by Sir Godfrey Kneller, the court painter, and he was an honored visitor to Oxford University, where he conferred and corresponded—using Latin as their common language—with the English savant Thomas Hyde.[6]

By the end of the seventeenth century the cult of things Chinese had spread to the extent that in an operatic performance of Shakespeare's *A Midsummer Night's Dream*, the stage directions ran as follows:

> While the stage is darkened, a single Entry is danced. Then a symphony is play'd; after the scene is suddenly illuminated, and discovers a transparent prospect of a Chinese garden, the Architecture, the Trees, the Plants, the Fruit, the Birds, the Beasts, quite different from what we have in this part of the World. It is terminated by an Arch, through which is seen other arches with close Arbors, and a row of trees to the end of the view. Over it is a hanging garden, which rises by several ascents to the top of the House; it is bounded on either side with pleasant Bowers, various Trees, and numbers of Strange Birds flying in the air, on the top of the Platform is a Fountain, throwing up water, which falls into a large basin.

In this enchanted setting, Chinese lovers sing duets to the stately harmonies of Purcell, six monkeys emerge from the wood to execute a dance, and the stage directions rise to a lyrical climax:

> Six pedestals of China-work rise from under the Stage, they support six large vases of Porcelain, in which are six China Orange Trees . . . the pedestals move towards the front of the Stage, and the grand dance begins of twenty four persons. Hymen then

appears on the scene to reconcile Oberon and Titania and then unite the Chinese lovers, a final quintet is sung and the opera brought to its close.[7]

Such extravagance of sentiment, with its cult of uncritical pro-Chineseness, found its first major antagonist in the novelist and pamphleteer Daniel Defoe. Born in 1660 to a London butcher, raised as a religious nonconformist, Defoe had made and lost his first fortune by the age of thirty, due to his own impetuosity and the chicanery of his business partners. Thereafter he earned a precarious and erratic living from his writing, achieving fame for his satirical portrait of "The True-Born Englishman" and the vigor of his claims that Britain should expand into the territories of the now-fading Spanish empire. His virulent political pamphlets were constantly getting him into trouble, and he was condemned to spells in the pillory and in Newgate Prison.

In his first references to China, which appeared in his fantasy "The Consolidator" or "World in the Moon" of 1705, Defoe had seemed to accept some of the prevalent favorable cult of the Chinese, calling them "ancient, wise, polite and most ingenious people," whose technical arts could be used to make up for the "monstrous ignorance and deficiencies of European Science."[8] But by 1719, with his publication of part 2 of *Robinson Crusoe*, Defoe had swung decisively to a hostile, openly contemptuous stance, either out of personal moral conviction or because he was now convinced such a stance would most appeal to his British middle-class readers.

Defoe rushed this second part of *Robinson Crusoe* through to the press in August 1719, to build on the prodigious success of the first volume, which had appeared in April. This extreme haste forced him to a concision and sharpness that he might have perhaps not attained had he felt he had more time. Thus, though the picaresque nature of Crusoe's landing in China has some echoes of Pinto's narrator's fortuitous arrival in China one hundred and fifty years before, Defoe does not ramble and reflect in as leisurely a fashion as Pinto, or spell out his reflections with any attempt at comparativist subtlety.

As Crusoe and his little party leave the south coast of China, where they have been accidentally forced to land, his first impression of China appears to be favorable:

> First, we went ten days' journey to see the city of Nanking, a city well worth seeing indeed; they say it has a million of people in it, which, however, I do not believe. It is regularly built, the streets all exactly straight, and cross one another in direct lines, which gives the figure of it great advantage.[9]

But this impression is promptly banished by a fully developed diatribe in which virtually every previously described positive aspect of China is negated, and every negative aspect of China is emphasized for Defoe's British readers:

> But when I come to compare the miserable people of these countries with ours, their fabrics, their manner of living, their government, their religion, their wealth, and their glory, as some call it, I must confess I do not so much as think it is worth naming, or worth my while to write of, or any that shall come after me to read....
>
> ... [W]hat are their buildings to the palaces and royal buildings of Europe? What is their trade to the universal commerce of England, Holland, France, and Spain? What are their cities to ours for wealth, strength, gaiety of apparel, rich furniture, and an infinite variety? What are their ports, supplied with a few junks and barks, to our navigation, our merchant fleets, our large and powerful navies?

It had been a commonplace in Western accounts ever since the time of Pereira to reflect on China's comparative military vulnerabilities. But Defoe outdid all his predecessors in the virulence of his views, and the range of details he adduced to support his arguments:

[A]s I have said of their ships, so may be said of their armies and troops; all the forces of their empire, though they were to bring two millions of men into the field together, would be able to do nothing but ruin the country, and starve themselves. If they were to besiege a strong town in Flanders, or to fight a disciplined army, one line of German cuirassiers, or of French cavalry, would overthrow all the horse of China; a million of their foot could not stand before one embattled body of our infantry, posted so as not to be surrounded, though they were to be not one to twenty in number; nay, I do not boast if I say that 30,000 German or English foot, and 10,000 French horse, would fairly beat all the forces of China. . . . They have firearms, 'tis true, but they are awkward, clumsy, and uncertain in going off; they have powder, but it is of no strength; they have neither discipline in the field, exercise to their arms, skill to attack, or temper to retreat.

The result, to Defoe, was an absolute dissonance between reality and perception so that, as he put it in Crusoe's words, "I must confess it seemed strange to me when I came home and heard our people say such fine things of the power, riches, glory, magnificence, and trade of the Chinese, because I saw and knew that they were a contemptible herd or crowd of ignorant, sordid slaves, subjected to a government qualified only to rule such a people."[10]

In passages of equal brevity and violence, Defoe's Crusoe dismissed China's so-called scholars as being "grossly, absurdly ignorant," and even the farmers' "husbandry" as being "imperfect and impotent" when compared to Europe. Here Defoe's satirical anger leads him not only to belittle Chinese rural industriousness but to overpraise the prosperity of British farming, a view he was to reverse with his *Tour Thro' the Whole Island of Great Britain* of 1724, written just two years after his equally compelling *Journal of the Plague Year.*

What seems to have particularly angered Defoe was his conviction that the Chinese were unshakable in their sense of superiority, and appeared incapable of understanding the fact that the West had surpassed them in many realms, not just in warfare. What he found "to the last degree ridiculous" was "their contempt of all the world but themselves."[11]

Perhaps the most concentrated expression of Defoe's anger can be found in his pen portrait of a member of China's ruling elite, whom Crusoe encountered on the road:

> [T]he state he rode in was a perfect Don Qixotism, being a mixture of pomp and poverty. The habit of this greasy Don was very proper for a scaramouch or merry-andrew, being a dirty calico, with all the tawdry and trapping of a fool's coat, such as hanging sleeves, tassels, and cuts and slashes almost on every side; it covered a taffeta vest, as greasy as a butcher, and which testified that his honour must needs be a most exquisite sloven. His horse was a poor, lean, starved, hobbling creature, such as in England might sell for about thirty or forty shillings; and he had two slaves followed him on foot, to drive the poor creature along.[12]

In Defoe's view, the Chinese man's eating habits and family life were as shameless as his modes of travel. Once again, Defoe underlined this by drawing a caricature that contradicted the values of British middle-class life in every detail:

> When we came by the country seat of this great man, we saw him in a little place before his door, eating his repast. . . . He sat under a tree, something like the palmetto-tree, which effectually shaded him over the head, and on the south side; but under the tree also was placed a large umbrella, which made that part look well enough. He sat lolling back in a great elbow-chair, being a heavy, corpulent man, and his meat being brought him by two women slaves. He had two more, whose office, I think, few gentlemen in Europe would accept of their service in, viz., one fed the squire with a spoon, and the other held the dish with one hand, and scraped off what he let fall upon his worship's beard and taffeta vest; while the great fat brute thought it below him to employ his own hands in any of those familiar offices which kings and monarchs would rather do than be troubled with the clumsy fingers of their servants.[13]

Though Defoe may have had various sources for this passage, or perhaps created it from whole cloth, it is hard not to see in it the shades of John Mandeville's fourteenth-century depiction of life as lived by a wealthy man under the Great Khan:

> This lord leads a marvellous life. For he has fifty maidens who serve him each day at his meals and his bed, and do what he wills. And when he sits at his meals, they bring him meat, always five dishes at once; and while bringing them they sing a lovely song. They cut up his meat in front of him and put it in his mouth as if he were a child; for he cuts none and touches none with his hands, which he keeps always on the table in front of him. . . . When he has eaten enough of the first course, they bring five other dishes before him, singing all the while. And so they do to the end of the meal. And in this way this lord leads his life, following the ancient custom of his ancestors, which custom his successors will follow in the same way. And thus they make their belly their god, so that they achieve no worthiness or bravery, living only in pleasure and delight of the flesh, like a pig in a sty.[14]

Every previous traveler, from Polo through Pinto to Ricci and Navarrete, had been at pains to delineate their routes through China, and as far as possible—in whatever mixture of romanized forms—to give some approximation to the Chinese names of the towns and provinces through which they passed. As if wearying of the task, however, Defoe's Crusoe failed to do so, giving a disarming and convincing explanation for his failure to record all the specifications that his readers might have wished. Falling off his horse, he explains, while crossing a small river by a ford, Crusoe was soaked to the skin: "I mention it because it spoiled my pocket-book, wherein I had set down the names of several people and places which I had occasion to remember, and which, not taking due care of, the leaves rotted, and the words were never after to be read, to my great loss as to the names of some places I touched at in this voyage."[15] There is, however, no loss to the narration in this loss of the pocket-book, because Crusoe has wearied of the joke and is impatient to leave China forever.

So with a few final passages of belittlement the caustic commentary comes to a close. The vaunted "porcelain buildings" of China, for instance, are "singularities" and nothing more, and the Great Wall may be "a very great work," but it is a "needless" one, running through terrain "where the rocks are impassible, and the precipices such as no enemy could possibly enter, or indeed climb up, or where, if they did, no wall could hinder them." "Needless" though the wall might be, Crusoe reflects, any British engineers could "batter it down in ten days" if they so chose, so that "there should be no sign of it left."[16]

In using the negative example of China to praise his native Britain—as Anson was to do twenty years later—Defoe was being deliberately polemical in his fiction, and in fact reversing the general direction of a trend that had usually gone the other way. The dominant trend had been to use positive features ascribed to Asia in order to highlight weaknesses lying at the heart of Western society. In the very first of all fictions that dealt in part with China, John Mandeville had also used the examples of exotic and distant societies to criticize the weakness of Christian values in his own mid-fourteenth-century world. Mandeville used the device of having his narrator engage in "a private talk" with a friendly Sultan who "spoke French wonderfully well" as a way to set the scene for his own profoundly iconoclastic religious views:

> And when they had all gone out, he asked me how Christians governed themselves in our countries. And I said, "Lord, well enough—thanks be to God." And he answered and said, "Truly, no. It is not so. For your priests do not serve God properly by righteous living, as they should do. For they ought to give less learned men an example of how to live well, and they do the very opposite, giving examples of all manner of wickedness."

The result of such negative examples was that the allegedly Christian society was filled with people who ate, drank, and fought "like beasts without reason":

"Christian men commonly deceive one another, and swear the most important oaths falsely. And they are, moreover, so swollen with pride and vainglory that they never know how to dress themselves—sometimes they wear short fashions of clothing, sometimes long, sometimes cut full, sometimes figure-fitting. You ought to be simple, meek and truthful, and ready to give charity and alms, as Christ was, in whom you say you believe. But it is quite otherwise. For Christians are so proud, so envious, such great gluttons, so lecherous, and moreover so full of covetousness, that for a little silver they will sell their daughters, their sisters, even their own wives to men who want to lie with them."[17]

Fictional devices such as Mandeville's became commonplace in sixteenth-century utopian fictions, from Thomas More's *Utopia,* which gave the genre its name, through to the *New Atlantis* of Francis Bacon (mentioned by John Evelyn) and Thomas Campanella's *City of the Sun.* At almost the same time that Defoe was rushing his negative version of China into print, in France, Montesquieu was writing *The Persian Letters,* published in 1721 to an instant success. Here Montesquieu stayed within the Mandeville tradition, by using two Middle Eastern visitors to comment frankly on the absurdities of French society, while also presenting as many of the realities of their own as Montesquieu could cull from his own voracious reading.[18] Within a few years, other French writers began to use China rather than the Middle East as the lever for their cultural critiques, and in Britain the struggling freelance writer Oliver Goldsmith decided to mine the same lode.

Oliver Goldsmith was an unlikely recruit to the pro-China forces. One might, rather, have thought he would have shared Defoe's aversion to the country, its people, its goods, and its philosophy. Goldsmith was born in Ireland in 1728 to the family of a clergyman, and managed to enroll in Trinity College, Dublin. But after a series of misadventures, including missing the vessel on which he had proposed traveling out to the American colonies to try his fortune, and gambling away all the money that well-inclined relatives had given him so that he could study law, Goldsmith joined the exodus of Irishmen from his native land. He traveled first to Scotland, where he studied medicine in Edinburgh, and then projected a trip to the Continent which fell through when he was arrested in Newcastle—apparently due to some misunderstanding—and managed again to miss the boat. By the late 1750s, having failed his medical exams, he was settled in London, earning a precarious living as an essayist and reviewer.[19]

As a professional writer, Goldsmith always kept a keen eye on the literary marketplace, and by August 1758—according to the evidence of a letter to his friend Bryanton—he resolved to write a work on Chinese philosophy. The cheerful yet sardonic letter is a good indication of Goldsmith's state of mind at this time: he was, he told Bryanton, tied to fortune's wheel "like an whore in a whirligig," though one day his innate "genius" would be recognized by all those who currently scoffed at his writings. Goldsmith could make up Chinese as well as anyone—"you see I use Chinese names to show my erudition"—but could equally well "make our Chinese talk like an Englishman." To amuse his friend, Goldsmith constructed the future encomium to his genius as it might be penned after his death by some Chinese man of letters:

> Oliver Goldsmith flourished in the eighteenth and nineteenth centuries. He lived to be an hundred and three years old . . . * age may justly be styled the sun of . . . and the Confucius of Europe . . . learned world, were anonymous, and have probably been lost, because united with those of others. The first avowed piece the world has of his is entitled an Essay on the Present State of Taste and Literature in Europe,—a work well worth its weight in diamonds. In this he profoundly explains what learning is, and what learning is not. In this he proves that blockheads are not men of wit, and yet that men of wit are actually blockheads.

* The ellipses are due to a damaged MS; they are not in Goldsmith's original.

Returning to his own persona, Goldsmith concluded the letter to Bryanton,

> Let me, then, stop my fancy to take a view of my future self; and, as the boys say, light down to see myself on horseback. Well, now I am down, where the devil *is I?* Oh Gods! Gods! here in a garret, writing for bread, and expecting to be dunned for a milk-score![20]

Less than a year later, Goldsmith was acting on his idea that he might be able to use China to pay the rent on his garret. In 1759, Goldsmith wrote his first essay on things Chinese in the form of a book review of a new play based on the Chinese drama *The Orphan of Chao.* The original play dated from the Mongol Yuan dynasty, in the days of the Polo familiy's Chinese adventures, though there is no evidence Goldsmith knew that. The English version was by Arthur Murphy, and prefaced with a poem by William Whitehead that—perhaps somewhat tongue-in-cheek—hymned the Chinese cult in Britain:

> Enough of Greece and Rome. The exhausted store
> Of either nation now can charm no more;
> Ev'n adventitious helps in vain we try,
> Our triumphs languish in the public eye;
>
> On eagle wings the poet of to-night
> Soars for fresh virtues to the source of light,
> To China's eastern realms: and boldly bears
> Confucius' morals to Britannia's ears.
> Accept th' imported boon; as echoing Greece
> Receiv'd from wand'ring chiefs her golden fleece;
> Nor only richer by the spoils become,
> But praise th' advent'rous youth, who brings them home.[21]

Despite this encomium, Goldsmith's review was cautious; he was not yet able to subscribe entirely to the abandonment of classical standards that some authors seemed to be advocating. Indeed he felt that, to the degree that Murphy had moved away from the "calm insipidity" of the original—a translation of which had appeared in the French Jesuit Jean du Halde's popular 1735 four-volume history of China—so was his work the better for it.[22]

Apparently now committed to a China course, Goldsmith began to write a series of "Chinese Letters," drawing the names of his Chinese protagonists from various other novels and pamphlets on China that he had seen.[23] The letters, which cumulatively formed an epistolary novel, dealt with the experiences of a Chinese scholar in London and the adventures of the scholar's son and true love in Asia. Published twice a week in the newspaper *The Public Ledger,* between 1760 and 1761, totaling ninety-eight in all, they became immensely popular. Supplementing these ninety-eight with some other miscellaneous essays, Goldsmith published the whole in 1762 as a two-volume novel. This was even more successful than the individual pieces had been, and made Goldsmith's literary reputation; he proceeded, over the next few years, to cement his renown as a major writer with the novel *The Vicar of Wakefield* (1766), the lengthy descriptive poem *The Deserted Village* (1770), and the play *She Stoops to Conquer* (1771). In 1772, based on these successes, he was even commissioned to write a history of China: but he farmed the job out to an acquaintance who produced a volume so full of errors that all the sheets of the proof had to be destroyed. Goldsmith died in 1774.[24]

Goldsmith's preface to *The Citizen of the World* is brief, but gives an admirable summary of his own skeptical view of the current mid-eighteenth-century attitudes to Chinoiserie. Posing as the "editor" of a Chinese scholar's letters, Goldsmith comments that that gentleman's learning and gravity would count on a scale of one to twenty as a resounding nine hundred and ninety-nine, and proceeds from that to an amusing comment on the kind of comparativist approach on which he was embarking:

> The truth is, the Chinese and we are pretty much alike. Different degrees of refinement, and not of distance, mark the distinctions among mankind. Savages of the most opposite climates have all but one character of improvidence and rapacity; and

tutored nations, however separate, make use of the very same methods to procure refined enjoyment.

The distinctions of polite nations are few; but such as are peculiar to the Chinese appear in every page of the following correspondence; the metaphors and allusions are all drawn from the East: their formality our Author carefully preserves; many of their favourite tenets in morals are illustrated. The Chinese are always concise, so is he; simple, so is he: the Chinese are grave and sententious, so is he. But in one particular, the resemblance is peculiarly striking: the Chinese are often dull, and so is he.[25]

Goldsmith proceeds to recount a dream he had while considering this vexed question of Chinese morality.

I imagined the Thames was frozen over, and I stood by its side. Several booths were erected upon the ice and I was told by one of the spectators, that Fashion Fair was going to begin. He added, that every author who would carry his works there, might probably find a very good reception. I was resolved, however, to observe the humours of the place in safety from the shore, sensible that ice was at best precarious, and having been always a little cowardly in my sleep.[26]

From this safe vantage, Goldsmith watched as cart after cart, many of them carrying enormous loads of "the furniture, frippery, and fire-works of China," ventured out across the ice without mishap, and soon sold all their wares. Emboldened, Goldsmith decided to edge on to the ice with a small wheelbarrow load of "Chinese morality." But the ice immediately cracked under even this light load of moral thought, and "wheel-barrow and all went to the bottom," as Goldsmith awoke from his dream in a terror.

There are, scattered through Goldsmith's re-creation of the Chinese scholar Lien Chi's letters, countless moments of shrewd social comment on British fashion, dishonesty, absurdity, and politics, and the book fully deserved its popularity. But the two letters that perhaps come closest to catching the elements of moral ambiguity to which Goldsmith was pointing so broadly in his preface are numbers 11 and 33. Letter 11 in the sequence that composes this picaresque epistolary novel is from Lien Chi to his friend Fum Hoam in Peking, and concerns the intersection of luxury, virtue, and happiness. It would have been a truism to Defoe that luxury corrupts, and certainly luxury in its more frivolous aspects was what Goldsmith seemed to mock in his own preface. But as Lien Chi asks his friend, "am not I better pleased in enjoyment, than in the sullen satisfaction of thinking that I can live without enjoyment?" Lien Chi continues:

> Examine the history of any country remarkable for opulence and wisdom, you will find they would never have been wise, had they not been first luxurious; you will find poets, philosophers, and even patriots, marching in luxury's train. The reason is obvious; we then only are curious after knowledge, when we find it connected with sensual happiness. The senses ever point out the way, and reflection comments upon the discovery. Inform a native of the desert of Kobi of the exact measure of the parallax of the moon, he finds no satisfaction at all in the information; he wonders how any could take such pains, and lay out such treasures in order to solve so useless a difficulty; but connect it with his happiness, by shewing that it improves navigation, that by such an investigation he may have a warmer coat, a better gun, or a finer knife, and he is instantly in raptures at so great an improvement. In short, we only desire to know what we desire to possess; and whatever we may talk against it, luxury adds the spur to curiosity, and gives us a desire of becoming more wise.[27]

Shared luxury encourages political unity; shared self-interest fosters good citizenship; high levels of consumption encourage full employment. Thus, in words that Lien Chi ascribes to Confucius, "we should enjoy as many of the luxuries of life as are consistent with our own safety"[28]

In Letter 33, however, Lien Chi is sharply reminded that what he might believe to be his own valid personal reflections about life are only acceptable to the English if they coincide precisely with English stereotypes. In this remarkable chapter, which opens with the apostrophe, "I am disgusted, O Fum Hoam! even to sickness disgusted," Lien Chi rails against the English, who "pretend to instruct me in the ceremonies of China." Lien Chi has been invited to dinner by a British "lady of distinction," but from the first moment of his entry into her house, everything goes awry. The lady expresses surprise that Lien Chi brought neither opium nor tobacco for his own solace; she gives him a cushion on the floor when all other guests were offered chairs; rejects his request for roast beef, serving him instead birds' nests and bear's claws; and protests, along with the rest of the company, when Lien Chi uses knife and fork instead of chopsticks. One could argue, here, that the hostess and her guests were simply against imposing their own cultural conventions on their honored guest out of politeness, but Goldsmith's Lien Chi rejects this interpretation. For the British not only tell Lien Chi how to sit and what to eat; a visiting savant also lectures him, ignorantly and at length, about China's cities, mountains, fauna, facial typology, language, and use of metaphor until, as Lien Chi pertinently observes, "he almost reasoned me out of my country."[29]

Lien Chi's response is rhetorically and philosophically powerful, as he points out the pretentious savant's ignorance of Chinese history, language, and culture, and his inability to comprehend that Chinese might be fully able to understand all the niceties of European philosophy and social life. Lien Chi concludes:

> The unaffectd of every country nearly resemble each other, and a page of our Confucius and your Tillotson have scarce any material difference. Paltry affectation, strained allusions, and disgusting finery, are easily attained by those who chuse to wear them; they are but too frequently the badges of ignorance, or of stupidity, whenever it would endeavour to please.[30]

But as he draws his discourse to a close, Lien Chi notices he has lost the company's attention: some are whispering or studying their fans, others yawning or already sleeping. Quietly, the Chinese guest of honor lets himself out. No one checks his going, and he is not asked again.

At the very end of Goldsmith's long novel, Lien Chi's son Hingpo, who has traveled with numerous adventures across Asia and the Middle East, reaches London and a joyful reunion with his father. The son is also, with the high coincidence common in eighteenth-century novels, reunited with his true love Zelis, who had been abducted long before by pirates and lodged in a Persian harem. The young lady, it turns out, is the niece of Lien Chi's closest English friend, and so, amid general rejoicing, the young couple celebrate an Anglo-Chinese wedding, and are settled into a "small estate in the country."[31]

Shortly after the publication of Goldsmith's novel, John Bell published the long-delayed account of his embassy to China. Goldsmith was not among the original subscribers, but the aristocratic aesthete Horace Walpole was. Walpole, in 1757, had been the author of a political squib in the form of a Chinese man's letter "To his friend Lien Chi at Pekin," and it was surely from this title that Goldsmith took the name of his protagonist Lien Chi. In a renewed turn of the circle, it may well have been the combination of Goldsmith's novel and Bell's memoirs that stimulated Walpole to return to a China image in one of his well-known *Hieroglyphic Tales*.[32]

Written to amuse a young female friend of his family, and published in 1785 in a small edition, Walpole's "Mi Li, A Chinese Fairy Tale" took the extravagances of Chinoiserie to their outermost limits, only to let them dissolve in their own absurdity. The story involves a Chinese prince named Mi Li (did Walpole expect readers to pronounce this "My Lie"?), who sets off round the world in search of his future wife, guided only by a mysterious prophecy uttered by his fairy godmother that he must find and marry "a princess whose name was the same with her father's dominions."[33] After various misadventures that take him from Peking to Canton, and Canton to Ireland in search of the elusive bride who will match this prophecy, Mi Li at last reaches England. There he hires a post-chaise to take him to Oxford, so that he can consult the wise men at the Bodleian Library, but the chaise breaks apart on the Henley road, and Mi Li enters the vast estate of a local landowner in search of help. This gives Walpole the chance to place Mi Li in an aristocratic setting, and at the same time to mock the excesses of the Chinoiserie gardens that were still much in vogue.

In Walpole's tale, Mi Li is taken in tow by a courteous gardener, who leads his Chinese visitor through deep woods, a menagerie, gloomy thickets, across rolling meadows offering magnificent vistas, and into artificial ruins. As they emerge once more into a sloping valley, Mi Li sees in the distance an attractive young woman in the company of her friends. He breaks into a run, and rushes toward her, shouting as he runs, "Who she? Who she?" This question receives the quiet answer, "Why, she is Miss Caroline Campbell, daughter of Lord William Campbell, his majesty's late governor of Carolina," and the ecstatic Mi Li realizes his quest is over and the prophecy is fulfilled. So, writes Walpole with becoming brevity, the young lady "became princess of China."[34] Like Goldsmith's Hingpo, Mi Li had found his happiness. And once again the reality of transcultural dissonance was shrouded, for a playful moment or two, in the softer light of romantic oneness.

Given the close intersections of the world of politics with the world of letters in the eighteenth century, we need not be surprised at the various overlapping impulses we have been observing. There was more here than just a shared ending to a fantastic story linking two creative writers. Defoe's Englishness had many similarities to Anson's. Many of Goldsmith's attitudes can be found in Bell, and vice versa. The two aristocrats at the end of the Age of Reason, Macartney and Walpole, both had the ability to combine their polemical arguments with a lighter-hearted view of the human condition. China, once again, had offered a focus for the most diverse tendencies, and the widest spectrum of contradictory impulses.

CHAPTER 5

Matters of Enlightenment

WHEN BELL NOTED THAT CONVERSATIONAL CHINESE was presumably easy because it was monosyllabic, Anson that the Chinese language was an elaborate pretense, and Macartney that Western children seemed to learn it without trouble, they were joining a discussion that had been going on for several hundred years. Polo had stated that he knew several languages, but never specified whether Chinese was or was not one of them. Mandeville sidestepped, by saying the potentates he talked to knew French. Pinto, with his usual casualness, managed in the space of a couple of pages both to state that he knew Chinese and that "he did not know how to communicate with them." Crusoe makes it clear that he relied on a Portuguese interpreter who "understood the language of that country and spoke good French and a little English."[1] Since the late sixteenth century a growing number of Western savants had been wrestling with Chinese grammar and written characters, trying to fathom the basic structures and the principles behind them. The result was an enormous accumulation of often erratic scholarship, and a group of alleged "keys" to the language, the most vaunted of which—never made available to others by its proud inventor— promised to teach the enlightened the Chinese language within a matter of weeks.[2]

In seeking to understand Chinese by uncovering its "keys," these scholars were reflecting the passionate belief in the existence of systems that became a central part of seventeenth-century Western intellectual life after the writings of René Descartes and Francis Bacon. From the idea that there was one central key to Chinese language, it was a logical step to try to find a key to the whole society of China, to see if there was some single system that explained the country, just as knowledge of other systems explained the physical universe. If China was to be understood, that system had to be explored, analyzed, and explained in precise terms.

It is not surprising that the first great generator of this approach should be Gottfried Wilhelm Leibniz, for his extraordinary brilliance in mathematics and his deep interest in religion and logic predisposed him to the quest. Leibniz was born in 1646, just before the nightmare of the Thirty Years War came to an end. He spent several years studying in Paris in the 1670s, before returning to a busy bureaucratic career in Hanover, which led finally to his appointment as court librarian. With this appointment he finally had time to pursue his many intellectual interests, among which were included the fields of binary arithmetic and geometry. At the same time, Leibniz came across Jesuit descriptions of the nature of the hexagrams that composed the venerable text (allegedly edited by Confucius) of *The Book of Changes,* which the Chinese used in divination and as a source of philosophical wisdom. The sixty-four hexagrams were arranged in a mathematically precise sequence, with each line containing one long or two short strokes.[3]

Intrigued by this similarity to the organizational principles of binary arithmetic, Leibniz began a protracted and erudite correspondence with several Jesuits living in China, and with others who had returned to Europe. He also explored the writings of many of the scholars who had been searching for the key to Chinese, as well as John Webb, who sought to prove that Chinese was perhaps the first or "primitive" language from which all others later sprang. And he read with close attention the writings and arguments of those Jesuits who had been pursuing lines of inquiry first suggested by Matteo Ricci in the attempt to trace elements of monotheism back into China's earliest classical texts.[4]

Leibniz had made it a central goal of his life to try to heal the vicious theological and political strife that wracked the society of his time. He believed in both the plurality and the essential harmony of matter, and in the power of pure reason to grasp ultimate truth if only it were guided by his organic philosophy. By such inquiry one would come to see that the indefinite number of substances or "monads" all in fact dance to a "pre-established harmony" that is the central manifestation of God.[5] China, to Leibniz, could play a significant part in this quest for understanding, since he felt his own ideas on the reconciliation of extremes were compatible with Chinese thought; thus, in seeking a middle ground of compatibility with Catholicism and Protestantism, Chinese beliefs could be fruitfully invoked. It was such a synthesis alone that could lead to an era of international peace and harmony. When Leibniz heard in 1692 that Emperor Kangxi had issued an edict of toleration for the Catholics, his sense of China's centrality seemed confirmed: for Kangxi's action contrasted so obviously with that of Louis XIV's 1685 Revocation of the Edict of Nantes, which for almost a century had protected the rights of Protestants in France.

The most extensive of Leibniz's writings on China appeared in 1699, in the preface to a volume he compiled called *Novissima Sinica,* or *Latest News from China.* In this volume, Leibniz presented the arguments he found most germane to the peaceful solution of the rites controversy in China, and appealed at the same time for the opening of a regular land route across Russia to China, and for the dispatch of Protestant missionaries to work along with the Catholics there. In a later letter to Peter the Great, Leibniz expressly warned the ruler how important it was to keep communications with China open and to keep information flowing in both directions, so as to prevent the Chinese from just taking a few elements from Europe that suited their purpose, only subsequently to close the door.[6]

Leibniz argued in his preface that in the closing years of the seventeenth century, "human cultivation and refinement" had come to be concentrated "in the two extremes of our continent," namely, Europe and China. This might indicate the hope of Divine Providence that these "most cultivated and distant peoples [would] stretch out their arms to each other," so that "those in between may gradually be brought to a better way of life." As things now stood, China and the West were posed "in almost equal combat, so that now they win, now we." Drawing up a complete balance sheet, Leibniz felt, was not particularly profitable, since in "the useful arts and in practical experience with natural objects we are, all things considered, about equal to them," and accordingly, "each people has knowledge which it could with profit communicate to the other."[7] But Leibniz then proceeded to attempt the kind of precise balance he had seemed to shy away from:

> In profundity of knowledge and in the theoretical disciplines we are their superiors. For besides logic and metaphysics, and the knowledge of things incorporeal, which we justly claim as peculiarly our province, we excel by far in the understanding of concepts which are abstracted by the mind from the material, i.e., in things mathematical, as is in truth demonstrated when Chinese astronomy comes into competition with our own. The Chinese are thus seen to be ignorant of that great light of the mind, the art of demonstration, and they have remained content with a sort of empirical geometry, which our artisans universally possess. They also yield to us in military science, not so much out of ignorance as by deliberation. For they despise everything which creates or nourishes ferocity in men, and almost in emulation of the higher teachings of Christ (and not, as some wrongly suggest, because of anxiety), they are averse to war. They would be wise indeed if they were alone in the world. But as things are, it comes back to this, that even the good must cultivate the arts of war, so that the evil may not gain power over everything. In these matters, then, we are superior.[8]

The Chinese, however, Leibniz believed, were far ahead in what he called "the precepts of civil life."

... [C]ertainly they surpass us (though it is almost shameful to confess this) in practical philosophy, that is, in the precepts of ethics and politics adapted to the present life and use of mortals. Indeed, it is difficult to describe how beautifully all the laws of the Chinese, in contrast to those of other peoples, are directed to the achievement of public tranquility and the establishment of social order, so that men shall be disrupted in their relations as little as possible.[9]

Chinese religious toleration, as evidenced since 1692, was proof of this discipline and morality, perfectly manifested in the person of China's current ruler Kangxi, "a prince of almost unparalleled merit." Leibniz was also fascinated by the news he had just received in a letter from China, that Kangxi's son and heir-apparent, continuing his father's openness and flexibility, "had acquired some knowledge of European languages." The logical corollary of these developments was that there should be a trade-off to the current Western obsession with sending droves of missionaries to China. If the West believed that was all that they should do, then, Leibniz feared, "we may soon become inferior to the Chinese in all branches of knowledge."[10]

What the West had to do was open itself to China, in an attempt to absorb from there those elements that would most strengthen Western society. Among these was the Chinese "practical philosophy" of everyday life, that might help redeem his own society, which Leibniz saw as slipping into "ever deeper corruption." Another was the intuitive moral sense of the Chinese, as expressed through Confucian and other values, that Leibniz felt constituted a "natural religion." Western Christianity seemed to be failing in the crucial task of organizing the people for moral life. It seemed to him, wrote Leibniz, "that we need missionaries from the Chinese."[11]

This dream was not to be, and the scattering of Chinese who managed to reach Europe at the end of the seventeenth and early in the eighteenth centuries were all Catholic converts, so they were unlikely to bring the kinds of insights about their own value system to Europe that Leibniz had hoped for.[12] In his later writings on China, Leibniz lost this view of a grander scheme, though he did explore more carefully what he termed "the civil cult of Confucius." He invoked this in support of those Jesuits in the rites controversy who argued that Confucianism was an ethical rather than a religious system of belief, and hence did not conflict with basic churchly doctrine. He acknowledged that Navarrete was probably correct in saying that "many Chinese inform all this pomp with superstition," but Leibniz felt that the rites themselves were "innocuous," and the superstitious elements were not the dominant ones. Matteo Ricci had surely been on the right path, even if he had made some errors in his interpretations—in this he had been like the earlier Church fathers in their attempts to interpret Plato in a Christian frame-work. "If we ever impute to Confucius doctrines that are not his," wrote Leibniz, "certainly no pious deception would be more innocent, since danger to those mistaken and offense to those who teach is absent."[13] Leibniz even held out the suggestion that someone like Ricci could in some cases understand the early Chinese texts better than the Chinese scholars themselves, for "how often strangers have better insight into the histories and monuments of a nation than their own citizens!"[14]

In his writings on China after the year 1708, Leibniz once more somewhat shifted his ground. He now paid more heed to the idea that the West might have philosophical skills to offer the Chinese, especially in terms of interpreting their own texts for them: "Among the Chinese, I believe, neither history nor criticism nor philosophy are sufficiently developed. No one at all has yet emerged who has produced a literary history of the Chinese and who has attributed the true works, meanings and sense to each author. I also fear that the ancient texts suffer interpolations."[15] He no longer suggested that the Chinese scholars he had once wished sent to Europe should be in charge of interpreting Western classical texts to the Westerners.

In his closing work on China, written in the year of his death,

1716, Leibniz roamed with great thoroughness across the whole sphere of what he called "the Natural Theology of the Chinese." Here, contrasting the newness of European civilization to the age of China, Leibniz concluded that it would be "highly foolish and presumptuous on our part, having newly arrived compared with them, and scarcely out of barbarism, to want to condemn such an ancient doctrine simply because it does not appear to agree at first glance with our ordinary scholastic notions."[16] And he proceeded to offer a spirited defense of the Chinese moral position:

> What we call the light of reason in man, they call command-ment and law of Heaven. What we call the inner satisfaction of obeying justice and our fear of acting contrary to it, all this is called by the Chinese (and by us as well) inspirations sent by the Xangti (that is, by the true God). To offend Heaven is to act against reason, to ask pardon of Heaven is to reform oneself and to make a sincere return in word and deed in the submission one owes to this very law of reason. For me I find all this quite excel-lent and quite in accord with *natural theology*. Far from finding any distorted understanding here, I believe that it is only by strained interpretations and by interpolations that one could find anything to criticize on this point. It is pure Christianity, insofar as it renews the natural law inscribed in our hearts—except for what revelation and grace add to it to improve our nature.[17]

In commenting on the moral excellence of the Chinese, Leib-niz had at one point mentioned a problem. While it was true that China's discipline, obedience, and such values as filial piety were indeed highly developed, some people might feel that these Chinese behavioral patterns "smack of servitude."[18] Leib-niz rejected this idea on the ground that Westerners holding such a negative view were "not enough accustomed to act by rea-son and rule." Yet he had hit a nerve, of the kind that was to be exploited to the full by Defoe with his talk of Chinese "slavish-ness." And in the writings of Montesquieu, this minor gloss as

Leibniz had seen it was transformed into a major component of a universal system.

It is impossible to guess what the effect might have been on European culture if Leibniz's recommended Chinese teachers had arrived in the early eighteenth century to proclaim their cultural values to all who would listen. But certainly the case of Montesquieu in the year 1713 suggests that the impact would have been ambiguous and might perhaps have been used in unexpected ways. Montesquieu was at that time a young man of twenty-four, broadening his mind and doing some legal work in Paris, when he heard that there was a Chinese man of some education living in Paris, by the name of Hoange. Through intermediaries, Montesquieu arranged a meeting. Hoange— brought to Europe from China by a French Catholic missionary who hoped he would enter the Church—had decided against a religious vocation, and instead found a job cataloguing Chinese books and working on a Chinese-French dictionary for the court. Montesquieu's notes from the talks he held with Hoange—he just says there were several conversations, not how many— enable us to gauge at least how one Chinese man responded to the kinds of questions that a French aristocrat with a lively mind chose to ask.[19]

The first questions Montesquieu posed were about the nature of Chinese religion. Hoange replied that there were three main sects: Confucianism, Taoism, and Buddhism. Confucius did not hold that the soul was immortal, but that a kind of vapor or spirit suffused our bodies and slowly dissipated at death. For this reason, the elite always chose execution by strangulation, rather than by beheading, which would split their spirit in twain. Chinese scholars did sacrifice to their ancestors, believing that the vapor from the sacrifice was joyfully commingled with the former vapor of the spirit on such occasions. They were atheist or Spinozist in doctrine, regarding heaven as the soul of the world. As to the enforcement of social custom, women were kept totally secluded, even from most of their in-laws, while punishments were savage, even against those officials whose duty it was to remind the emperor of any faults he had committed. Details of ordinary life were so enshrouded by geomantic practice that misunderstandings and even struggles were a constant occurrence—so much so, wrote Montesquieu, that he doubted "if the Chinese could ever be fully understood." Dress was now a matter of personal choice, no longer dictated by sumptuary laws. Families held their property in common, and shared the guilt and punishment for crimes committed by family members, the result being remarkable family durability and strength.[20]

Montesquieu and Hoange spent a great deal of time discussing the nature of the Chinese language. Grammatically it was simple, and despite a few very unusual sounds—one, for example, *qu,* was similar to the sound that French "carriage-drivers used to check their horses"—posed no particular problems. One especial difficulty was in the number of characters, over eighty thousand in total, though with eighteen to twenty thousand one could get by, and a European could probably learn to read pretty fluently in three years.

Montesquieu suspected that the origins of this writing system might lie in some secret confraternity of long ago, like the "cabalists" of his own time, who rejected the simpler system of hieroglyphics for those more abstract forms. Hoange explained, correctly in terms of the language reforms widely spread by Emperor Kangxi, that there were 214 radicals that singly or in combination—up to a maximum of around 33 separate strokes— formed the basic components of most Chinese characters. With a dictionary writer's precision, he gave Montesquieu a number of examples of character composition, and recited the Lord's Prayer and sang a popular song to Montesquieu to demonstrate tonal differences. Hoange and Montesquieu also discussed the problems of writing interesting novels about a Chinese world where "there is no contact between men and women . . . and it takes extraordinary contrivances for the girl to get a glimpse of her swain, and then another four or five years for them to get a chance to speak to each other."[21]

In argument and discourse, the Chinese appeared muted and

well-mannered, but in actual fact, "someone who has higher status than another can beat the other person without that person daring to defend himself." Montesquieu and Hoange moved logically from such social or legal distinctions to discuss the civil service and military exams of China and their respective hierarchies, before considering the nature of the state itself. It had not been unchanging, Hoange explained. Long ago, before the Christian era, there had been as many as three rulers at once, for the country was often fragmented, and there were even periods of republican government. Now, the second Tartar conquest had "completely disfigured if not abolished the Chinese government," "the most sacred laws of the state had been violated," and the Chinese people "were still groaning under their tyranny." The emperors were now more powerful than they had ever been, and the country remained isolated and secure behind its Great Wall and its desolate border regions and deserts. Clearly, though, the Chinese government had atrophied before the Tartar conquest, for never had such a huge country been so swiftly conquered as China was in 1644. Montesquieu added that he pursued this question of the nature of the Chinese government further with Hoange, and came to this conclusion: "The ruler's authority there is completely unlimited, he combines ecclesiastical power with secular power, for the Emperor is the head of the school of literati. Thus the goods and the lives of his subjects are always at the sovereign's disposition, exposed to all the caprices and untamed whims of a tyrant."[22]

Their conversations concluded by probing a wide range of other topics: the severity of the justice system, the castration of eunuchs, the selection of concubines, the nature of the Manchu military organization, the limitations of Chinese scientific discoveries, the absurdity of the ritual gestures and conventions with which the Chinese interlarded their conversations, and the length and the sophistication of the Chinese written historical record. One final grace note, Hoange told Montesquieu, was that the Manchus had somewhat loosened the tyranny previously exerted over women. Progress would be even swifter if the Manchus were allowed to intermarry with Chinese, but that was still forbidden.[23] Hoange himself had recently married a French woman, and the Catholic Montesquieu was shortly to marry a Protestant, so each may have been reflecting on such comparative freedoms.

It was to take Montesquieu many years to digest all these ideas, for he was still a young man when he talked to Hoange and conceived the outline of his great work, *The Spirit of the Laws,* even though it was not completed until 1748. In the meantime he had written *The Persian Letters* (1721) and a history of *The Roman Greatness and Decline* (1734), as well as traveling extensively in England, marrying, caring for his estates, and reading voraciously on all aspects of human political and legal history. Montesquieu's goal was to isolate empirically certain specific principles of laws, rather than relying on general theories of natural law or universal principle, and certainly Hoange's comments must have helped him on his way.

In *The Spirit of the Laws,* Montesquieu divided governments into three main blocks—Monarchies, Despotisms, and Republics—which were directed, respectively, by the principles of honor, fear, and small-scale government linked to principles of virtue. The monarchy and its principles of honor led to rigorous hierarchies of institutions; despotisms and their principle of fear led to a lone ruler, a slave to his passions; and the republic with its small scale and its virtues led to growth of equality among citizens. In subsidiary portions of the argument, Montesquieu reflected on the balance of power within certain societies such as the British monarchy that arose from the separation of the legislative, the judicial, and the executive branches of government. He analyzed the effect of different forces on typologies of government, such as climate, temperament, family structure, commerce, religion, and history. And he discussed the relationship between three forces that were often confused: *mores,* which regulated internal conduct and could not be imposed from above or without; manners, designed to regulate external conduct; and laws designed to regulate specific personal actions.[24]

Montesquieu's numerous comments on China were scattered throughout his lengthy and carefully orchestrated work, but cumulatively they added up to an indictment of China that showed how far he had moved away from the more favorable assessments of the Jesuits on which he had initially drawn, and nearer to the harsher critiques found in Defoe's fiction—which he may have read—and Anson's account, which he definitely had. Many of these facets flowed together in his concluding chapter 21 to Book 8, "On the corruption of principles of the three governments," which Montesquieu headed "On the Chinese Empire." Montesquieu first addressed the question of whether the example of China contradicted his wider theories: "Our missionaries speak of the vast empire of China as of an admirable government, in whose principle intermingle fear, honor, and virtue. I would therefore have made an empty distinction in establishing the principles of the three governments." But he rejected the missionaries' interpretation on the grounds that the realities of Chinese society demonstrated an absence of the idea of honor that was central to other monarchies: "I do not know how one can speak of honor among peoples who can be made to do nothing without beatings." Similarly, the virtue that informed republican government was equally lacking, for "our men of commerce, far from giving us an idea of the same kind of virtue of which our missionaries speak, can rather be consulted about the banditry of the mandarins. I also call to witness the great man, Lord Anson." The missionaries in their letters, by detailing the murderous politics that accompanied the naming of an heir-apparent in China, gave further force to such arguments, he felt. It looked to him as if "the missionaries were deceived by an appearance of order," not its reality.[25]

Montesquieu was willing to admit that China had special

characteristics that explained its current form, so that almost ironically: "Particular and perhaps unique circumstances may make it so that the Chinese government is not as corrupt as it should be. In this country causes drawn mostly from the physical aspect, climate, have been able to force the moral causes and, in a way, to perform prodigies." China's favorable climate had led to the growth of a huge population, since "women there have such great fertility that nothing like it is seen elsewhere on earth. The cruellest tyranny cannot check the progress of propagation." Yet the vast numbers led to frequent famines, and the famines in turn led to a rise in banditry. Though most bandits were wiped out, an occasional group would survive, grow stronger, march on the capital, and overthrow the ruler. The result was a curious form of fatalism, for the Chinese ruler would "not feel, as our princes do, that if he governs badly, he will be less happy in the next life, less powerful and less rich in this one; he will know that, if his government is not good, he will lose his empire and his life."[26]

The ruler's fear for his throne, the people's battle for subsistence, formed a symbiotic whole. The outline of the system began to emerge:

> As the Chinese people become ever more numerous despite exposing their children, they must work tirelessly to make the lands produce enough to feed themselves; this demands great attention on the part of the government. It is in its interest for everyone at every moment to be able to work without fear of being frustrated for his pains. This should be less a civil government than a domestic government.
>
> This is what has produced the rules that are so much discussed. Some have wanted to have laws reign along with despotism, but whatever is joined to despotism no longer has force. This despotism, beset by its misfortunes, has wanted in vain to curb itself; it arms itself with its chains and becomes yet more terrible.
>
> Therefore, China is a despotic state whose principle is fear. In

the first dynasties, when the empire was not so extensive, perhaps the government deviated a little from that spirit. But that is not so today.[27]

Elsewhere in his analysis, Montesquieu probed how geography and environment flowed together in a particular way in China, and gave the country less chance to develop healthily than Europe. In Asia, strong and weak nations were neighbors, "the brave and active warrior peoples are immediately adjacent to effeminate, lazy and timid peoples; therefore, one must be the conquered and the other the conqueror." Whereas in Europe, adjacent states had similar levels of courage. This increased the tendency "for the liberty of Europe and the servitude of Asia: a cause," Montesquieu proudly added, "that I think has never before been observed. This is why liberty never increases in Asia, whereas in Europe it increases or decreases according to the circumstances."[28]

On the problem of the rites, which Leibniz had also spent much labor trying to understand, Montesquieu concluded that the Chinese had fatally blurred the four key forces—religion, laws, *mores* (or customs), and manners—that should cumulatively give the moral structure to society. By lumping all these four distinct elements together and calling them rites, the state at one level "triumphed: One passed all of one's youth learning them, all of one's life practicing them. The scholars taught them; the magistrates preached them." The difficulty of Chinese written script ensured that Chinese youth would be totally immersed in learning their texts, while the comparative simplicity of the package of values thus created seemed to make ethical learning intellectually easy. They also gave Chinese society a spurious permanence, since those conquering China's land or its armies could never replace the four elements that composed the rites. "As either the vanquisher or the vanquished must change, in China it has always had to be the vanquisher; for, as the *mores* of the vanquishers are not their manners, nor their manners, their laws, nor their laws, their religion, it has been easier for the vanquishers to bend slowly to the vanquished people than for the vanquished people to bend to the vanquishers." For similar reasons, Christian missionaries would find it as impossible as the foreign conquerors had to convert the Chinese to their own beliefs.[29]

These critiques of Chinese values were not echoed by Montesquieu's slightly younger contemporary, Voltaire. It is true that in his witty novel *Candide,* written in 1758 or 1759, Voltaire mocked what he considered the excessive optimism of Leibniz that all would turn out for the best in the best of all possible worlds. But from perhaps as early as his own schooldays with Jesuit teachers, Voltaire had been saturated with the moralistic literature on China, and the praises of the natural goodness of that civilization. It was his particular genius to see the force of divorcing these favorable analyses from the Christian context in which they were placed, and to argue that in fact the very presence of such morality in a non-Christian China pointed to the relativity of morality itself and nullified arguments on the need for Christian institutions in imposing moral systems. Starting in the 1740s, Voltaire pursued his Chinese thoughts along two parallel tracks, both critical of contemporary interpretations, one in the field of drama, one in history.

In drama, he focused on the recently translated Chinese play, *The Orphan of Chao,* a moral and family tragedy of loyalty and conquest set in the period of the Yuan dynasty. (Goldsmith had reviewed the slightly later English reworking of the play.) Voltaire wrote that he learned more about China from this play than from all the history books he had read. In his own stage version of 1755, *Orphelin de la Chine,* Voltaire went back to the thirteenth century for his setting, but chose to recast the play entirely as a proof of the comparative superiority of Chinese moral values over the innate cruelties of the conquering Mongol lord Genghis Khan. Voltaire also condensed the plot so as to highlight the clash between aspects of Mongol violence and contrition, a major point in the play being the impassioned speech

by Octar, one of Genghis Khan's senior officers, who pleads with
the Khan to carry out absolute vengeance against the Chinese
who have flouted the Mongol's will:

> Can you then admire their weakness?
> What are their boasted arts, the puny offspring
> Of luxury and vice, that cannot save them
> From slavery and death? the strong and brave
> Are born to rule, the feeble to obey.[30]

Genghis, however, torn by his emotions of love and admiration for the courage of the Chinese heroine Idame, and by the
loyalty of her husband, weakens in his resolve to subdue them
by violence and cruelty, and at length comes to acknowledge the
reality of China's moral superiority.

> Ye've done me ample justice, be it mine
> Now to return it: I admire you both;
> You have subdued me, and I blush to sit
> On Cathay's throne, whilst there are souls like yours
> So much above me; vainly have I tried
> By glorious deeds to build myself a name
> Among the nations; you have humbled me,
> And I would equal you: I did not know
> That mortals could be masters of themselves;
> That greatest glory I have learned from you:
> I am not what I was; to you I owe
> The wondrous change . . .
> At length you may confide in Genghis; once
> I was a conqueror, now I am a king.[31]

In his dedicatory essay to the play, Voltaire made it clear that
he thought his version of the *Orphan* was far superior to the Chinese original. The Chinese however didn't really care. Not only
would they not learn from the West, but they did not "so much
as know whether we have any history or not."[32] This Chinese dis-
interest in Western history was not matched by Voltaire's disin-
terest in theirs. At just this time in the mid-1750s, indeed, he was
completing his own major work on world history, the *Essai sur les*

Moeurs et l'esprit des nations or *History of the Manners and Spirit of Nations,* which he had commenced writing in 1740, and revised for final publication in 1756. In the preface to this massive history, he wrote that the West had the duty "to learn the genius of those nations which our European traders have constantly visited, ever since they first found out the way to their coasts,"[33] and true to his words, Voltaire began his book with China. By so doing, he gave a new twist to Western historiography.

Despite the pride of place he gave to China, his praise was muted and qualified. China had grown long and steadily, wrote Voltaire, and enjoyed great prosperity; the Manchu conquerors of 1644 (like Genghis Khan in *The Orphan of Chao*) had "submitted, sword in hand, to the laws of the country they invaded."[34] Yet China had failed to develop to its fullest potential a single one of the great inventions to which its people could lay claim in the recesses of their past:

> It is surprising that this people, so happy at invention, have never penetrated beyond the elements of geometry; that in music they are even ignorant of semitones; and that their astronomy, with all their other sciences, should be at once so ancient and imperfect. Nature seems to have bestowed on this species of men, so different from the Europeans, organs sufficient to discover all at once, what was necessary to their happiness, but incapable to proceed further: we, on the other hand, were tardy in our discoveries; but then we have speedily brought everything to perfection.[35]

In pursuing the root causes of this stagnation, Voltaire's analysis focused on the very reverence for the past that suffused China's culture, and on the nature of their language. Both of these impeded China's inclusion in the force that could now be seen as driving the West onward, that of progress:

> If we inquire why so many arts and sciences, so long cultivated without interruption in China, have nevertheless made so little progress, perhaps we shall discover two causes that have retarded their improvement. One is the prodigious respect paid by these

people to everything transmitted from their progenitors. This invests whatever is antique with an air of perfection. The other is the nature of their language, which is the first principle of all knowledge. The art of communicating ideas by writing, which should be plain and simple, is with them a task of the utmost difficulty. Every word is represented under a different character; and he is deemed the most learned, who knows the greatest number of characters.[36]

Voltaire, in the following pages of his discussion, invoked both Commodore (by this time Admiral) Anson, on Chinese commerce, and Navarrete on the Chinese concept of the soul. He was cautious about following either too far, and clear about the comparativist reasons for his care. On Anson, Voltaire asked if it was ever fair "to judge the government of a mighty nation by the morals of the populace in its frontier places?"[37] And on the theological fulminations of "the famous archbishop Navarrete"—for Navarrete too had received elevations after returning from China—Voltaire offered a different and elegantly critical warning note:

> We have calumniated the Chinese, merely because they differ from us in their system of metaphysics. We should rather admire in them two articles of merit, which at once condemn the superstition of the pagans, and the morals of the Christians. The religion of their learned men was never dishonored by fables, nor stained with quarrels or civil wars. In the very act of charging the government of that vast empire with atheism, we have been so inconsistent as to accuse it of idolatry; an imputation that refutes itself. The great misunderstanding that prevails concerning the rites of the Chinese, arose from our judging their customs by our own; for we carry our prejudices, and spirit of contention along with us, even to the extremities of the earth.[38]

As the idea of placing China in a world of systems took ever firmer hold in the later eighteenth century, the modifications that Montesquieu and Voltaire in their different ways had tried to impose began to fade, until they ultimately were lost without

trace. The idea of Chinese stasis or lack of progress was succeeded by the ideas of exhaustion or even petrification. Perhaps
picking up on a curious phrase of Montesquieu's, that "servitude always begins with drowsiness," the German polymath and
historian Johann Gottfried von Herder described the Chinese
empire as having the "internal circulation of a dormouse in its
winter sleep."[39] This sentence appears in Herder's major life
work, *The Outline of a Philosophy of the History of Man,* published in
1784, a work purportedly drawing together all his thoughts on
the nature of man and his experience in history. To Herder, the
Chinese nation was like "an embalmed mummy, wrapped in
silk, and painted with hieroglyphics," governed by "unalterably
childish institutions."[40] There was nothing the Chinese could
do to alter their destiny. They were "planted on this spot of
the Globe," and even if they wished, they "could never become
Greeks or Romans. Chinese they were and will remain: a people
endowed by nature with small eyes, a short nose, a flat forehead,
little beard, large ears and protuberant belly." Presiding over this
hollow society was an emperor "harnessed to this yoke" of imitation and superficiality, doomed to "go through his exercise
like a drill corporal."[41]

As Herder moved to condemn their language along with their
cupidity and their guile, all the pent-up grievances of his predecessors seemed to boil and seethe within him, even as the
individual phrases of his diatribe seem to point back to specific sources and offer a clue to his undeniable erudition and
assiduity:

> What a want of invention in the great, and what miserable
> refinement in trifles, are displayed in contriving for this language,
> the vast number of eighty thousand compound characters from
> a few rude hieroglyphics, six or more different modes of writing
> which distinguish the chinese from every other nation upon
> Earth. Their pictures of monsters and dragons, their minute care
> in the drawing of figures without regularity, the pleasure afforded
> their eyes by the disorderly assemblages of their gardens, the

naked greatness or minute nicety in their buildings, the vain pomp of their dress, equipage, and amusements, their lantern feasts and fire-works, their long nails and cramped feet, their barbarous train of attendants, bowings, ceremonies, distinctions, and courtesies, require a mungal [Mongol] organization. So little taste for true nature, so little feeling of internal satisfaction, beauty, and worth, prevail through all these, that a neglected mind alone could arrive at this train of political cultivation, and allow itself to be so thoroughly modelled by it. As the chinese are immoderately fond of gilt paper and varnish, the neatly painted lines of their intricate characters, and the jingle of fine sentences; the cast of their minds resembles this varnish and gilt paper, these characters and clink of syllables.[42]

Nothing in his account, wrote Herder, should be seen as "coloured by enmity or contempt." Everything he was saying had been said already by China's "warmest advocates." Thus he claimed his analysis to be a totally neutral one, designed to show nothing more or less than "the nature of the case." One could continue to admire Confucius, as others had, and Herder noted that "Confucius is to me a great man." But the trouble with Confucius was that he was shackled by "fetters," which, "with the best intentions, he rivetted eternally on the superstitious populace," leaving to China and its people a "mechanical engine of morals for ever checking the progress of the mind." As a consequence, no "second Confucius" having arisen to move them forward, "Ancient China stands as an old ruin on the verge of the World."[43] The implication seemed too simple to be even poignant any more. A push to those on the verge, and over they tumble, into the abyss.

CHAPTER 6

Women Observers

FOR MANY IN THE WEST, LORD MACARTNEY'S EXPERI-
ences acted as a kind of summation for the ambiguities of China,
its strange mix of pressure and profit, of arrogance and bland-
ishment. In her 1814 novel *Mansfield Park,* Jane Austen makes it
clear that Macartney's China experiences were also applicable on
the wider stage of life: they offered a metaphor for the interplay
of power and personality, with Macartney's final refusal to kowtow before Qianlong being emblematic of true strength of character. Austen's heroine Fanny Price has the recently published
volume of Macartney's journal lying on her work table in the
East Room at the novel's central moment, and as Edmund in his
mental agitation leafs quickly through the massive book, he
shares his thoughts with Fanny: "*You* in the meanwhile will be
taking a trip into China, I suppose. How does Lord Macartney
go on?" Fanny, from reading the journal, knows the decision
Macartney had made. Could she resist as well? "Was she *right*
in refusing what was so warmly asked, so strongly wished for?
What might be so essential to a scheme on which some of those
to whom she owed the greatest complaisance, had set their
hearts? Was it not ill-nature—selfishness—and a fear of exposing
herself?"[1]

Jane Austen's knowledge of China was not just limited to
published works. Her own brother Frank had spent almost half
a year in China in 1809, on a naval mission, and while there had
experienced the same mixture of threats and delays experienced
by Macartney. Frank Austen's level of exasperation had reached
such a pitch that he had turned on his heels and left the Canton

viceroy's office, throwing the parting shot—not unlike Anson's before him—that the Chinese knew where to find him if they wanted him.[2] Certainly his tales would have regaled his family after his return in 1810.

By the early nineteenth century the interest of women in China, and discussions of Chinese women's lives, were becoming more extensive. Again it was Macartney who had broached the subject first in an extended fashion. In a passage of reflections appended to the account of his embassy to China, he included a passage on the absence of women from Chinese social occasions, and on the effects of that exclusion on social life. "Where women are excluded from appearing," he wrote, "all delicacy of taste and sentiment, the softness of address, the graces of elegant converse, the play of passions, the refinements of love and friendship must of course be banished. In their place gross familiarity, coarse pleasantry, and broad allusions are indulged in, but without that honesty and expansion of heart which we have sometimes observed to arise on such occasions among ourselves." The result of this, he noted, was that the expressions of morality among Chinese men became, in the absence of their womenfolk, "a mere pretence." It was in this moral vacuum, accordingly, that Chinese men had developed two of their cardinal vices, their passion for gambling and their appetite for opium.[3]

Though Macartney was pointing these remarks at the Chinese themselves, everything he wrote in this passage had reference also to the small community of Westerners—dominated numerically by the British—that was beginning to carve out a life for itself on the southeast edge of the Chinese empire, outside the walls of Canton. Barred from living in any other region, prevented from entering the city of Canton itself, forbidden to bring any womenfolk with them, and forced to return at the end of every trading season to Macao or some more distant settlement, the members of this male community had developed their own peculiar patterns of conduct in order to retain their sanity. A reckless desire for gain was often combined in them with an intense religiosity, and even as they crammed their outpost's little chapel they were scheming how to expand their opium sales—one of their surest means to speedy affluence.

Already in his *Citizen of the World* of 1760, Oliver Goldsmith had mentioned that a polite English lady wishing to make a visiting Chinese feel at home would expect him to bring either his opium or his tobacco box, as if the two habits were parallel in familiarity.[4] But in fact tobacco had been a passion in China since the late sixteenth century when plants were imported from Latin America, and John Bell had noted tobacco shops all over Peking in 1720, whereas in Goldsmith's and even in Macartney's time opium was still a considerable rarity, and expensive. By the 1840s, however, the rhythms of life were changing rapidly in coastal China. By a brief but violent war between 1839 and 1842 the British had forced the Chinese to abandon the old exclusive system and allow Westerners (both men and women) to settle, trade, and preach at five selected ports, and also to travel peacefully in the surrounding countryside. In addition, the British seized and occupied the then almost deserted island of Hong Kong, on which to establish a naval and commercial base.

The trade monopoly of the East India Company had been abolished by Parliament, and the importation and sales of opium—grown mainly at this time in India—had risen immensely. The number of Chinese Christian converts had risen dramatically as well, through the labors of a new generation of Protestant missionaries, especially the Americans and the British. And as a result new types of legal and jurisdictional conflicts were becoming apparent between Westerners, their converts or employees, and the Qing state, while entirely new kinds of social problems emerged. It was in the 1840s, for instance, that a Chinese Christian convert formed his own sect of "God-worshippers" in the southeast, and during the following decade led an immense politico-religious insurrection and founded a "Heavenly Capital" in Nanjing city on the Yangzi River, almost bringing down the dynasty.[5]

In such a changed environment it became possible for the first time in Chinese history for a sizable contingent of Western women—whether married or single—to reside in China. As early as the mid-fourteenth century, we noted above, there was a small community—mainly of Italians—living and trading in Yangzhou in Central China, on the Grand Canal, and among them was a young woman, Katerina Yllioni. But with the collapse of the Mongol Yuan dynasty in 1368, these small clusters of West-erners, if they were ever common in China, had come to an end. They were not revived under the first two centuries of Qing rule, and the only female Western visitors to China seem to have been a few intrepid tourists or spouses of merchants who slipped into the foreign settlement outside Canton in defiance of the Qing ban—often dressed as men, to deflect the authorities' atten-tion. Books on moral and Christian themes in Chinese and Malay were already being written by Western women in the early 1830s—for instance, those by Elisabeth Medhurst and her sister Sophia.[6] But the first Western woman to live extensively in China, and to record her feelings in detail, was the American Eliza Jane Gillett, who reached Hong Kong in the spring of 1845. After marrying the experienced missionary and U.S. government interpreter Elijah Bridgman later that year, she spent most of the next two decades with him in China, either in Canton or in Shanghai. Her first book, *Daughters of China,* was published in the United States in 1853.[7]

Eliza Jane gained access to a source of information that had been denied to all the previous male travelers or analysts of China, namely, the half of China's population who were female. At first put off by what she could only see as "a certain inane expression" which Chinese women shared with their menfolk, she found—as her language abilities improved, and she was able to penetrate their seclusion—that their attitude to her was "singularly confiding and affectionate," and that they entered into conversation "with sprightliness and vivacity." As she summarized her early impressions:

> ... when the Chinese lady is favored with an interchange of sympathies with one of her own sex from another country, there is light in her eye and joy in her heart; it is not the flash of a bright and highly cultivated intellect,—for alas! she is not considered worth the pains, time and money, of being taught to read; but the women of China have souls; and there are deep fountains there, sending out, as far as their situation admits, streams of maternal and sisterly affection.[8]

There was also, she was honest enough to note, something darker, which she ascribed to their religion rather than their nature:

> ... there are fountains of evil too, and the courses that issue from them are broad and deep. Ungovernable temper often spreads discord in the domestic circle, and the strong folds of idolatrous superstition bind her tender offspring by an oath of perpetual fidelity to the altars of false deities.[9]

Such passages, despite their prejudgments, gave a more nuanced picture of Chinese women as a whole than anything presented before. In particular, Eliza Bridgman moved away from the merely physical description of dress, hair, and feet that had preoccupied earlier travelers. She also rejected the two main fictional stereotypes about Chinese women that had been established in the eighteenth century. One, as found most clearly in Voltaire but prevalent amongst his precursors, was the highly virtuous Chinese woman of impeccable courage, like Idamé, able to melt the heart even of a Genghis Khan. The other was the portrayal of the Chinese woman as indomitably proud, deeply suspicious of all men, a portrait that received its most passionate rendering in the Venetian playwright Carlo Gozzi's portrayal of *Turandot, Princess of China,* which was published the same year as Goldsmith's *Citizen of the World.* As Turandot tells one of her suitors, it is not at all that she is "mean-spirited and cruel" but just that she "loathes constraint and submission." To her, "all men are liars, inconstant, and treacherous. They pretend to love us so that we will yield to them; and they abandon us once they have made us their own." So she swears "by Confucius" to remain forever free.[10]

But these fictional forays into the drama of women's mental worlds were brought firmly back to earth by Eliza Bridgman, as she courteously lulled the Chinese women she met into comfortable conversations. One sure topic was her age and her children, another her clothes and hair ornaments, a third her "large feet." Each of these would lead, easily and naturally, to questions of a similar kind about the Chinese women's experiences. There were a host of other domestic and religious topics to cover, and sometimes those as dark as the infanticide of unwanted female children.[11]

The satisfaction of such approaches naturally depended on some knowledge of Chinese language, and Eliza Jane added a new perspective on this problem to that attempted by her varying male precursors, aiming her remarks especially at those who feared the problems would be "insurmountable." She separated language study into three components: the dominant spoken language, which could be learned through steady drill and application as the student "added to [her] little stock of Chinese words and phrases" by conversing with anyone available and willing to respond; the "local phraseology," some knowledge of which was "indispensable" as one moved from place to place, which could be learned if one was willing to "mingle with the people, hear them talk, and learn as the little child does." And then there was the written language, though again this could be thought of from two angles. From the point of view of the missionary's primary goal, "to impart a knowledge of the simple truths of the gospel," one did not need even "one half or one quarter" of the "copious number" of Chinese written characters; and to achieve this level, "a few hours of study each day on the written character"—as long as not drawn out too long—"is pleasant, and will afford a variety of occupation." There were several remarkably successful Christian preachers, she observed, "whose knowledge of the character is very limited."[12] The real sufferers were those who tried to get to too high a scholarly level too fast:

> The health of several persons has been seriously injured, and some have lost it entirely, by too close indoor application, to Chinese during the first or second year of a residence in the East, and then too, if a feeling of discouragement takes possession of the mind in the outset, it acts like an incubus—induces sedentary habits, and often the individual disheartened, sinks under the pressure of disease, or returns to his native land.[13]

Eliza Bridgman was too honest to see the problems of advanced language study as being the most serious that confronted the Westerners. There was a darker current of "hatred and hostility to foreign influence" that flowed in China, and it was this that she presented, with great narrative skill, in her account of an outing she made on a rented boat into the countryside outside Canton on a broiling late July day in 1846.

Initially, the Chinese people's friendliness seemed so spontaneous that the little party of voyagers were quite off guard. Although they all knew that there had recently been armed clashes in the area between Western merchants and the local Chinese that had left several dead, the menfolk went ashore when opportunity offered and "distributed tracts, and copies of the Testament."[14] Between such moments, they lazed in the reclining chairs of the boat's cabin and through the dangling venetian blinds watched the countryside glide past. After some four miles of this, they turned into a small creek, where there was an easy landing spot.

> There we walked up a hill, and came to a farm-house; it was a mere shed, but there was a poor woman there who understood the rites of hospitality. She prepared Tiffin* in her humble way, gave us a rough bench, the best she had, and begged us to be

---

* "Tiffin" was the slang word for a noon or evening meal, commonly in use among the English expatriates.

seated at the table and take some tea. There was something in her manner particularly attractive, because her politeness seemed to proceed from real kindness of heart. While we were partaking of her good tea, a crowd of people came round to look at us. My costume especially attracted their attention, and I took off my bonnet, and allowed them to see the style in which my hair was dressed; I was quite willing to gratify their curiosity, as they seemed very respectful.[15]

From that point on her account needs no commentary, except to say that the Sze Ping she mentions was a young man working in the missionary printing office, drawn to Christianity but not yet converted, who had helped Eliza in her early language studies and accompanied the missionaries and their families—at their request—on this outing.

We re-embarked, and proceeded on our way, along the creek, passed under a bridge, and came to a Chinese village; the sun was declining; the lengthened shadows of the shrubbery upon the water gave indications of the approach of evening. It being a warm summer's day, I put off my bonnet, and went outside on the deck of the boat to enjoy the cool air. I had not stood there but a moment before Sze Ping said to me, "You had better come inside, those are bad people on the shore."

I observed a crowd of boys and others making a noise; and presently heard the sound of pebbles against the sides of the boat. Sze Ping looked alarmed, and closed the blinds; there came small stones with more force. The excitement seemed to increase; there was quite a mob; pieces of mud, and heavier stones came; we barricaded the windows with anything we could find. . . .

The two boatmen were sadly cut, and I took my pocket handkerchief and with some cold water tried to staunch the blood—the storm of stones increased; our Venetians were getting broken, and we were expecting every moment to be knocked down by the heavy stones that came in quick succession.

One man with a demon-like expression, plunged into the water, and filched away an oar; and two or three of the boatmen escaped to the shore with fright.

The tide was against us, and we had to pass under another bridge before leaving the creek. There was one young man, about seventeen, left in the bow of the boat, who remained firm at his post. The mob gathered on the bridge, and as the boat emerged from under it, threw down a stone large enough to sink the boat, or kill any person upon whom it might fall. It struck upon a beam of the boat, cracking the beam, but harming none of us. The young hero of our battered craft took the stone and sat upon it, still rowing with all his might. . . .

It was nearly dark when we arrived at the landing; a favorable hour, for we were in a sad plight; my dress was covered with the blood of the wounded boatmen, the others were covered with dirt, though not a hair of our heads was injured.

The heavy stone, which no doubt was intended as our death-blow, was taken home, and weighed nearly one hundred pounds.[16]

No Westerner had written about China like this before. What was most new was the frank depiction of fear, and the acceptance of blame for that flaunted hair, about which Eliza had been lulled into false complacency in the friendly environment of the peasant lady's hut. The flowing hair, the mess of blood and mud, the cold water and the hard stones, the shouts and smashing blows, all images evoking a passionate New Testament resonance, became in their turn an integral part of Eliza Jane's Chinese landscape.

For Jane Edkins, who arrived in Shanghai at the age of twenty in 1859 from her native Scotland, with her husband Joseph, the prospect of China was even fairer than it had been for Lord Macartney with his short-lived rhapsodies over the "brave new world." "The Chinese"—she wrote to her mother in September in her excitement just after landing—in their light, cheerful clothes, and bustling energy, "are cleaner and more pleasing and winning-looking than I ever thought they should be," and there was no doubt in her mind that they "add to the beauty of the scene."[17] By mid-October, her pen flowed even more freely, in a letter to her father about a just-completed boat trip on the nearby Wusong River, in which all the echoes of eighteenth-century Chinoiserie seemed to have found their current place in the reality of her mind.

> On each side hung weeping willows, dropping their bending branches into the limpid stream. Back from the river were numerous fields waving with golden corn, and many a neat farmhouse peeped out amid a very luxuriance of trees. We were now nearing a beautifully arched bridge, green with flowering creepers. The sun by this time had warmed this lovely scene, and we waited anxiously a turn in the river to see to greater advantage the principal feature in the landscape. On the top of a pretty green hill stood a time-worn pagoda, its numberless corners and juttings, edged with bronze and brass, catching a glow from the morning rays, and glittering in the fair sunlight. Beyond us lay a bustling village, teeming with inhabitants. Already we were within the arched gateway, and coursing our way through the little town. Crowds of people came to look at us, and many a pair of chopsticks were arrested in the act of conveying the rice to the mouth, that they might gaze at the "barbarians." We soon passed through this village. I wish I could vividly picture the scene. I want to put baskets crowded with cackling ducks before you, tables spread with tempting fruit, bales of red cotton, with an endless diversity of men, women, and children, some pretty, some plain, all jabbering, talking, traversing narrow streets, crossing old crazy little bridges, and standing in crowds to gaze at us. Many a pretty face I noticed among the women, but in general the men of China are more interesting-looking than the females.[18]

"The more I see of China the more I love it," she added, "and my heart warms to the people already. . . . I think I should put 'China is beautiful' at the end of each page, I am so in love with 'the flowery land.'"[19] Yet in the midst of paradise, the crowds, already noticed a month before as intrusive and potentially troublesome, took on an oppressive feel:

> Crowds now began to collect around and look at us, and Mr. Edkins thought it best that Mrs. John and I should stay in the

cabin. Half reluctantly I assented, but I was soon thankful I did. What a collection of people gathered all round the water's edge to gaze at us. We had hove-to. Fifties, or hundreds rather, had come together, and talking so fast, but quite peaceable. We remained until the noise was perfectly deafening, and the heat from so many breaths most oppressive, so we pushed off, and steered for a quiet spot three miles farther on.[20]

At other times the Westerners were subject not to overt hostility, but to a jarring, raucous laughter, or had to confront groups of women and children in their faded cotton clothes "shouting as they came."[21] And on one occasion, though the experience was not as terrifying as Eliza Bridgman's, it was all Jane Edkins could do to keep her dignity in place.

We landed, but such a shouting, and gathering together of all the youngsters of the place, to see the "barbarians." The crowd became immense, rolling on behind us, and the shouting and whooping was something harassing to the ears. . . . [T]ier after tier of human heads were gazing at us, a right round circle swelling up, and babies high above all, quite like a gallery of people. How they managed to elevate themselves so I cannot think; chairs, I have no doubt, did their part. Such a gathering of people I have seldom seen before, even in China. We found the longer we stayed the more would come, so Mr. Burdon took me to the boat, I being the principal attraction, while Mr. Edkins stayed in peace. Once in the boat, I put up an umbrella, and sat doggedly hiding my face, but they got on their knees on the river bank, peered under my hat, umbrella, and all. I turned to the opposite side, and there, through tall rank weeds and rushes, dozens of faces were gleaming.[22]

Jane Edkins was more forthright than most male observers had been in expressing moral doubts about her presence in China. Among incidental intelligence, she learned that many of the American missionaries were "favourable to slavery in America, and I know one lady who is a slaveholder. This is very melancholy; it seems fearful to me."[23] And listening to the endless prayer meetings and preachings, an unworthy thought entered her mind: "Am I right in thinking that religion should not always be on the lip?" She spent more and more time on her Chinese language study, for which she felt "daily a growing love," despite their difficulty. "If it were not for the present disturbances" she wrote, in reference to the Taiping Rebellion which raged all around them, "and if I could bear solitude better, I should like, above all things, to go into the interior and mix thoroughly with the Chinese. That is the only way of acquiring the language at present." But as it was, she and her husband contented themselves with preaching to the refugees who had fled the rebels' "Heavenly Capital" of Nanjing, and raising money for their food from the Western merchants.[24]

In the summer of 1860, Jane Edkins got a sharper taste of the excitement of imminent warfare, as she wrote in a letter to her brother John:

> Yesterday a rumour ran the round of Shanghai, "The rebels are coming." The news reached us, and while Mr. Edkins walked quietly away to learn the truth, boats were pushed off from the Bund, living [sic] with men and women, with fear depicted in every face. Coolies, singing along the road *aho*, in a quiet, morning humour, heard the noise, stopped, listened, and, dropping their bundle, flew to the boats, and rowed away. Those who were in chairs were speedily placed on the ground, and the affrighted coolies rushed to the river. The literary man, walking along in his own peculiar, calm, dignified way, hears the affrighted cry, "Dy ong m'ah," "lac," etc., and at first hastens his speed, then dignity, scholarship, all are forgotten, and he gathers his skirts, and runs.[25]

Confident that she herself was safely guarded by British soldiers and by God, Jane felt secure: "It is almost sweet sometimes to feel a little danger," as she told her mother in August 1860. Her ambivalence about the rebels deepened. "I profess to be a rebel at heart somehow, and have a secret wish to welcome them," she told her father.[26] The desire faded, after the rebels had been driven back from Shanghai and Jane took an excursion into the countryside with her husband and some other missionaries:

> It is most sorrowful to see the perfect desolation all around. Houses burnt to the ground, stones scattered in endless confusion, mingled with tiles and mortar, a melancholy sight. Scarcely a house bounding the river is entire, all a mass of ruin for at least a mile. We passed up and through the silent streets, and, instead of busy activity, the lonely barking of the dogs, and the echo of our footsteps only resounded. The bridge, once lined with the busy passers-by, now utterly deserted, the tall rank weeds rendering the steps almost impassable; the closely shuttered windows, showing that no inmate was within; the barricaded door, and sometimes the doorless house, and the windowless house too, met our gaze.[27]

But Jane was too weak for the life of China, with its unremitting tensions and infections, diarrhea and headaches, heat and cold. Sick by mid-July of 1861, despite a move to the more salubrious north, living on beef tea, blackcurrant water, or champagne, when she could keep it down, by August 5 she had been sent to Taku, to try the sea air, still obsessed by the beauty of the scenery, as she walked on the veranda of her "sea-side temple house," a "pale-faced English lady, wrapped in a great brown plaid." She died on August 24, 1861, a little before her twenty-third birthday. Her husband "robed her in her bridal dress" and packed her body in ice for the long hot journey to the Westerners' burial ground in Tientsin.[28]

Published in London in 1863, Jane Edkins's letters gave a far fuller account of China than Eliza Bridgman had managed to do, and raised more difficult issues, despite the many lyrical descriptive passages that encased them. In particular, the relationship between the missionary work and the terrible suffering of the country haunted her. At times overwhelmed by the sense of being an outsider, she was tugged deeper and deeper into the foreign community, rather than into the Chinese one she had sought so dearly to enter. Still childless at her death, despite what was clearly a loving and passionate marriage, she was spared the worst fears that other women felt, that of the loss of their children. Forced too, by war and circumstance, to stay in a community filled with missionaries, she was spared the terrible sense of isolation that brought other Western women to despair in China.

For Mary Crawford Fraser, approaching Peking in 1870 by boat, after the Taiping Rebellion had been suppressed and nominal order restored to the country, the sight of a "smart, friendly, British Constable" was a major moment: "The sight of him was almost too much for my feelings after a week of those hideous, and as I fancied, hostile, Chinese faces around me. How gladly I scrambled out of the horrible little boat and into the luxurious palanquin which had been sent down for me."[29] Just as the alliteration of the three adjectives beginning with "h" in these two short sentences betrayed her agitation, so did Mary Fraser's sense of landscape immeasurably differ from that of Jane Edkins or Eliza Bridgman:

> As we approached the town, the everlasting fields of millet stubble gave way before vast spaces of yellow dust, beyond which the enormous walls of the Manchu City stretched as far as I could see, four miles in an exact square, with huge outstanding buttresses all along their length and triple-roofed watch towers at every corner. It looked like a great sulky monster waiting to spring.[30]

Even on the subject of footbinding, which had aroused at least some sympathy on the part of Western observers, Mary Fraser was sardonic rather than compassionate, as shown in her discussion of a visit of Manchu women to her temporary Peking home:

> It was something of an ordeal to have the wife of a great dignitary arrive at eleven or twelve o'clock and stay till sunset. All her female relations accompanied her and brought two maids apiece, so that the Compound seemed filled with palanquins and mule carts. The maids were supposed to support their mistresses' tot-

tering footsteps when they descended from their chairs—a piece of affectation which always particularly amused me. The Manchus do not make cripples of the baby girls, and all the court ladies have natural feet which they can use as well as anybody else. But the praise and fame of the "Golden Lilies" has filtered from Chinese tradition into theirs, and though they have been spared the sufferings and disabilities of their less fortunate sisters, it is the correct thing to simulate the latter and hobble along with an attendant gravely supporting each elbow.[31]

She found the women themselves irritating, as they "flit about from room to room fingering everything, trying on one's clothes, turning out wardrobes and asking the use of every article, and, strange to say, carrying off all the toilet soap in sight." She was not mollified to learn that the visiting women had thought the soap to be "a palatable sweetmeat and cut it up in little squares to distribute to their friends."[32]

In one of her most startling metaphors, which echoed the initial fear she had felt at the sight of Peking, the yellow roofs of the Imperial Palace became the focus of her deepest terrors. Mary Fraser had been told that the priceless art treasures stored there were constantly pilfered by robbers or secretly smuggled out by court officials for sale. If such imperial treasures were not sacrosanct, what of other treasures? "Grim tales of cruelty floated over the walls to us and when I became the proud mother of little Britishers I was always haunted by the fear that they would be spirited away and lost to me forever in the silent, populous labyrinth beyond the trees."[33]

There was nothing particularly British about such feelings. They were shared in part by Sarah Conger a few years later, when she arrived in Peking in her turn as the wife of the American minister. The opening sentences of a letter to her sister, written in Peking on June 3, 1899 (and later published), caught Sarah's ambivalences to perfection:

I am going to tell you of a few things that I have seen in Peking since I last wrote. It seems strange to find all that the Chinese do is part of a system. How I should like to know something of this system! Everything I learn urges me on to learn more.

I am not afraid of the Chinese. There is nothing about them to create fear in me, but they can annoy me if I oppose their thought and their customs of propriety.[34]

Then without digression, she describes her fear—which she has just said she does not have—in all its rawest form:

The city wall is a quiet, clean walking place; Chinese are seldom allowed upon the wall, and you feel safe and free. To-day daughter Laura started out alone with our guests. They walked to the tower over the Ch'ienmen, meeting no one but a wall-keeper and they threw him cash. They sat down to rest and watch the people below. A beggar came and asked for cash; they had none and paid no attention to him. Then another and another came, half clad in their filthy rags. This was a new phase on the wall. Laura, seeing the situation, said, "I don't understand this; let us move on, or retrace our steps." They retraced. The beggars followed, gathering more in numbers as they went. These half-covered wretches would run in front of them, form lines, fall upon their knees at their feet, kotow (bump their heads on the bricks), and yell and cry in the most horrible way. They stood on their heads, turned over and over, and kept up a loud noise all the while. These people kept increasing in numbers and yells, until the foreigners reached the place to leave the wall and descended upon the ramp, leaving their train of twenty native escorts looking down upon them. Where these dirty, ragged people came from is still a mystery.[35]

In another passage of the same letter, Sarah Conger lingered on an aspect of China that had been largely ignored by earlier travelers, but now had come to appear as a central feature of China: a disregard for those in misery, caused by a mixture of social convention and fear of getting involved. Here Sarah does not fear for herself or her daughter Laura, but rather, like a latterday Montesquieu, ponders whether there is a system that can somehow explain the Chinese to themselves in the barren harshness of their lives:

The Chinese never interfere with one another. For their own safety they dare not. We saw a man hauling sacks of grain; one sack was broken and the grain was flowing out in the street. Many Chinese saw it, but it was not their business and they did not interfere by telling him. Again we were passing and saw that a man with his two baskets on the end of a pole had fallen and could not get up. The Chinese on the street passed by him and so did we; on our return the man was still lying there but was lifeless. His baskets and pole were beside him undisturbed. The authorities alone had the right to touch that dead man and his belongings. Upon another occasion we were going through the crowded streets in the Native City. An obstruction was lying in the centre of the thoroughfare; this obstruction was a dead man covered from public view with reed matting. Each person's rights are so positively and so rigidly observed that no one interferes; these systems are "as old as the hills."[36]

Sarah Conger never did learn to understand that "system," as she had hoped, though she did learn to overcome her fear and to develop compassion and understanding of China. She came to this stance during the nightmare period of the Boxer Uprising in the summer of 1900, when she, her husband, and their daughter Laura were besieged along with the other foreign diplomats in China—and their Chinese staffs—behind the walls of the Legation Quarter. As she helped to fill the sandbags for the defenses, doused the incessant fires set by the besiegers, cared for the wounded, and practiced the small dishonesty of bargaining with the cooks to keep Laura's pony as the last one to be slaughtered for food, Sarah reflected on how the Chinese, once mocked for their refusal to fight at all in the dark or the rain, had now become "reckless, fierce, cruel and determined."[37] And when the nightmare was over, she refused to join the cries of those demanding vengeance.

Eliza Bridgman, Jane Edkins, Mary Fraser, and Sarah Conger had all spent their Chinese years surrounded by friends and fellow workers, in large cities, and with a deep and bustling sense of community that could buttress them against the Chinese world when they found it too harsh or fearful. But to be truly isolated was something else again, and it was a feeling that most of the earlier Western travelers to China had never experienced, and the fiction writers had been unable to conceive. Eva Jane Price knew what it entailed, when she, her husband, Charles, and their two children reached the small mission station of Fenzhou in the inland province of Shanxi in late 1889, six days by poled boat from the nearest city, followed by a fourteen-day trek through the mountains, with four litters, and thirteen pack mules. The country-town life was utterly different from that most other Westerners had known, Eva wrote in a December 1889 letter home to her family in Des Moines, Iowa:

> We have a large outer gate or door in our street wall which is kept shut and fastened except when we go in and out. The gatekeeper has a little room near the gate and the rest of the servants sleep there too. We have a small court about fifty feet square, paved with brick and walled in with our rooms so that all the outdoors we get is the sky and air and dust. The rooms are not all together but are built around other little courts and connected by little gateways and it is quite like a little village. Some of the places look spooky after dark. The whole premises cover about two acres but many of the rooms need repairs and are not used now. It is all enclosed by a high wall with only the one outer gate, so we are pretty well shut in. I have been outside the gate only three times since we came.[38]

It was not easy, after Iowa, to get used to the opium-smoking men, and the bound-foot women, with their faces painted white and red, while "their necks are left brown and dirty." Attempts to evade the isolation proved emotionally troubling: "There is a stone stairway leading to the roofs where we can walk and look off over the walls to get a view of the city and mountains. But the city is so depressing with everything so woefully dilapidated that I get down again very quickly and am glad to get back inside our rooms."[39]

If people were hostile on the rare occasions when she did go out, she could get used to it by keeping a sense of perspective: "It is the common thing for us to be yelled at by children and sometimes stones are thrown and 'foreign devil' is often heard. But it is no worse than a certain class of our people would do at home if a strange people were to come in their way. We hope to live before them uprightly, and quietly gain their confidence and esteem."[40] When one matched up these inner and outer worlds, the protection afforded her children seemed to outweigh the isolation:

> We have a pleasant place to live here, quiet and safe for the children. They have not played with any of the Chinese children yet because there have not been any come here except once or twice with their mothers, and they are afraid of us. As we walked out one afternoon we came suddenly upon some little fellows and they ran screaming at the top of their voices, crying and yelling as though we were going to take their heads off. And you must remember too that we are shut and locked in a compound that is surrounded by a wall fifteen feet high. This is the way everyone lives in China if they can afford a wall.[41]

Eva could not help it if at times her only wish was for one of her mother's big aprons, so she could put her head down on it, cry, and imagine it was her mother's lap. Her husband was often away, preaching, traveling, and attending mission meetings. As she waited behind her walls with her two sons, Stewart and Don, she could only hope "they will be spared to each other and to us as long as we are here. It would be terribly lonely without them."[42] By October 1890,

> Every week here is just about like the one before—no place to go, no friends to visit, no callers coming in (only our Chinese friends occasionally); one day so much like another that we hardly know them apart. . . .
> I bought some chrysanthemums which I set up on the window ledge outside the sitting room and they are refreshing. If we stay

here another year I am going to have some flowers if possible. By tearing up some of the brick pavements I think I can have quite a flower garden.

But in the meantime fate had taken an odd turn, by removing her one source for an internal view of the world outside: "The old stone stairway by which we climbed to the roofs to walk and get a view of the city and mountains fell down with a crash one night and since then I can't get a squint at the rest of the world unless we go outside the compound."[43]

Eva did learn to travel outside her compound. She learned the language. She began a school for the local women and girls, but her early nightmares eventually became real. On May 16, 1892, three-year-old Donnie had a bad sore on his face which made Eva nervous. A week later, her boy was dead. Her son Stewart died in February 1897 of kidney disease. He was twelve and a half.[44] She had given birth to a new daughter, Florence, in November 1893, but the pressures were hard to bear, and the memories of the lost sons hard to erase:

> March 15, 1899. I get pretty lonesome here, in fact I'm really blue. Did you think missionaries always were bright and happy and hopeful? Well, there may be some of that kind but they are not out here. It is only by taking a wide look out over the whole general missionary field and seeing what has been done and what seems to be God's purpose that we can stand to live here at all. Mrs. Atwater and I went to call on a friend in the south suburb last Friday. The streets were fearful because of mud and stench and the places and people seemed dirtier than ever and a flea jumped into Mrs. Atwater's cup of tea.
>
> We had a terrible dust storm several weeks ago and when the gale came it just whirled and swirled around the house and into every crack and crevice of our poorly made doors and windows. I even felt the grit on my teeth. There had not been any snow yet this winter and no rain since last September so you may know there was plenty of dust. Then when the wind fell it began snowing and when we got up on a Sunday morning everything was white and clean.[45]

The drought that Eva Price referred to was protracted and terrible, leading to countless deaths from starvation in the nearby countryside. In this context of misery, the Boxer rebels with their message of antiforeignism and national renewal found ready and enthusiastic followers. The attacks on Eva's family had already begun the year before—jostling, shoving, hooting, throwing mud and stones.[46] In February 1900, as Eva saw Florence through a protracted crisis with whooping cough, she heard that the first missionaries had been killed by the Boxers, and in the summer the killings became commonplace.[47] In August 1900, the Price family's own walled compound was in danger of attack and Qing troops moved in, allegedly to protect them. Eva, her husband, and daughter Florence, were promised that they would be escorted out of the city and taken to safety. But once they had been conveyed by cart some distance beyond the walls, all three of them were killed. Their bodies were stripped and left lying in a ditch. Shortly before their deaths, when they left their compound and jogged out into the open countryside toward what they hoped, but hardly dared believe, would be freedom, the whole community lined the narrow streets to see them off.[48]

CHAPTER 7

China at Home

WHEN CHARLES PRICE FIRST ARRIVED WITH HIS LITTLE family at the Shanxi mission station in Fen-zhou late in 1889, he found it an unattractive place, and was deeply unsure about what the future might offer. But he had the honesty to notice that the Chinese in Fen-zhou, poor and desperate as many of them were, and ravaged by disease, nevertheless were instinctively generous to him and his family. It was hard not to draw an implicit contrast with the United States, as he wrote to his father in a letter of March 1890: "They are very kind to us and usually treat us as though they are glad we have come to live among them. They treat us much better than Chinamen are sometimes treated in America."[1]

Such attempts to apply a comparative scale of judgment had existed among Western travelers in China ever since the time of Pereira in the mid-sixteenth century, but they had remained abstract, because there were no comparable Chinese travelers in the West. By the later nineteenth century this was no longer the case, and though Chinese communities in Europe were small and scattered, in the United States the Gold Rush of 1849 and the subsequent expansion of the railways had brought tens of thousands of Chinese immigrant laborers—mostly men—to the West Coast. By the 1890s "Chinatowns" were commonplace in many American cities, and pockets of Chinese workers could be found all across the country, from the Pacific Northwest, the Midwest, the deep South, to the Eastern Seaboard.

The attitudes of white Americans to this new influx were

mixed, as one might expect, but initially tolerance was high. A Chinese boy like Yung Wing, from a poor family in Southeast China, brought to the United States by generous missionaries with merchant support, could go to prep school in New England, graduate from Yale in 1854, and marry a local woman from Hartford, all without creating much of a stir.[2] More surprisingly, Chinese "Siamese Twins" like Chang and Eng (1811–1874), fastened inseparably to each other at the chest, after an initial period as "circus freaks" exhibited by Barnum & Bailey, could also lead lives as normal as their circumstances could permit. They settled in North Carolina, took the American name of Bunker, married white sisters—Adelaide and Sarah Ann Yeates—from the local community, built two homes where they alternated residence, bought land, shared their wedding present of a black slavewoman they called "Aunt Grace," and had between them twenty-one children.[3] Other Chinese ran fruit farms, formed charitable organizations, fished for shrimp and oysters, worked abandoned mines for leavings, labored in shoe or cigar factories, and ran laundries and restaurants.

By the late 1860s, however, the pressures that Charles Price alluded to were already becoming apparent. As the Chinese fanned out from San Francisco into new kinds of work in the mines and on the railroads, they moved from being objects of amused curiosity into targets of sarcasm, economic discrimination, legal harassment, and outright violence, sometimes ending in murder by lynch mobs. Two early chroniclers of this trend were Bret Harte and Mark Twain. As young men from the East who had traveled west in search of good copy, along with fame and fortune, they encountered Chinese for the first time in the late 1850s and early 1860s in Nevada and California. Perhaps the first fairly detailed evaluation of a Chinatown community by any American is that written by Mark Twain for the *Enterprise*, the newspaper of Virginia City in Nevada, where he lived and worked as a reporter from 1861 to 1864, while in his late twenties.

There were about one thousand Chinese in Virginia City at the time, Twain reported, mostly working at washing clothes, though a few were houseboys and cooks, jammed together in a small "Chinese Quarter" a "little removed from the rest of the town."[4] As one can see from the way Twain sets the scene for his piece, he had already absorbed many of the negative stereotypes that were beginning to gain force in the country as a whole:

> The Chinese have built their portion of the city to suit them-selves; and as they keep neither carriages nor wagons, their streets are not wide enough, as a general thing, to admit of the passage of vehicles. At ten o'clock at night the Chinaman may be seen in all his glory. In every little cooped-up dingy cavern of a hut, faint with the odor of burning Josh-lights and with nothing to see the gloom by save the sickly, guttering tallow candle, were two or three yellow, long-tailed vagabonds, coiled up on a sort of short truckle-bed, smoking opium, motionless and with their luster-less eyes turned inward from excess of satisfaction—or rather the recent smoker looks thus, immediately after having passed the pipe to his neighbor—for opium-smoking is a comfortless opera-tion, and requires constant attention. . . . John likes it, though; it soothes him; he takes about two dozen whiffs, and then rolls over to dream, Heaven only knows what, for we could not imagine by looking at the soggy creature. Possibly in his visions he travels far away from the gross world and his regular washing, and feasts on succulent rats and birds'-nests in Paradise.[5]

But in individual pen portraits of three of the Chinese he encountered, Twain showed himself a somewhat more compas-sionate observer, though harsh comments could still be found. "Mr. Ah Sing" of "No. 13 Wang Street," for instance, "lavished his hospitality upon our party in the friendliest way. He had var-ious kinds of colored and colorless wines and brandies, with unpronounceable names, imported from China in little crock-ery jugs, and which he offered to us in dainty little miniature wash-basins of porcelain." Ah Sing "had in his store a thousand articles of merchandise, curious to behold, impossible to imagine the uses of, and beyond our ability to describe." But he also offered his journalist guest "small neat, sausages," which Twain wrote that he declined to sample, suspecting "that each link contained the corpse of a mouse."[6]

"Mr. Hong Wo," of "No. 37 Chow-chow Street," a former cook for the newspaper's staff, known to all as "Tom," ran the local lottery for the Chinese community. The workings of this lottery system he explained to the journalist in what Twain, his sarcasm returning, referred to as "faultless English." As Tom put it, "Sometime Chinaman buy ticket one dollar hap, ketch um two tree hundred, sometime no ketch um anyting; lottery like one man fight um seventy—maybe he whip, maybe he get whip heself, welly good."[7] While "Mr. See Yup," who ran a "fancy store on Live Fox Street" which Twain found a delightful place to browse, "sold us fans of white feathers, gorgeously ornamented; perfumery that smelled like Limburger cheese, Chinese pens, and watch-charms made of a stone unscratchable with steel instruments, yet polished and tinted like the inner coat of a sea-shell. As tokens of his esteem, See Yup presented the party with gaudy plumes made of gold tinsel and trimmed with peacocks' feathers."[8]

There was also a small Chinatown restaurant that entranced Twain, even down to the totting up of the bill on an abacus:

> We ate chow-chow with chop-sticks in the celestial restaurants; our comrade chided the moon-eyed damsels in front of the houses for their want of feminine reserve; we received protecting Josh-lights from our hosts and "dickered" for a pagan god or two. Finally, we were impressed with the genius of a Chinese bookkeeper; he figured up his accounts on a machine like a gridiron with buttons strung on its bars; the different rows represented units, tens, hundreds, and thousands. He fingered them with incredible rapidity—in fact, he pushed them from place to place as fast as a musical professor's fingers travel over the keys of a piano.[9]

Moving to California from Virginia City in 1864, Twain began to absorb more information about the Chinese and their living habits, and to note the discrimination against them with a sharper eye. "As I write," he recorded of the grim flare-up of racial hostility in the San Francisco of 1869, "news comes that in broad daylight in San Francisco, some boys have stoned an inoffensive Chinaman to death, and . . . although a large crowd witnessed the shameful deed, no one interfered."[10] He noted how "any white man can swear a Chinaman's life away in the courts, but no Chinaman can testify against a white man," how the new mining taxes were levied only on the Chinese trying to rework the abandoned claims of their white predecessors, and how quack doctors working for the immigration department took a ten-dollar fee for vaccinations on the wharf from every arriving Chinese.[11]

The Los Angeles riots against the Chinese in 1870, in which over twenty Chinese were killed, further shocked Twain, and other sensitive observers in the West. But the fact that the most famous of all American poems about the Chinese, Bret Harte's "Plain Language from Truthful James," was written in 1870, was pure coincidence, according to its author. As Harte told his friend Ambrose Bierce, who had written and was to write passionately in support of the Chinese, "he meant nothing whatever by it."[12] Harte had included references to "John Chinaman" and other Chinese migrant laborers in some of his pieces in the 1860s, but "Plain Language" was simply one of a number of poems Harte was writing at the time to encapsulate his memories of the tough gold-mining camps in which he had lived in the 1850s and 1860s.[13]

Yet it was surely because of the context of discrimination and killing that the poem had such an impact when it appeared. Harte gave the work a bold and mysterious beginning, as if he had caught Truthful James in the middle of a sentence, proceeding at once to set the scene of Ah Sin's gambling with the other white miners:

PLAIN LANGUAGE FROM TRUTHFUL JAMES
(*Table Mountain, 1870*)

Which I wish to remark,
    And my language is plain,
That for ways that are dark
    And for tricks that are vain,
The heathen Chinee is peculiar,
    Which the same I would rise to explain.

Ah Sin was his name;
    And I shall not deny,
In regard to the same,
    What that name might imply;
But his smile it was pensive and childlike,
    As I frequent remarked to Bill Nye.

It was August the third,
    And quite soft was the skies;
Which it might be inferred
    That Ah Sin was likewise;
Yet he played it that day upon William
    And me in a way I despise.

Which we had a small game,
    And Ah Sin took a hand:
It was Euchre. The same
    He did not understand;
But he smiled as he sat by the table,
    With the smile that was childlike and bland . . . [14]

In the heart of the poem, Truthful James makes it transparently clear that he and his friend Bill Nye have been cheating outrageously, in order to fleece Ah Sin, who has confessed his total ignorance of the game. Their astonishment is directed at Ah Sin's successes despite this cheating, and their growing realization that he must be cheating better than they are. The final straw, to them, is when Ah Sin wins the game by artfully palming a hand that Nye had meant to deal to Truthful James, and a fight ensues in which "twenty-four jacks" fall from Ah Sin's sleeve. This brings Truthful James back, in his last stanza, to the poem's opening:

> Which is why I remark,
>   And my language is plain,
> That for ways that are dark
>   And for tricks that are vain,
> The heathen Chinee is peculiar,—
>   Which the same I am free to maintain.

The poem appeared in the 1870 *Overland Monthly*, and produced something of a sensation, due to its originality and its content. One bookshop in New York reported sales of twelve hundred copies within a two-month period, several well-known newspapers ran the poem twice, two illustrated editions were closely followed by two musical versions, and a "Heathen Chinee Songster" appeared in 1871.[15]

Having by his own testimony intended nothing by the poem, Harte found himself caught up in the need to launch a defense of the Chinese, since so many Americans interpreted the poem as anti-Chinese. If the poem had an ideology, it was surely to attack the cupidity and greed of white miners, with their swiftness to take offense at other races who might emulate their own uncouth ways. Yet even if many people misinterpreted it, the poem brought Harte a good deal of money, and by publishing continuations that served in a way as rebuttals, he not only made yet more money but also established a stance of moral purity.

The character Ah Sin had attained a rare resonance, and Harte sought to capitalize on this in a follow-up poem, "The Latest Chinese Outrage." Here, a violent group of white miners who have refused to pay their laundry bills are bested by a group of Chinese led by Ah Sin, who raid the miners' livestock and possessions to claim the money owed to them. More startlingly, the Chinese capture Joe Johnson, one of the white miners who had cheated them, and subject him to their own form of vigilante justice: After catching Johnson, they induced him to take opium, and then "shaved off his eyebrows, and tacked on a cue," dressed him in Chinese clothes, painted his face with a coppery dye, and after stuffing him into a bamboo cage with a label announcing, "A white man is here," they "left him there hanging/Like ripening fruit."[16]

Mark Twain returned to the topic of the Chinese migrant population in the year Harte's famous poem appeared. Yet he chose to continue his treatment of the Chinese not through direct reportage, but in the form of an epistolary novel serialized in the local newspaper, the *Galaxy*. He placed himself firmly in a literary tradition that he clearly assumed would be familiar to newspaper readers by titling his work "Goldsmith's Friend Abroad Again."

Goldsmith had designed his letters so that they constituted a fundamental critique of English society, and only as a secondary criterion sought to show how the British treated Lien Chi. Lien Chi suffers little discrimination at the hands of Goldsmith's Londoners, and if he does, it is less out of malice or cruelty and more from the standpoint of the "innocent from abroad" being gulled, as when he offers his cherished watch to a friendly lady who turns out to be a prostitute and of course fails to return it. Lien Chi is never jailed, or beaten, or even yelled at, though, as we have seen, his right to speak definitively for his own Chinese culture is denied him by his eighteenth-century London society hostess and her guests. Twain's critique is leveled, similarly, against the society in which his Chinese letterwriter Ah Song Hi happens to be, but the plot is constructed more specifically around the individual outrages that Ah Song Hi has to endure.

In abandoning the name Lien Chi which Goldsmith had chosen for his protagonist—a name in any case taken from Horace Walpole—and adopting Ah Song Hi, Twain perhaps hinted at some connection with Ah Sin, but Ah was the name most commonly ascribed to emigrants at the time, especially those from the Canton delta region.

In the first letter of the series, addressed to a friend, Ching-Foo, Twain has Ah Song Hi set the scene for his high expectations of his soon-to-be-adopted land:

> Dear Ching-Foo: It is all settled, and I am to leave my oppressed and overburdened native land and cross the sea to that noble realm where all are free and all equal, and none reviled or abused—America! America, whose precious privilege it is to call herself the Land of the Free and the Home of the Brave. . . . We know how America has welcomed the Germans and the Frenchmen and the stricken and sorrowing Irish, and we know how she has given them bread and work and liberty, and how grateful they are. And we know that America stands ready to welcome all other oppressed peoples and offer her abundance to all that come, without asking what their nationality is, or their creed or color.[17]

In the second letter, written on shipboard, Ah Song Hi, with similar naïveté, describes the way his promised wages of twelve dollars a month are already being whittled away: two dollars have gone into the American consul's pocket; the passage money is being deducted from all his future wages; his wife, son, and two daughters have been pledged as security. Upon landing in San Francisco, he loses most of what he still has: his luggage is muddled with an opium smuggler's, and confiscated; his best friend is jailed; and Ah Song Hi is forced to give his last ten dollars of cash to be vaccinated against smallpox by an officially appointed doctor, even though he had just been vaccinated in China, and the going rate for such vaccinations elsewhere in San Francisco is two dollars.[18]

Twain places Ah Song Hi in the context of one of the stranger sides of the immigration experience: the post–Civil War attempt of some labor procurers to ship large numbers of Chinese to the South, to work the plantations once worked by black slaves. But when the plantation plan fails—as most such plans did in actuality—Ah Song Hi, who has been held with fellow Chinese immigrants "massed together in some small houses up to that time, waiting," is set free on guarantee of repaying his sixty-dollar passage money. He has, he tells his friend Ching-Foo, been learning "a little of the language every day," and reflecting on his good fortune in being in "the heaven-provided refuge of the oppressed and the forsaken" when catastrophe strikes:

> Just as that comforting thought passed through my mind, some young men set a fierce dog on me. I tried to defend myself, but could do nothing. I retreated to the recess of a closed doorway, and there the dog had me at his mercy, flying at my throat and face or any part of my body that presented itself. I shrieked for help, but the young men only jeered and laughed. Two men in gray uniforms (policemen is their official title) looked on for a minute and then walked leisurely away. But a man stopped them and brought them back and told them it was a shame to leave me in such distress. Then the two policemen beat off the dog with small clubs, and a comfort it was to be rid of him, though I was just rags and blood from head to foot. The man who brought the policemen asked the young men why they abused me in that way, and they said they didn't want any of his meddling. And they said to him:
>
> "This Ching divil comes till Ameriky to take the bread out o' dacent intilligent white men's mouths, and whin they try to defind their rights there's a dale o' fuss made about it."[19]

Ah Song Hi is arrested by the police for "being disorderly and disturbing the peace" and taken off to jail "with a jeering crowd of street boys and loafers at [his] heels." As the key turns in the cell door, the policeman yells after him, "Rot there, ye furrin spawn, till ye lairn that there's no room in America for the like of ye or your nation." The subsequent three letters deal with the grim experiences of Ah Song Hi's night in jail and his farcical trial, in which he learns for the first time the reality of a world in which whites can testify against Chinese, but Chinese cannot testify against whites, and is duly convicted, with a fine of five dollars or ten days more in jail. The letters end with Ah Song Hi in a crowd of around fifteen other arrested Chinese, all doomed to suffer similar fates.[20]

Mark Twain's story, heavy-handed from the beginning, bogged down in its own rhetoric and legal details, and it is not surprising that he abandoned it after seven "letters." Twain left no doubt that the Irish brogue of both the vicious youths and the uncaring police marked the realities of a racial and legal situation against which there could be no appeal.

But though he clearly felt comfortable with rendering the Irish brogues of Ah Song Hi's persecutors, Twain held off here from trying to convey Ah Song Hi's own diction in the "Pidgin English" form that he had used in the *Enterprise* piece on Virginia City's Chinatown. Instead, he adopted a flowery version of the English language, as if that would somehow convey the cadences of the Chinese visitor's predicament. Twain attempts a version of Ah Song Hi's Chinese diction in the courtroom phase of his fragmentary novel, when the judge finally asks Ah Song Hi if he has anything to say. Expecting that his remarks will be translated for him by the court-appointed interpreter who is present at the trial, Ah Song Hi begins: "Hear, O high and mighty mandarin, and believe! As I went about my peaceful business in the street, behold certain men set a dog on me, and—" but his speech is cut short by the cry of "Silence" from the judge, and the whispered comment of the interpreter that no statements of Ah Song Hi's would be accepted by the court.[21]

Americans, however, were now getting ready to accept the linguistic validity of that "pidgin" or business English, originating in the commercial ports in the eighteenth century, that Commodore Anson had found so ridiculous a century before. Transposed into European settings, the burden of language had been transferred to the Chinese, and both firsthand and fictional records show the range of decisions that could be made. In the late seventeenth century Shen Fu-tsung had spoken in Latin to Thomas Hyde at the Bodleian Library. Montesquieu's 1713 informant, Hoange, spoke decent French. John Hu, a Chinese Catholic who came to France in the company of a French Jesuit shortly after Hoange, was never able to learn French or any other language, and in a sad but early prefiguration of Twain's Ah Song Hi, was finally incarcerated in the madhouse of Charenton because he could not explain the reasons for his actions to the authorities.[22] Oliver Goldsmith's Lien Chi is presented as knowing perfect English, though no explanation is given as to how he learned it. Horace Walpole's Mi Li spoke in broken English, as when he cried out, "Who she, who she?" on seeing his future bride Caroline Campbell.

Pidgin English was clearly well established among the Californian and Nevadan Chinese camps that Harte and Twain knew, and the first semiformal guide to its usage appeared in 1860 in the *Knickerbocker* magazine.[23] The first well-publicized long passage of pidgin was written anonymously by an American naval officer and published in *Harper's* in 1869.[24] The charm of this offering was that it gave a "translation" into pidgin of what was then almost certainly the most popular poem in America, Longfellow's "Excelsior" of 1842. No one in 1869 would have needed reminding of the poem's most famous stanza:

> The shades of night were falling fast,
> As through an Alpine village passed
> A youth, who bore, 'mid snow and ice,
> A banner with the strange device
>   Excelsior!

The pidgin English version, replacing the Latin "excelsior" or "higher" with the pidgin for the same word, "topside," came out as follows:

> That nightee teem he come chop chop
> One young man walkee, no can stop;
> Colo maskee, icee maskee;
> He got flag; chop b'long welly culio, see—
>   Topside Galah![25]

So did Ah Sin, in Bret Harte's poem of the 1870s, harangue the assembled miners in self-confident tones:

> Then we axed for a parley. When out of the din
> To the front comes a-rockin' that heathen, Ah Sin!
> "You owe flowty dollee—we washee you camp,
> You catchee my washee—me catchee no stamp;
> One dollar hap dozen, me no catchee yet,
> Now that Flowty dollee—no hab?—how can get?"[26]

The leader of the miners, a tough rousterbout named Johnson, responds at once, and forcefully:

> "Are we men?" says Joe Johnson, "and list to this jaw,
> Without process of warrant or color of law? . . ."
> "Shall we stand here as idle, and let Asia pour
> Her barbaric hordes on this civilized shore?
> Has the White Man no country? Are we left in the lurch?
> And likewise what's gone of the Established Church?
> One man to four hundred is great odds, I own,
> But this 'yer's a White Man—I plays it alone!"[27]

It was in 1875, after the success of these poems with a Chinese theme, that Harte wrote his most eloquent and effective assault on white American bigotry against Chinese immigrants, "Wan Lee, the Pagan." In this piece, Harte first introduces his friend, the wealthy storekeeper Hop Sing, with language redolent of Goldsmith, as "that most sombre of all humorists, a Chinese philosopher."[28] He then proceeds to an affectionate and dignified sketch of Hop Sing whom, he observes, he has known since 1856:

> He was, on the whole, a rather grave, decorous, handsome gentleman. His complexion, which extended all over his head except where his long pig-tail grew, was like a very nice piece of glazed brown paper-muslin. His eyes were black and bright, and his eyelids set at an angle of 15°; his nose straight and delicately formed, his mouth small, and his teeth white and clean. He wore a dark

blue silk blouse, and in the streets on cold days a short jacket of Astrakhan fur. . . . His manner was urbane, although quite serious. He spoke French and English fluently. In brief, I doubt if you could have found the equal of this Pagan shopkeeper among the Christian traders of San Francisco.[29]

Through Hop Sing, Harte employs his friend's ten-year-old adopted son Wan Lee in his newspaper office. Wan has had a mixed Chinese-American education—"he had gone through the Tri-literal classics," says his father, "knows but little of Confucius, and absolutely nothing of Mencius"—and speaks in pidgin. He is a mischievous, sparkling boy, "with happiness beaming from every tooth and satisfaction shining in his huckleberry eyes," who loves to set minidiatribes against himself in type, to insert insulting Chinese sentences into the midst of some passage of fulsome praise for some unworthy local politician.

A little later, enrolled in the San Francisco school of a retired China missionary, Wan Lee studies joyfully and befriends the daughter of his Western landlady, who becomes his inseparable companion. At the peak of his vitality and joy, with a yellow ribbon given to him by the girl tied round his queue and the little porcelain god he always carried with him tucked under his shirt, Wan Lee is suddenly, pointlessly, slain.

Harte closes his story sharply:

> Dead, my reverend friends, dead! Stoned to death in the streets of San Francisco, in the year of grace, eighteen hundred and sixty-nine, by a mob of half-grown boys and Christian school-children!
>
> As I put my hand reverently upon his breast, I felt something crumbling beneath his blouse. . . . It was Wan Lee's porcelain god, crushed by a stone from the hands of those Christian iconoclasts![30]

By the mid-1870s, Harte—at the apogee of his fame as a writer—developed ambitions as a dramatist. His first play, a convoluted comedy entitled *Two Men of Sandy Bar*, dealt mainly with economic and social battles between elitist Anglo-Saxon Americans and wealthy Spanish rancheros, but included a part for a Chinese named Hop Sing. Harte had obviously borrowed the name of his own friend Hop Sing from "Wan Lee, the Pagan" to serve for a Chinese laundryman in the play. In a literal sense, Hop Sing has only a bit part in *Two Men of Sandy Bar,* but it is a crucial one, since the drama hinges around problems of mistaken and deliberately concealed identities, and Hop Sing—as the only laundryman in the area—is also the only man who knows the crucial secrets of the key participants, since to avoid confusion he always marks every shirt on the tail with the owner's name in indelible ink. In a key moment of the play, Hop Sing's irritation boils over into contempt for the Americans who refuse to pay their bills: "Me no likee 'to-mollow!' Me no likee 'next time John!' Allee time Melican man say, 'Chalkee up, John!' 'No smallee change, John.'"[31]

The play ran to mixed reviews and success, but it did make money. Furthermore, the small part of Hop Sing was played with such amusing panache by the actor Charles T. Parsloe that it aroused widespread praise that could be exploited. Harte, having noted Mark Twain's rising fame, and his interest in evoking Chinese themes, persuaded Twain to join him in writing a new play, in which a longer Chinese part for Parsloe would be included. The result was the 1877 play called *Ah Sin,* a deliberate attempt to go Hop Sing one better and exploit the now six-year-old success of Harte's earlier poem, "Truthful James." The play was a rambling comedy about western mining camp life and Ah Sin's gambling prowess, and the playbills deliberately linked poem and play by showing a picture of Ah Sin, in Chinese silk jacket with flowing pigtail, balancing an ace of clubs on his nose while holding four other aces in his hand.[32]

The jointly authored play opened quite promisingly in Washington, D.C., and proceeded to New York City to patchy success in the late summer of 1877; it played thereafter with ever-declining audiences in St. Louis and at a number of one-night stands in upper New York State until it closed at the end of the year. There was no further collaboration between Harte and Twain. Indeed, the tensions of the experience ended their friendship. In doing the best that he could with the part of Ah Sin, Parsloe, however, had found his niche as a Chinese, which he continued to create successfully in other plays, as in the role of "The Chirping Chinaman" in Bartley Campbell's 1879 play *The Partner*.[33]

As Harte achieved greater and greater success as a lecturer on the circuit in the 1880s and early 1890s, he apparently tried to undo any damage he might have brought to the cause of Chinese tolerance by including more favorable appraisals of the Chinese in the United States. In 1896, he put these thoughts into print for the introduction to a new edition of his work, *The Argonauts*, a collection of his early writings on the pioneers who opened up the American West. But even here, there remained a profound ambiguity in Harte's portrayal:

> The Heathen Chinee was *not* an Argonaut. But he brought into the Argonaut's new life an odd conservatism. Quiet, calm, almost philosophic, but never obtrusive or aggressive, he never flaunted his three thousand years in the face of the men of to-day; he never obtruded his extensive mythology before men who were skeptical of even one God. He accepted at once a menial position with dignity and self-respect. He washed for the whole community, and made cleanliness an accessible virtue. . . . He worshipped the devil in your household with a frank sincerity and openness that shamed your own covert and feeble attempts in that direction. Although he wore your clothes, spoke your language, and imitated your vices, he was always involved in his own Celestial atmosphere. He consorted only with his fellows, consumed his own peculiar provisions, bought his goods of the Chinese companies, and when he died, his bones were sent to China![34]

And Harte concluded the passage with a series of reflections that left the Chinese immigrants firmly outside the mainstream of American life, just as eighteenth-century thinkers from Montesquieu to Herder and Hegel had placed them outside history.

> He left no track, trace, or imprint on the civilization. He claimed no civil right; he wanted no franchise. He took his regular beatings calmly; he submitted to scandalous extortion from state and individual with tranquillity; he bore robbery and even murder with stoical fortitude. Perhaps it was well that he did. Christian civilization, which declared by statute that his testimony was valueless; which intimated by its practice that the same vices in a pagan were worse than in a Christian; which regarded the frailty of his women as being especially abominable and his own gambling propensities as something originally bad, taught him at least the Christian virtues of patience and resignation.[35]

Out of these works by Twain, Harte, and others of their contemporaries, with their curious blending of stereotype, myth, and self-fulfillment, developed a whole range of general fictions about China, and thence a newer genre that one might call specifically "Chinatown fiction." The fictions often had an undercurrent of fact. As one can see from the works of the late nineteenth-century Chinatown photographer Arnold Genthe, most Chinese men kept their queues of hair, even as they adopted Western dress in other ways, often coiling the queues around their heads and tucking them under their derby hats. Some Chinese men certainly brought their opium habits from China, and spent much of their hard-earned money on gratifying their needs. Traveling from China alone, or with other men, they cooked their meals from what they could find and formed all-male communities, with only prostitutes for sexual diversion. Discriminated against by complex webs of commercial, educational, and occupational laws, which might take years and great expense to fight through the courts, they formed packed communities within their allotted Chinatown space. The former "benevolent societies" often consolidated into predatory organizations or "tongs" that gave some protection in a strange land,

and offered them backers speaking their own native dialects. But the societies also extorted money through protection rackets, controlled drugs, prostitution, and gambling, and indulged in venomous wars with their rivals. Sometimes bitterly hostile, at other times bemused or intrigued, their host society constructed their own rationales for Chinese behavior along a multitude of tracks.[36]

Elements that had lain tucked between the often funny or at least lighthearted lines of plays like Twain and Harte's *Ah Sin* now became the molders of entire plots. Though the two authors seemed sympathetic to many of the Chinese immigrants' travails, their play was filled with examples of the patent hostility to the Chinese expressed by the white mining men or their women. Within a few pages chosen at random, one can find Ah Sin described by his antagonists as a "slant-eyed son of the yellow jaunders," a "sinful old sluice robber," "jabbering idiot," "moral cancer," "unsolvable political problem," a "mental vacuum" with the "monkey faculty of imitating," and as possessed of "a glittering ignorance."[37]

From such elements, and countless others in the press, political rhetoric, and popular perceptions, emerged an increasingly harsh series of portrayals of Chinese scheming, danger, unreliability, and viciousness that dominated the fiction about China of the last years of the nineteenth century. It was in the Boxer year of 1900 that C. W. Doyle, an expatriate British physician living in California, began to produce the first in a series of Chinatown fictions that showed how Chinese ruthlessness could threaten white values. Doyle's stories focused on a villainous Chinese racketeer called Quong Lung—a name faintly evocative to some readers, perhaps, of the Chinese emperor Qian Long who had received Macartney. Quong Lung is described as having been educated at Yale—as had been the real-life pioneer among Chinese students in America, Yung Wing—and imbued by his white roommate Ray with a love of "Shakespeare and

Byron and the Psalms of David." Quong Lung has rewarded Ray by turning him into an opium addict, providing Chinese sing-song girls to minister to him, and compelling him to turn his great skills as an electrical engineer into the construction of engines of destruction. Quong Lung runs the San Francisco Chinatown with an iron hand—he kills those who dispute his authority, and has the power to break families asunder at will, and to steal their womenfolk. "'Accidents are constantly happening in Chinatown,'" he tells Ray "in an indifferent tone of voice" when Ray questions one of his instructions.[38]

Doyle touched a chord that was to be more fully elaborated with the creation of the character Fu-Manchu in 1910 by the British writer Sax Rohmer (Arthur S. Ward). With Fu-Manchu, the depiction of the evil Chinese took on an enduring and definitive international form. Fu-Manchu, even more than Quong Lung or his various other precursors, is a brilliant man—"the greatest and most evil genius whom the later centuries have produced"—and his goal is to establish a "universal Yellow Empire." His slavegirl, evoking many earlier stereotypes, wears "the gauzy dress of the harem, her fingers and slim white arms laden with barbaric jewelry," and has "eyes like pools of mystery to taunt the thirsty soul."[39] But these eyes are nothing beside the eyes of Fu-Manchu, as depicted by his ever clumsy British antagonist Dr. Petrie:

> In the high-backed chair sat Dr. Fu-Manchu, wearing a green robe upon which was embroidered a design, the subject of which at first glance was not perceptible, but which presently I made out to be a huge white peacock. He wore a little cap perched upon the dome of his amazing skull, and with one clawish hand resting upon the ebony of the table, he sat slightly turned toward me, his emotionless face a mask of incredible evil. In spite of, or because of, the high intellect written upon it, the face of Dr. Fu-Manchu was more utterly repellent than any I have ever known, and the green eyes, eyes green as those of a cat in the darkness,

which sometimes burned like witch lamps, and sometimes were horribly filmed like nothing human or imaginable, might have mirrored not a soul, but an emanation of hell, incarnate in this gaunt, high-shouldered body.[40]

Such stories drew their popularity from the clash of innocence—"divine simplicity," Fu-Manchu called it—on the part of the clumsy Western protagonists, with a kind of timeless "yellow peril" and Oriental cruelty that Westerners could trace back to the early tales of Mongol conquests in the age of Marco Polo, or down to the Boxer Uprising of their own time. As Petrie realized, in lying bound in the presence of Fu-Manchu, "he lay at the mercy of this enemy of the white race, of this inhuman being who himself knew no mercy, of this man whose very genius was inspired by the cool, calculated cruelty of his race, of that race which to this day disposes of hundreds, nay! thousands, of its unwanted girl-children by the simple measure of throwing them down a well specially dedicated to the purpose."[41] To emphasize this grim aspect of the Chinese, the word "Mongol" was commonly used in American political speeches and legal cases to refer to those who had previously been known as "Chinese." "A Chinaman is not a Caucasian," runs one such legal brief. "We cheerfully admit this fact. A Chinaman is a Mongolian."[42]

The mystique of a super-Chinese intelligence was of course a paradoxical one in the light of China's humiliations at the hand of foreigners both at home and abroad, and other writers were aware of this. Jack London, for example, who had begun in his fictions by depicting the desperado type of Chinese who poached in other people's rightful fishing grounds off the West Coast, and ended up by praising the suave subtlety of Chinese self-made millionaires in Hawaii, between these two extremes sketched portraits of the Chinese he had encountered during his travels in the South Seas, in which their simplicity of nature was exploited blindly yet cruelly by the dominant French.

Whereas London's first stories of California Chinese fishermen, published prior to 1905, had emphasized their toughness and dishonesty,[43] his tale of "The Chinago," published in *Harper's Monthly* in 1909, sought to go back to the earlier theme of Chinese innocence. London was going against the trend, and eleven magazines rejected the story before *Harper's* at last accepted it.[44] London injected the reader straight into a court-room scene that Twain's Ah Song Hi would have instantly rec-ognized:

> Ah Cho did not understand French. He sat in the crowded court room, very weary and bored, listening to the unceasing, explosive French that now one official and now another uttered. It was just so much gabble to Ah Cho, and he marvelled at the stupidity of the Frenchmen who took so long to find out the murderer of Chung Ga, and who did not find him at all. The five hundred coolies on the plantation knew that Ah San had done the killing, and here was Ah San not even arrested. It was true that all the coolies had agreed secretly not to testify against one another; but then, it was so simple, the Frenchmen should have been able to discover that Ah San was the man. They were very stupid, these Frenchmen.[45]

True to this common sense of solidarity, the twenty-two-year-old Ah Cho, already a three-year veteran of plantation life, had automatically "blocked and obfuscated" the inquiry when the cotton plantation overseers sought to find the murderer. But now that he himself was accused of the murder, he confidently awaited his own acquittal, knowing that he was innocent. In his mind, the French would learn the truth even faster if they used torture in the investigation, but they were too stupid for that as well. Ah Cho cannot know what the reader has already learned, that in this Tahitian plantation, owned by an English consor-tium, managed by the French, and supervised by the German overseer Karl Schemmer, the concept of law is attenuated and unclear.

As Ah Cho listens to the testimony he cannot understand,

his thoughts are fixed on the elsewhere that will follow his inevitable release:

> He would be a rich man for life, with a house of his own, a wife, and children growing up to venerate him. Yes, and back of the house he would have a small garden, a place of meditation and repose, with goldfish in a tiny lakelet, and wind bells tinkling in the several trees, and there would be a high wall all around so that his meditation and repose should be undisturbed.[46]

In Ah Cho's mind, it is the whites who represent irrational and violent forces on the island, not the Chinese:

> There was a curtain behind the eyes of the white devils that screened the backs of their minds from the Chinago's gaze. And then, on top of it all, was that terrible efficiency of the white devils, that ability to do things, to make things go, to work results, to bend to their wills all creeping, crawling things, and the powers of the very elements themselves. Yes, the white men were strange and wonderful, and they were devils.[47]

Condemned to twenty years of penal servitude for his alleged part in the killing, Ah Cho "was not perturbed. Twenty years were merely twenty years. By that much was his garden removed from him—that was all. He was young, and the patience of Asia was in his bones. He could wait those twenty years, and by that time the heats of his blood would be assuaged and he would be better fitted for that garden of calm delight. He thought of a name for it; he would call it The Garden of the Morning Calm."[48]

Even when Ah Cho is taken to the guillotine, his name wrongfully written on the death sentence by a drunk French magistrate, he is calm. As he explains to the French gendarme, in the Kanaka language that both of them have learned to speak in Tahiti, it is simply a mistake that can be easily corrected. The Frenchman smiles and agrees, but does nothing to reverse the flow of events. Only when the blade of the guillotine falls onto his neck on the executioner's orders does Ah Cho get a small surprise. "The knife did not tickle. That much he knew before he ceased to know."[49]

Ah Cho would never see his Garden of the Morning Calm, but the reader had been reminded that such visions could and did exist. Whatever the discriminations to which the Chinese had been subjected in their sojourns overseas,* a central thread of hope and nostalgia continued to hold firm.

---

* In fact, though such discriminations were commonplace, appeals were possible, and successful ones can be tracked through to the Supreme Court of the United States, as in cases like *Yick Wo* v. *Hopkins* of 1886. In this case Yick Wo, a Chinese laundryman in San Francisco who had come to the United States in 1861, protested his fine of ten dollars, or one day in jail per dollar of the fine if he could not pay, for violating a new city ordinance against conducting a laundry business from a building not made of brick or stone. After careful review, the Supreme Court reversed Yick Wo's conviction, on the grounds that the ordinances had been directed solely at Chinese rather than white laundries: In firm language, the justices told the San Francisco authorities that though the ordinance might "be fair on its face, and impartial in appliance, yet, if it is applied and administered by public authority with an evil eye and an unequal hand, so as practically to make unjust and illegal discriminations between persons in similar circumstances," then there had been a denial of justice.

In the case of Yick Wo, and over two hundred other laundrymen who had petitioned with him, "the conclusion cannot be resisted that no reason for it exists except hostility to the race and nationality to which the petitioners belong"— *Supreme Court Reporter,* 1886: 118 U.S. 356, p. 1073.

CHAPTER 8

The French Exotic

WITH THE PASSAGE OF TIME, PEOPLE FROM VIRTUALLY
every Western land had been involved with China in one way
or another: as traders, missionaries, diplomats, soldiers or sailors, physicians, teachers, technicians. Their reports in turn had
encouraged scholars and theorists to place China in world history, to divine its future fate, and to see if they could discover
among the shards of evidence the outlines of an explanatory system. Writers of fiction found in this accumulation of fact and
opinion a rich vein of material, which they mined in different
fashions according to their own inclinations and their sense of
the market. Among the growing numbers of those occupied
with China almost none were emotionally neutral, no matter
whether they had spent years there working and traveling, had
merely visited briefly, or were desk-bound speculators. Instead,
they wavered between and across waves of emotions, from awe
to amusement, from irritation to infatuation.

It seems to have been a peculiarly French genius, however, to
draw out of this welter of overlapping themes a central core of
mutually reinforcing images and perceptions that by the later
nineteenth century coalesced to form what we can call a "new
exotic." The antecedents for this new exotic were rich and complex, beginning in the reign of Louis XIV, when for reasons of
religion and international prestige the king invested heavily in
the expansion of the French China missions. This policy brought
some of France's most talented Jesuit fathers to the court of
Emperor Kangxi, where they had good opportunities to explore
Chinese mathematics and philosophy. Their findings fed the

imagination of thinkers as different as Leibniz, Montesquieu, and Voltaire, and played a part too in the expansion of the craze for Chinoiserie, which found its most flamboyant manifestations in eighteenth-century France. From this movement grew not only impulses for new artistic forms, but also the French decision to ground the formal study of Chinese language and history in the academy, leading to the West's first great flowering of what came to be called sinology.

Looking back from our present vantage, we can see that by the mid-nineteenth century the emerging cult of the Chinese exotic in France had come to combine four main realms or elements. One was an appreciation of Chinese grace and delicacy, a sensitivity to timbre and texture, that spread from the initial stimuli of silk and porcelain and temple architecture to become the basis of an entire aesthetic. One was an awareness of Chinese sensuality, initially tied to this new aesthetic, but rapidly moving out to embrace something harsher and ranker, something unknowable, dangerous, and intoxicating, composed of scent and sweat, of waves of heat and festering night air. Separate from this, though inescapably linked to it, was the sense of a realm of Chinese violence and barbarism, of hidden cruelties, threats of ravishment, uncontrollable impulses. And lastly was the idea of China as the realm of melancholy, as a land that stood for something forever lost—lost to the West through uncaring materialism, lost to China through the weight of its own past, compounded by its weakness and its poverty. Opium was the natural accompaniment to this fourth realm, the narcotic of langor and of longing.

An initial stage in the drawing together of these four realms can be seen in the journal of Prosper Giquel, penned in 1864. Giquel was a French officer, loaned by his government to the Qing armies seeking to suppress the Taiping insurgents. His assigned task was to destroy the last remnants of the Taiping rebels, who still held out in certain bastions of Central China after their "Heavenly Capital" of Nanjing had fallen. He and his

company of veteran French troops performed this task professionally and successfully. But Giquel recorded more than a roster of battles fought and won. He showed life amid the smell of
war under the burning Chinese sun, and wrote of the mutilated
corpses strewn along the roads, his men splashing in the muddy
creeks and beckoning to the watching Chinese women to join
them. He told how he had a billiard table hauled up the slopes
of a hill near the battle zone, so his men could play as they
watched the enemy's preparations. And he shared the dreamy
drunkenness that came at nightfall, as the soldiers under the
Chinese stars drank their chilled and clouded absinthe, and
watched the lights of the flickering campfires.[1]

Giquel was first and foremost a soldier, and if we can see here
all the elements of the emerging Chinese exotic, they are still
presented in a raw, undigested form. With an artist like Giquel's
contemporary, Gustave Flaubert, the components of the new
exotic are already being assembled with almost schematic precision. In his novel of love in the midst of revolution, *Sentimental
Education* (1869), Flaubert uses Chinese images as markers for
the major shifts in his characters' lives. Thus in the deep sensuality of Frédéric's first visit to Madame Arnoux's home, he finds
her hallway "decorated in the Chinese style." The lascivious
world of the dance hall and gardens at the top of the Champs
Elysées is under "a sort of Chinese roof," and at Frédéric's crucial assignation with Rosanette she carries a parasol of lilac satin
"rising to a point in the middle like a pagoda."[2]

Chinese lanterns and porcelain, screens and curios, yellow
silks and Chinese blinds, provide their own rhythms as objects
of beauty and regard. In the moments of deepest romantic
melancholy, Frédéric will go to "a lecture on Chinese or political
economy" or finds himself at an old pantomime of "a slave-
market in Peking."[3] Images of violence are present in the "trophy
of Mongol arrows" that Madame Arnoux examines on her first
visit alone to Frédéric's home and the "Chinese weapons" on
offer at the tragic auction of the Arnoux possessions. And when

Frédéric, suffused with lust, takes Rosanette to the love nest he had prepared for Madame Arnoux, "Chinese lanterns were hanging from the houses, looking like garlands of fire," the bayonets of the guards "gleamed white against the dark background," and the murderous fusillade that kills so many innocent people on the Boulevard des Capucines was "like the sound of a huge piece of silk being ripped in two."[4]

Despite the specificity and apparently deliberate placement of these items from China and their relationship to the plot, Flaubert's China remains entangled with a broader group of images from the Middle East that cumulatively remind us that this is still in part the mid-nineteenth-century world of a more generalized "Orientalism," an "Orientalism" that had received a further boost in France after the Napoleonic campaigns in Egypt. Again, Flaubert seems aware of this by his choice of juxtapositions: the dance hall with the Chinese roof is called the "Alhambra" and also boasts "two parallel arcades in the Moorish style"; the pantomime of the Peking slave market is replete with "bells, drums, and sultan's wives"; and Rosanette, even as she clasps her pagoda-parasol, shows Frédéric that she "thought that Lebanon was in China."[5]

But by the end of the nineteenth century, Chinese images and metaphors were being isolated more sharply, and under the pens of a number of remarkable French writers the Chinese exotic came into its own. Pierre Loti was among the first to set the new mood, in his immensely popular book *The Last Days of Peking*, based on his reminiscences serving as a French naval officer and attache during the suppression of the Boxer Uprising in 1900. Loti (Julien Viaud, 1850–1923) was already famous as a novelist for his tales of the South Seas, the Middle East, and Japan. Short, scrawny, and weak as a youth, Loti had transformed his body through a harsh regimen of physical exercise, culminating in learning the arts of the circus acrobats who traveled through his home district. Subsequently joining the French Navy, he transformed his sexual and emotional experiences into the self-image of the passionate romantic and reckless lover, with a taste for excess. In his novel *Aziyadé* (1879) he astonished French readers with the dazzling language and bravado of his love affair with a harem beauty in Istanbul; in *Le mariage de Loti* (1882) it was his sensual experiences in Tahiti that ravished his readers; in *Madame Crysanthème* (1887) he had become the companion of youthful Japanese geishas.[6]

Along with these tales of amorous endeavors, tales where the fictional and the real can no longer be disentangled, Loti had shown himself to be a precise observer of the constantly rediscovered exotic. In 1884, the Goncourt brothers wittily categorized him as "the genius of the nose," worthy successor to Gautier (genius of the eye), and Fromentin (genius of the ear).[7] They had perhaps been confirmed in this judgment by reading the accounts of Asia that Loti sent back to the journal *Le Figaro,* based on his observations of the bombardment of Annam by the French in 1883, in which Loti participated as an officer on the cruiser *Atalante.* (The harsh precision of these accounts of French brutalities led to Loti's recall from active duty and enforced return to France aboard a freighter.) For Loti, at age thirty-three, the Orient was "yellow, scurrying, rapacious, ape-like and obscene . . . a smell of yellow sweat, incense and filth, over all, the stench of musk, irritating, sickening, intolerable."[8] Loti introduced Annam to his French readers as a land illuminated by the flickering light of its burning villages, while the French officers who watched the carnage from their armchairs on the ship's decks seemed to him like modern-day simulacra of "Attila and Genghis Khan." When struck by French exploding shells, the gaily-colored Chinese-style houses, with their bamboo frames and porcelain decorations, writhed and twisted in the intense heat of their own fire, giving off a light "dark as blood" and a "black acrid smoke with a trace of musk," as the terrified village survivors zigzagged frantically in search of cover, or burrowed themselves like rats into the sand.[9]

By the year 1900, now aged fifty and comfortably settled in a

French country home flamboyantly decorated with Oriental motifs, Loti had given up all thought of returning to the East. But the order from his government to return to uniform as a member of the French contingent to the eight-nation expeditionary force being sent to suppress the Boxer Uprising struck him as a wonderful bounty of fate, a chance to return for a last time to a way of life he had believed vanished forever. As he wrote home from shipboard:

> I have found once more the person I used to be; I am twenty years younger. The delicious calm of this cloister has made everything at peace within me. I recall my torments and anguish as if they had gone for ever. I love noone anymore, nor any thing, except for this air and sea. Supremely detached from everything, I am once more the man of those earlier campaigns, but with less of the vague despairs of those days, the tormenting regrets, the desolated tenderness. I am on my way, transformed, amnesiac, carefree, young.[10]

Pierre Loti's most celebrated depiction of a Chinese exotic thus grew from this sense of euphoric, late-life rejuvenation, one in which the senses and the witnessing of violence were inseparably blurred. As an experienced observer, he knew that the scenes of destruction and carnage that greeted him when he reached Peking had been brought on by the Boxers, by the Qing dynasty troops who had sided for a time with the Boxers, and by the allied troops themselves. As a senior naval officer with the French forces, attached to the admiral's staff, Loti traveled in comparative comfort, the dangers of infection and the fatigues of the journey eased by a case of Evian water he kept by his side.

His first Chinese home was a palace compound on the north lake, just on the edge of the Forbidden City itself. The walls of Peking, as he approached them, had seemed to him "the color of mourning,"[11] and once inside he understood why: he saw acres of ruins, he smelled the death and the smoke, he watched dogs tugging at the corpses of dead Chinese children buried in the rubble, and in one image of incomparable horror saw an initially unrecognizable object that turned out to be "the lower half of a woman's body, shoved into a bucket, legs in the air." The top of the torso was missing, but the head, "a black bundle of tangled hair, lay under an armchair, next to a crushed cat."[12] Unforgettable for Loti was the night in China: as he lay in bed in his huge chamber, he could see glinting through the darkness around him, and up in the eves, the eyes of countless rats; and as he pulled the coverlet around him he could hear the tinkling sounds the rats made as they hunted for scraps among the porcelain bowls in which he had been served a late-night snack.[13]

Amid the horrors, the possessions of the once-great dynasty lay all around him, for the picking. His French and Chinese servants disported themselves in the palaces, clowning away in embroidered palace robes. Loti himself, we know from his journal, shipped home at least ten crates of loot, though he played this down in the published accounts, and informed his wife that—at least in the case of the furs he was sending her—he had not looted them himself but had bought them for her from Chinese looters.[14] He also toured around the city and the palaces, writing the careful and elaborate descriptions of Peking that helped project his book into fifty printings between its initial publication in 1902 and the outbreak of the world war in 1914.

As he told his wife in a letter just before his departure, he would never again have such a place in which to write:

> I leave Peking tomorrow, and this will be the end of my little imperial dream. . . . I will miss this time; the parks were exquisite in spite of the corpses and the crows. It is fun to open cupboards and chests every day to explore the marvels there. I have a little study room, and I shall never find peace like that again, in a rotunda beloved by the empress, where at times one of her former cats came to visit me. I am under a porcelain roof, in front of a lotus lake. For company I have a great jade goddess in a golden robe, who was meant to ensure the safety of the Chinese empire. I left home with a single suitcase. I will return with a huge load of baggage.[15]

As a living souvenir to go with the baggage, Loti brought home with him to France one of those prowling cats who—in his mind at least—had once belonged to the empress of China. He made the cat a visiting card, on yellow pasteboard, bearing the full name he had bestowed on her: "Madame Moumoutte—Chinoise, 2ème chatte chez Monsieur Pierre Loti." That way there would be no confusion between her and her predecessor, his beloved "Madame Moumoutte Blanche," who would be forever his "première chatte."[16]

On his return to France, Loti mourned the lost magic of China, "its prestige gone, its mystery unveiled." The Forbidden City had been to Loti "a last refuge of the unknown and the marvellous; it was one of the remaining bastions of ancient humanity, as incomprehensible to us as it was fabulous." Loti had seen how, "in the golden throne rooms, the sumptuous carpets were covered with bird droppings." And yet a new China might somehow emerge from the faded splendors; what would the future hold, Loti wrote, if "all these myriad young peasants such as I have seen, sober and lean and muscled" were given the "modern methods of destruction" that the French already possessed?[17]

Loti let the thought drop, and when he returned to Chinese themes it was to the even remoter past, to the theme of the thwarted love of a Chinese princess for her Tartar emperor, in a play, La fille du ciel (The Daughter of Heaven) that he wrote with Judith Gautier. He had hoped his friend Sarah Bernhardt would play the Chinese princess, but she refused to conceal her bright red hair under a black wig, as Loti demanded, and the idea was shelved. The play was bought by American producers and appeared briefly on Broadway in 1912, just after the Qing dynasty had fallen. Loti traveled to New York for the opening, a somewhat pitiable figure now, his face rouged and hair dyed against the passing years, his small body raised on high-heeled shoes. He disliked the feel of New York—"houses pushed up beyond all measure, like asparagus in April"—but he liked the lavish props in the production, and was astonished at the numbers of Chinese available in New York to play the bit parts: he learned they were students, trying to decide what to do next now the dynasty had fallen.[18]

Whereas Loti's creative career was virtually over when he visited New York—and the play was a failure—the lifelong interest in China of the French poet and dramatist Paul Claudel seems to have been initially sparked by his experiences in the same city. Born in 1868, and undergoing a profound conversion experience to the Catholic faith in 1886, Claudel had already created a satisfying life that combined poetry and drama with the foreign service when he received a posting as French vice consul at New York in 1893. Before New York, Claudel's knowledge of the East had been restricted to the Japanese prints that had captivated many of his contemporaries in Paris, and to some Annamese plays that he had seen staged in Paris at the great exposition of 1889.

But shortly after arriving in New York, Claudel discovered the Chinese theater. As he wrote to a friend in Paris: "Here in Mott Street there is a Chinese quarter, with its bright red placards, its sinister basements that serve as opium dens, its theater to which I intend to go soon, and a temple with its 'Joss' gods." The specific theater he referred to was probably the one at number 5 Dyers Street, formerly the Chinese Mission Sunday School building, now transformed for this new medium, with separate blocks of seats for Chinese and "Americans."[19] Though he does not tell us which plays he saw, Claudel was clearly struck by the complex plot structures and protracted performances, by the ritual gestures and diction, ebullient costumes, and strident on-stage musicians. "There is nothing in the world more beautiful than the Chinese theater," he told a friend in 1895, "and when one has seen that one need see nothing else." A play that Claudel himself wrote in 1893, *The Exchange*, has some similarities in plot and structure to the most popular of the Chinese plays that was running in New York at the Dyers Street theater that year.[20]

When a summons came from the French foreign office to

Claudel in 1895 posting him to be a consul in China, he later observed, "I was absolutely delighted. There was no country I wanted to see as much as China. But then, I had no exact idea of the Orient at that time." His China thus initially remained a vague and timeless one: as he wrote to his friend the poet Mallarmé after his arrival, "life here has not been touched by the modern sickness," and China remained "an ancient land" that could still teach "its own dreams."[21]

Claudel was to spend most of the years between 1895 and 1909 in China, and almost from the first week he began using the country as inspiration for a new genre of prose-poem that he was exploring. His vision was softer than Loti's, and had a dreamladen quality, yet Claudel's words also retained a remarkably sharp and observant edge. His Chinese prose-poems were usually plotless, content to seize and hold a fugitive moment. One of the first was called, simply, "Theater," and gave first full expression to the view of Chinese drama that he may have started to understand in New York: As then, so now in China, encased in their draperies, faces covered with masklike makeup, hidden amid "the plumage of their roles," each actor was revealed only as "a gesture and a voice. The Emperor weeps over his kingdom, the unjustly accused princess flees to shelter among monsters and savages, armies maneuver, battles are waged, the years and the distances are surmounted by a gesture." While amid the crashing or plaintive chords of the on-stage orchestra the audience, totally absorbed, takes in every movement and sound; it is as if the theater "were paved with heads, with round and yellow faces, jammed together so tightly that one could see no limbs or bodies—all were glued together, the hearts in the heap beating one against the other."[22]

In "The City at Night," a piece written on a visit to Shanghai in January 1896, and published that summer in a Paris review, Claudel moved out beyond the stage to try to seize the essence of this Chinese city that so deeply attracted and repelled the West:

The narrow tangle of streets, where we are involved in the midst of a shadowy crowd, is lit only by the deep open booths which border it. These are the workrooms of carpenters, engravers; the shops of tailors, shoemakers, and venders of fur. From innumerable kitchens, behind the display of bowls of noodles and soup, the sound of frying escapes. In a dark recess some woman attends a crying child. Among stacked-up coffins is the gleam of a pipe. A lamp, a sidewise flicker, shows strange medleys. At the street corners, at the bends of heavy little stone bridges, in niches behind iron bars, dwarfish idols can be seen between two red candles. After a long progress under the rain, in the darkness and filth, we find ourselves suddenly in a yellow blind alley which a big lantern lights with a brutal flare.[23]

Despite the narrowness of these lanes and alleys, the dead ends, the dark, the stench, "the city forms a coherent whole" to Claudel; it is "an industrious honeycomb communicating in all its parts, perforated like an ant-hill." In this perforated honeycomb, his China waits:

An opium den, a market of prostitutes, these last fill the framework of my memory. The smoking den is a vast nave, empty all the height of two stories which superimpose their balconies inside. The building is full of blue smoke, one breathes an odor of burning chestnuts. It is a heavy perfume, powerful, stagnant, strong as the beat of a gong. . . .

On narrow benches, their heads helmed with flowers and pearls, clothed in wide blouses of silk and full embroidered trousers, motionless, with their hands on their knees, the prostitutes wait in the street like beasts at a fair, in the pell-mell and the dust of passers-by. Beside their mothers and dressed like them, also motionless, little girls are seated on the same bench. Behind, a flare of petrol lights the opening to the stairway.[24]

It is an overpowering introduction, and the eye of the reader lingers, as Claudel intends it to, on those prostitutes with their blouses of silk, the solemn girl-children beside them on the narrow benches, the flare of lights beckoning to the stairway. Does

Claudel succumb? "Je passe," he writes in the next line, untranslatably ambiguous—"I go up"? "I go on my way"? "I proceed"? "I let it be?"—"Je passe," and that is all. Then the words, still beautiful but hectic now, jerk the reader and the narrator out of the reverie into the bright clarity of the International Concession which the foreign powers have been steadily making their own since the post–Opium War treaties of 1842.

> Je passe. And I carry the memory of a life congested, naïve, restless; of a city at the same time open and crowded, a single house with a multifold family. I have seen the city of other days, when, free of modern influences, men swarmed in an artless disorder; in fact it is the fascination of all the past that I am leaving, when, issuing out of the double gate in the hurly-burly of wheelbarrows and litters, in the midst of lepers and epileptics, I see the electric lights of the Concession shine.[25]

Claudel was hopelessly careless about his manuscripts and his page proofs, and it was to Victor Segalen, his close friend and admirer, that we owe a corrected and fairly definitive edition of this and other works.[26] Segalen himself was to become perhaps the greatest French interpreter of the China exotic. Born in 1878, ten years Claudel's junior, Segalen trained as a physician, and in a curious echo of Claudel's induction, first encountered the Chinese in the San Francisco Chinatown, which he passed through in 1902 on his way to a posting in Tahiti. Segalen's attraction to China became deep and total. In Paris, he studied the Chinese classical language and culture with one of France's first great sinologues, Edouard Chavannes, who became one of the formative influences on his life. Chavannes had been an activist scholar, roaming China's sacred sites, examining and transcribing inscriptions, sketching tombs and decorative motifs. Segalen was able, thanks to his professional postings, to spend most of the time between 1909 and 1917 in China. Inspired by his teacher's example, despite the demands of his life as a physician, Segalen made three protracted journeys across China,

investigating archeological sites and sketching and photograph-
ing Chinese stone sculpture, for which he developed a scholar's
passion and a connoisseur's eye, sharing his discoveries with
Chavannes through regular letters.[27]

Segalen's beautiful series of poems, entitled simply *Steles,* conceived and written in 1909, published in 1912, drew its title and
some of its content from the stone steles, some millennia old,
that he came across on his travels. Segalen dedicated the series
to Paul Claudel—whose work he loved—but perhaps more totally
than Claudel or any other of the Western writers of the time
Segalen caught all four elements of the exotic, the passionate,
the aesthetic, the melancholy, and the violent. Drawing inspiration from the fact that the Chinese often placed giant stone
steles, bearing incised texts or poems, along their roadways, or
near ancestral temples, Segalen determined to create his own
offerings in the same genre. He constructed a convincing and
emotionally satisfying fiction that Chinese steles always bore a
different type of message according to the direction in which
they were facing: thus steles of love face toward the east; steles of
friendship face toward the north; the emperor's instructions are
pointed toward the south; and the steles of war and death will
face the "blood-soaked west, the palace of red" and the setting
sun.[28] One other group face downward into the earth. These are
the steles of the center; without direction yet full of meaning,
they press the seals of their messages into the soil itself. "They
are the decrees of another—singular—empire."

"Supplication," one of the love poems from the "Steles Facing
East," shows the pureness of the diction Segalen created to capture his chosen Chinese mood:

SUPPLICATION

You will be wooed with smiles, looks, sudden
     effusions, and gifts, which you will refuse on
     principle, being as yet but a girl;

You will be implored to say what you yearn
    and thirst for, what ornaments please you
    most—red wedding clothes, poems, songs,
    sacrifices . . .

This unworthy man—myself—unworthy even to
    beg, entreats you to grant him nothing but
    your appearance, the form which haunts you,
    the gesture, dancing bird, you alight in.

Or your inflectionless voice, or that blue reflection
    in your hair. But your soul, which is ten
    thousand times precious in the eyes of the Sage,

Let it be well concealed in the depths of your
    disconcerting presence,
        Beautiful young girl, and be silent.[29]

In savage contrast to the limpid eroticism of the invocation to
the young woman in "supplication," in one of the poems to war
and death in the "Steles Facing West," Segalen conjured up the
ferocity of all China's past conquerors and violators:

At Sword Point

We horsemen astride our horses, what do we know
    about sowing? But any field that can be
    plowed by horse hooves, any meadow that
    can be galloped across,

    We have trampled.

We do not stoop to build walls or temples,
    but any town that will burn, with its temples
    and walls,

    We have burnt down.

We honor and cherish our women who are all of
    high rank; but the others, those who can
    be tumbled, spread apart and possessed,

    We have taken.

Our seal is a spearhead: our ceremonial dress,
    armor starred with dew; our silk is woven
    from manes. The other kind, which is softer
    and fetches a price,

    We have sold.

Having no boundaries, and some of us no names,
    we do not rule, we move. But whatever
    can be hacked and gashed, whatever can be
    spiked and split,

    Whatever can be perpetrated at swordpoint,

    We have done.[30]

In a poem from the fifth cycle of *Steles*, Segalen explored another theme, that of the steles of the "middle," pressed down under their own weight and breathing their message into the soil. This poem came from the region outside—or within—the other four, trapped in their emotional categories dictated by the cardinal points of the compass. Here Segalen presented China's central city as constructed in layers, each concealing the other, as in his own way Claudel had done for Shanghai in his prose-poem of 1896. Segalen called this stele "Forbidden Purple City":

Built in the image of Pei-king, the capital of the
    North, in a climate either extremely hot or
    colder than extreme cold.

Ringed by merchants' houses and inns open to one
    and all, with their one-night beds, mangers,
    and dung heaps.

And, standing back from that rabble, the proud
    outer wall, the Unassailable, with its forbidding
    ramparts, its redans, its corner forts for
    my stout defenders.

In the center: this red wall restricting its quadrangle
    of perfect friendship to the elect.

But there, central, subterranean, superior, filled with
palaces, lotuses, lifeless pools, eunuchs, and
porcelain—stands my forbidden Purple City . . .[31]

Of all the poems in Segalen's *Steles,* this one seems to have had
the deepest resonance for him, as it captured the many levels of
reality he himself had encountered in China.[32] One can clearly
see in these lines the genesis of his extraordinary and beautiful
novel, *René Leys,* which he began to write just afterwards. Segalen was in Peking during 1911 and 1912 when China's last
dynasty, the Qing, was brought down by its own incompetence,
the ceaseless pressures and wars of the foreign powers, and the
recurrent assaults of its own revolutionaries seeking to establish
a republic. Segalen's vision of China, like that of every Westerner
up to 1912, had been an imperial one, colored by spectacle and
glamorous memories that spanned over two millennia. But
now, once penetrated, the Forbidden City lost its mystery. Loti
had been a precursor to this process, Claudel had mourned it,
but both had now departed, Loti to France (and New York),
Claudel to continued diplomatic work in Frankfurt. So it was
left to Segalen to record the final disintegration of the last
dynasty, the shocking image of the president of the new republic arriving by train to dispossess the Manchu regents and their
child emperor Pu-yi.

For those who loved the exotic, it had to be a time of loss.
Segalen possessed his own "vision of China," he wrote to his
friend Debussy at this time, and to hold on to that vision he
turned to the poems of the "middle," and in particular to the
figure of a young Belgian man he had met in Peking, Maurice
Roy.[33] Roy was the son of the director of postal services in
Peking, and spoke Chinese admirably, so Segalen hired him, for
a time, as a language teacher. Handsome and impressionable,
gliding between the cultures, Roy opened up the possibilities
that Segalen created for his fictional René Leys: bilingual sensu-
alist, close confidant to the young and indolent Manchu princes
with their love of theatrical performances and the entertain-

ment quarters, drawn by coincidence and lust into the very chambers of the boy emperor's widowed mother, accidental witness to the revolution, discoverer of the secret life of the real city beneath and within the apparent city of Peking, the surface city that was all other Westerners knew or could know.

Apparently first drafted in a few weeks during 1912, in an extraordinary burst of creative energy—allegedly for a bet, to show that he could master the newly emergent form of the virtually "plotless" novel—and revised in 1919, just before Segalen's death, *René Leys* cannot readily be summarized in any way that would do it justice. But it is not hard to find within it aspects of the many exoticisms that Segalen and his contemporaries sought and found in China.

One passage that makes the link to the stele facing the middle most immediate comes at the center of the novel, when the narrator and his young friend are out riding their horses together in Peking, just two days before the revolution erupts: They rein in their horses at a spot near the Forbidden City, above a batch of paving that sounded oddly hollow, and René Leys lets the narrator into the secret that only he has unraveled:

> Pei-king is not, as one might think, a chessboard whose game, fair or foul, is played on the surface. No—there is an Underground City complete with its redans, its corner forts, its highways and byways, its approaches, its threats, its "horizontal wells" even more formidable than the wells of drinking and other water that yawn up at the open sky. . . .

What Leys has opened up for the narrator is a "Palace of Dreams" to be set besides the other breathing, yet hollow city

> All the unknown, thrice immured behind twenty-foot-high walls, has taken on ten times the mystery in being furnished with this vertical abyss at their base—the Profound City with all its subterranean cavitations! Beneath the broad, flat expanse of the capital anything that even nibbles at the dimension of depth is unexpected . . . disturbing. . . . [34]

In other passages in the novel, Segalen reflected aloud, with more forthrightness than other Westerners had done, on the possibilities of physical love between East and West. At a dinner party with his elderly language teacher, the narrator appraises the youngest consort of his host. Such a mixed company dinner would have been unthinkable in China until the idea of a Westernized "modernity" began to filter into the courts of the late Qing, part and parcel of the new trends in education, technology, journalism, and business that were slowly transforming the traditional society. Segalen's description of the woman, with the constant interruption of the ellipses he uses so lavishly, is breathless and hot, like the summer evening:

> Her seasonal toilet (it is summer) was all slender lines; vertical yet supple; straight, yet rippling at the slightest movement, almost at the merest breath . . . A barely opaque material through which the air filtered, cooling the skin . . . A blouse with a round collar from which emerged a neck without perceptible anatomy, I mean with neither muscles nor leannesses, a round, moving, living column . . . Beneath the blouse, two modest breasts, precise of angle. And lastly a pair of legs that were incontrovertibly long. In fact I let my gaze linger on them the better to gauge their length . . . [35]

Segalen goes on to reflect more specifically on the possibilities of an affair.

> After the meal the evening really began. An evening spent in the finest company of promises, adventure, ventures, and refusals . . .
> I looked at her. She was laughing at some gesture of mine. I amused her. I entertained her. But it amused me in my turn to wonder whether she considered physical love and all that goes with it as a childish game too (and it is a hypothesis) or as a shameful necessity, a service, a function, an adventure, a fashion, a moment, a habit, a well-drilled mannerism, a ceremony, a sacrifice, or as a ritual governed by chapter and verse. . . . [36]

The affair never progressed, but Segalen's fictional narrator had made his attitudes clear: China was a boundless adventure ground, in which the Westerner from his privileged and protected post-Boxer terrain could take his ease and plan his moves at leisure. When the revolution triumphs, and the Qing court is forced to abdicate the throne completely, keeping, however, the Forbidden City palaces and their contents in its private hands, Segalen realizes he has to end his novel. There has been no catastrophe. Merely the end of an era:

> A winter morning just like any other. Nothing happened in the night. Nothing at all. For the first time Pei-king has disappointed me: the City did not burn last night. . . .
>
> It may be indiscreet or clumsy of me to wake at this hour . . . for all that it is an historic one. And to be suddenly as lucid as the "great dry winter sky." It is a deep, deep sleep I am waking from. For the first time the day is not what I expected. Pei-king is no longer the haunt of my dreams. My bad mood invading and besieging the very Palace itself, I even begin to doubt that I ever wanted to set foot inside it! . . .
>
> Tonight or tomorrow I shall pack my bags.
>
> I have just reread the first sheet of this manuscript and found myself underlining—the gesture was involuntary—the words: *"I shall know no more . . . I shall retire from the field . . . "*
>
> And adding in a quite different hand: " . . . and I do not wish to know any more."[37]

In the last year of his life, the novel revised to his satisfaction, and now back in France, Segalen turned again to his book on Chinese sculpture, which despite his passions for poetry and fiction had continued to absorb him. His teacher Chavannes had died recently, and he felt the weight of the stone past he had tried to make his own. It was up to the Europeans, he felt, in the midst of the chaotic yet surely temporary revolution, to hold on to the Chinese values that mattered, even though inevitably the magic was gone: "The people who carved them and placed them are dead. Nor do we ourselves live in the days when the chimeras, unicorns, or lions weighing ten thousand weight, towed along on stone wheels, miraculously began, when they neared their destination—generally a princely tomb—to sniff the wind, to shake themselves, and leap onto the site reserved for them."[38]

In the more prosaic world, all that was left was the purity of rediscovery, the shaking loose of the earth and the maintenance of our sense of wonder. "When a European eye beholds, for the *very first* time, a stone shape that bears witness to two thousand years in the Chinese past, when each blow of the pickax makes a little more of the earthen mantle fall from it, an impression of personal possession, personal achievement, swells such that the mere description, long afterwards, vibrates with the thrill of personal adventure."[39]

Segalen died in 1919, of a mysterious, attenuating illness that he could neither diagnose nor cure, before he could ready his sculpture book for the press. But the China that he had enfolded so tightly within him endured, challenging with the richness of its multilayered exotic the pile of shattered fragments out of which he had composed it.

CHAPTER 9

An American Exotic?

DESPITE THE AESTHETIC STRENGTH OF SEGALEN'S vision, by the early 1920s the great French fascination with China as representative of the exotic began to fade. It was undercut in part by the realities of World War I. More than one hundred thousand Chinese laborers worked in France during that war, brought over by contractual agreements so that they could perform unskilled labor such as unloading arms and shells in the docks, clearing the battlefields of the dead, and bringing supplies up to the front lines. But this experience in no way contributed to the play of the exotic—if anything, it lent support to an opposing set of impressions, for the Chinese were only there to release more able-bodied French (and English) men from non-military tasks so they could be sent into active combat against the Germans. Illiterate, homesick, dirty, bored, the Chinese did not present a glamorous image. At the same time the other Chinese in France, the children of wealthier middle-class families who had come over on various forms of scholarships or work-study programs, were drawn into the organized worlds of radical politics—including the Communist Party—and presented a front of committed social seriousness-of-purpose that was also antithetical to their exotic image.[1]

As if picking up the slack, however, the creative exploitation of moods and images from China found a new source of energy in the United States. There, the panorama was a mixed and complex one, as it had been in France, but with different and sometimes conflicting components. A legacy of sensuality and violence had come down from the Chinatown fictions, but in the first decade of the twentieth century—in response to the horrors of the Boxer Uprising—there emerged a heightened sense of moral obligation toward China, particularly evident in the Protestant churches and their missionary arms, which began to pump massive funding into Chinese medical and educational facilities.

The final collapse of the Qing dynasty in 1912 spread the sense of moral commitment to Chinese politics, inducing strong American support for the development of democratic institutions in China. As more Chinese students began coming to the United States, there was also a growing sense of shame over the anti-Chinese discrimination still prevalent there. American business interests created their own portrayals of the Chinese as potential consumers within an expanding global market. And finally, the rapid growth of modern sectors in Chinese cities—cars, movie theaters, electric lights, bobbed hair, department stores, phonographs—brought an emotional backlash among some Americans for what they believed to be the fundamental values of traditional Chinese culture. The combination of these varying trends led in the period of World War I and after to a new patterning: a revived fascination with the lifestyle and philosophy of traditional Confucian thinkers, nostalgia for earlier Chinese artistic forms, a sympathy for the Chinese as innocent victims of unthinking Western materialism, and a sentimental respect and affection for the Chinese peasant farmer as the fruit of the soil and the fount of immemorial wisdom.

The film directed by D. W. Griffith and released in 1919—*Broken Blossoms*—drew together a number of these transitional elements, as well as others that went back centuries earlier. It followed closely after three other films made in 1915 that had achieved notoriety by their portrayals of interracial relations and tensions: Griffith's own *Birth of a Nation*, Cecil B. de Mille's *The Cheat*, and Sidney Olcutt's *Madame Butterfly*. The first dealt with white/black hostilities, and the other two with Japanese themes: in *The Cheat*, the Japanese male was the dominant force and threat to white womanhood; in *Madame Butterfly*. Cho-

chosan (played by Mary Pickford) represented abused Japanese womanhood.[2] Griffith set *Broken Blossoms* in London's Limehouse district, following the original short story by Thomas Burke, somewhat less sentimentally entitled "The Chink and the Child."[3] Limehouse was as near as England came to having a Chinatown, and had already been fictionally visited by Conan Doyle in the Sherlock Holmes stories.

By keeping the setting for the film overseas, Griffith blunted the sense that he was criticizing his own society. Thus freed from the merely topical, he gave himself the opportunity to present his story of the intense love of a Chinese man for a white woman in the universalist context of human compassion. The Chinese protagonist, Cheng Huan, is at once voyeur, aesthete, and victim. He has traveled from China (almost like one of Leibniz's putative Chinese missionaries) with the dream of bringing a message of Buddhist peace and love to the war-torn West, but all he finds is impotent loneliness in a single room above a Chinese curio shop where he works, and occasional sating of his opium addiction among the Western prostitutes and other addicts in the squalid Limehouse taverns where he goes for company. His heart is wrenched by the terrible abuse that he can see and hear his near neighbor Lucy enduring from her vicious, drunken father, Battling Burrows. When she is in danger of death, Cheng takes her in, and gives her warmth, food, and shelter. But he does more than that: he clothes her in Oriental finery from the curio shop, and surrounds her with Chinese luxury so that she becomes the potential concubine and he the potential ravisher. The lines between protectiveness and menace are deliberately blurred. When Battling Burrows discovers that his daughter has taken refuge with a "Chink," he breaks his way into Cheng's room, shreds the Oriental trappings, and forcibly takes Lucy home, where, in a terrible scene, he beats her to death. Cheng shoots Burrows, and then, after reverently laying out Lucy's dead body in his ravaged room, stabs himself to death at her side.

Broken Blossoms is as much a critique of Western violence and insensitivity as it is a hymn to Chinese virtue, but it gives a number of twists to the old theme. Battling Burrows, for example, is without a single redeeming feature; Cheng may be sensitive but he is fatally indecisive and his heart is tinged with lust, even though he controls it; Lucy herself knows nothing of China and seems to know little of the West. The film's other characters are shrouded. It is clear that Griffith—who presented the film, through a lavish publicity campaign, with special reserved seating at inflated prices—intended the work to be seen as "high art" with a "universal message."[4] Yet later viewers might feel, in language that Goldsmith had once used so well, that Griffith's frail wheelbarrow load of Chinese morality would crack the thick ice of conventional life.

Less portentous, though equally earnest in its intent, was the series of poems constructed around Chinese motifs that Ezra Pound began creating shortly before the release of *Broken Blossoms*, and was to continue writing for the following thirty years. As a resident in turn of London, Paris, and Rapallo after he left the United States in 1908, Pound made himself a citizen of the world, and was the friend or editor (often both) to a wide array of remarkable writers—Yeats and Joyce, D. H. Lawrence and T. S. Eliot, Frost and Hemingway—and pioneer of the new sparse school of poetry known as "Imagist." Yet he was drawn deeply to Chinese culture, especially to its early Confucian philosophical traditions, the flowering of classical poetry in the Tang dynasty, and the great summation of Chinese history known as *The Comprehensive Mirror for Aid in Government* of the eleventh century.

Pound never visited China, though he taught himself some Chinese characters in this period, and continued to study the language off and on, but his leads-in to this Chinese literature came mainly from translations. He began his work on the Chinese poetic tradition in 1913, when he was given the accumulated notes and papers of the recently deceased distinguished Orientalist and art historian Ernest Fenollosa. Though Fenollosa had published mainly on Japanese art, his papers contained many notes on Chinese poets such as the Tang dynasty's Li Bo (701–762), which Pound could explore and use. Pound's intensive work on Confucian thought was made possible when he acquired in 1917 or 1918 the translation by the French sinologue M. G. Pauthier of the *Four Books,* regarded in China as the basic works for studying the Confucian canon. Similarly, his detailed treatments of Chinese history were made possible by his readings in the eighteenth-century French Jesuit Joseph de Mailla's rendering of *The Comprehensive Mirror,* a meticulous chronological overview of Chinese politics and economics from the earliest days down to the eighteenth century.[5]

Pound's first brief book of Chinese poems appeared in 1915 under the title *Cathay.* Most of the book was drawn from the famous Tang poet Li Bo, via Fenollosa's renderings, and they are fairly literal translations, designed to catch the lyric structure of the Chinese original, to transpose the true flavor of the poem without overt intrusion. But the first two poems of *Cathay* have a vibrant originality, even though also drawn from early Chinese models. Pound took the first of these, the "Song of the Bowmen of Shu," from the *Book of Poetry,* the earliest anthology of Chinese verse, allegedly edited in the fifth century B.C. by Confucius himself. The poem emerges from Pound's hands with the same kind of violent and restless energy that so fascinated Segalen in the same years:

Here we are, picking the first fern-shoots
And saying: When shall we get back to our country?
Here we are because we have the Ken-nin for our foemen,
We have no comfort because of these Mongols.
We grub the soft fern-shoots,
When anyone says "Return," the others are full of sorrow.
Sorrowful minds, sorrow is strong, we are hungry and thirsty.
Our defence is not yet made sure, no one can let his friend return.
We grub the old fern-stalks.
We say: Will we be let to go back in October?
There is no ease in royal affairs, we have no comfort.

Our sorrow is bitter, but we would not return to our country.
What flower has come into blossom?
    Whose chariot? The General's.
Horses, his horses even, are tired. They were strong.

We have no rest, three battles a month.
By heaven, his horses are tired.
The generals are on them, the soldiers are by them.
The horses are well trained, the generals have ivory arrows
    and quivers ornamented with fish-skin.
The enemy is swift, we must be careful.
When we set out, the willows were drooping with spring,
We come back in the snow,
We go slowly, we are hungry and thirsty,
Our mind is full of sorrow, who will know of our grief?[6]

The second poem, "The Beautiful Toilet," was an utterly different type, from a later period (perhaps around the second century B.C.), and showcased Pound's most mournfully lyrical view of China:

Blue, blue is the grass about the river
And the willows have overfilled the close garden.
And within, the mistress, in the midmost of her youth,
White, white of face, hesitates, passing the door.
Slender, she puts forth a slender hand,

And she was a courtezan in the old days,
And she has married a sot,
Who now goes drunkenly out
And leaves her too much alone.[7]

By the end of World War I, or just after, Pound had embarked on the grandiose plan that was to be his central life's work, the creation of a lengthy sequence of Cantos that would constitute a poetic narration of the history of the world. He did not, like Voltaire, start his venture with China, but China came in very early, in Canto XIII, which represents Pound's strongest attempt to catch the central aspects of Confucian teaching. The Canto starts with what to the Chinese was one of the best-known pas-

sages in the *Analects of Confucius,* the collection of conversations
and sayings of the sage collected shortly after his death by his
disciples. (Here Pound, correctly, substitutes the true Chinese
transcription "Kung" for the Western form "Confucius.")

Kung walked
     by the dynastic temple
and into the cedar grove,
     and then out by the lower river,
And with him Khieu, Tchi
     and Tian the low speaking
And "we are unknown," said Kung,
"You will take up charioteering?
     Then you will become known,
Or perhaps I should take up charioteering, or archery?
Or the practice of public speaking?"
And Tseu-lou* said, "I would put the defences in order,"
And Khieu said, "If I were lord of a province
I would put it in better order than this is."
And Tchi said, "I would prefer a small mountain temple,
With order in the observances,
     with a suitable performance of the ritual,"
And Tian said, with his hand on the strings of his lute
The low sounds continuing
     after his hand left the strings,
And the sound went up like smoke, under the leaves,
And he looked after the sound:
     "The old swimming hole,
And the boys flopping off the planks,
Or sitting in the underbrush playing mandolins."
     And Kung smiled upon all of them equally.
And Thseng-sie† desired to know:
     "Which had answered correctly?"

* By oversight, Pound omitted Tseu-lou from the other young scholars in lines 5
and 6.

† This time Pound has muddled up the sequence of Confucius' questions and the
answer, and has not realized that Thseng-sie is an alternate name for Tian.

> And Kung said, "They have all answered correctly,
>   That is to say, each in his nature."[8]

Such a poem seems to be both a moral and political document, and so the Chinese would have perceived it. But by strongly putting his own gloss on the reading of the passage, Pound alters the ending completely. In the original Chinese, and in all accurate translations, the text does not say, "Kung said, 'They have all answered correctly, that is to say, each in his nature.'" Instead, the Chinese goes, "The Master sighed and said, 'I am all in favour of Tian.'"[9] By having Confucius agree with everyone, Pound gives him a less dogmatic look, but also loses the sage's judgmental character, which was one of his great strengths. In the attempt to universalize Confucian appeal, Pound has weakened it.

Such a distortion of the text, geared to ideological rather than poetic needs, is especially poignant in the context of the Canto's ending, which is a montage of several passages in the *Analects*:

> And Kung said, "Wang ruled with moderation,
>   In his day the State was well kept,
> And even I can remember
> A day when the historians left blanks in their writings,
> I mean for things they didn't know,
> But that time seems to be passing."
> And Kung said, "Without character you will
>   be unable to play on that instrument
> Or to execute the music fit for the Odes.
> The blossoms of the apricot
>   blow from the east to the west,
> And I have tried to keep them from falling."[10]

Pound has not been content to leave a blank for something he did not understand, or disagreed with, but has insisted on inserting his own words. Similarly, the billowing last three lines of his Canto XIII are Pound's sharpening of what in Confucius' *Analects* is a deeply problematic stanza about the effect of fruit tree blossoms in stirring longings for home. Both the precision of the word "apricot" and the directional sharpness of "east to the west"—with all its possibilities for cross-cultural inferences about China and the West, are Pound's own contributions.[11]

As Pound's vision of *The Cantos* grew to be a vision of a universal history of the human race, he was more than ever determined to make China part of the global story. Unlike Voltaire, he sought to march China on parallel tracks down through the ages alongside Western civilization. In Canto LVI, for instance, his linear presentation of history already growing almost too dense for interpretation, Pound offered his own version of Mongol power and goals, a new rendering to be set alongside Polo's and Voltaire's:

> Kublai before him
>> and about him damned rascals, courtezans, palace women
> Cliques, easy wars without justice.
> And Kublai said: Sung laws very beautiful
>> unlike their conduct. . .
> War scares interrupt commerce. Money was now made of brass
> and profit on arms went to the government
> wine taxed high, settlers licensed.
> KUBLAI was a buggar for taxes
>> Sangko stinking with graft
> Ouantse made a law code
>> eliminated 250 tribunals, that mostly did nowt* but tax
> KUBLAI died heavy with years
>> his luck was good ministers, save for the treasury.[12]

By Canto LX, Pound's narrative was becoming an ever more literal paraphrasing of his historical readings. Thus his passage on the rites controversy of Kangxi's reign, with its naming of the key Jesuit missionaries and listing of the main issues, could have served virtually unchanged as the backdrop for Leibniz's *Novissima Sinica:*

* English slang for "nothing."

KANG HI was pleased with the pasture land,
delayed his return to the capital,
stayed stag-hunting outside the great wall. . .
1699 peace year in all Tartary
Grimaldi, Pereira, Tony Thomas and Gerbillon
sent in their *placet* sic:
European litterati
having heard that the Chinese rites honour Kung-fu-tseu
and offer sacrifice to the Heaven etc/
and that their ceremonies are grounded in reason
now beg to know their true meaning and in particular
the meaning of terms for example Material
Heaven and Changti meaning? its ruler?
Does the *manes* of Confucius
accept the grain, fruit, silk, incense offered
        and does he enter his cartouche?
The European church wallahs wonder if this can be reconciled.[13]

Because of his decision to stay on in Italy under the Mussolini
regime, and even to speak up for it in the dark hours of the
Allies' battle with fascism, Pound was forcibly committed to a
psychiatric hospital after World War II and his reputation went
into decline. Giving a new twist to the old idea of China offering
a model for Europe, his later Cantos, many written in the Mussolini period, treated the Confucian values of Chinese society as
being compatible with the new values of social order, rigor, and
cohesion demanded by Italian fascism. One has to be a committed Poundian indeed to find some of these renderings either
poetically persuasive or ideologically convincing. But in the teens
and twenties, Pound was widely respected and his influence
enormous: in the dedication of *The Waste Land* to Pound, Eliot
called him "Il miglior fabro" ("the better craftsman") and in
the introduction to Pound's *Book of Songs* renderings, a distinguished Chinese scholar quotes with approval Eliot's judgment
that Pound was "the inventor of Chinese poetry for our time."[14]

Pound had based his China on Confucius and was to slide
it in the direction of fascism. His almost exact contemporary,

Eugene O'Neill (Pound was born in 1885, O'Neill in 1888), drew his China from Marco Polo and slid it toward a harsh critique of capitalism. O'Neill wrote his play *Marco Millions* in 1927, after *Anna Christie* and *Desire Under the Elms* but before *Mourning Becomes Electra* and *The Iceman Cometh*. O'Neill's play about Polo was never as popular as those others, and seems to a current reader almost unactable on account of its didacticism. But it is certainly an original reading of the Sino-Mongol past, and one that made a reprise of earlier themes and put them on view in contemporary American society.

O'Neill's starting point would appear to have been a few lines from Polo's *Description of the World* in which Rusticello writes of Marco, his father, and his uncle being named by Kublai Khan to escort a new bride to the recently bereaved Khan of the Levant, Arghun. According to Polo's text, the new bride was "a lady named Kukachin, of great beauty and charm," seventeen years old, from the lineage of the deceased queen. Furthermore, the three Venetians watched over Kukachin and her fellow women travelers "as if they had been their own daughters. And the ladies, who were very young and beautiful, looked upon them as their fathers and obeyed them no less." Kukachin's affections, in particular, were "so deeply attached to the three men" that there was "nothing she would not have done for them as readily as for her own father"; and accordingly, when the journey was completed and the Venetians continued on their way home, "she wept for grief at their going."[15]

O'Neill used these passages as the trigger for his drama. The prologue to the play sets the scene by showing that "Marco Polo, of Polo Brothers and Son, Venice," has been planning to exploit this fortunate friendship, and has been counting on selling Kukachin and her husband a "whole fleet load of goods."[16] The action then fades back twenty years, as Marco Polo travels toward China with his uncle and his father. Marco is presented as naive, a bumbling teller of sexual and ethnic jokes, easily seduced by prostitutes after his initial shyness has been rubbed off, and relentlessly absorbed by money and its acquisition. As the Polos cross at last into China in Act One, scene six, O'Neill has a lengthy stage direction that summarizes his own personal views of China's past: it seems to flow directly from the conclusion of that earlier play by Voltaire, *The Orphan of Chao*, in which Genghis had succumbed at last to an acceptance of the superiority of Chinese moral values over Mongol barbarity. In O'Neill's words:

> Music from full Chinese and Tartar bands crashes up to a tremendous blaring crescendo of drums, gongs, and the piercing shrilling of flutes. The light slowly comes to a pitch of blinding brightness. Then, as light and sound attain their highest point, there is a sudden dead silence. The scene is revealed as the Grand Throne Room in the palace of Kublai, the Great Kaan, in the city of Cambaluc, Cathay—an immense octagonal room, the lofty walls adorned in gold and silver. In the far rear wall, within a deep recess like the shrine of an idol, is the throne of the Great Kaan. It rises in three tiers, three steps to a tier. On golden cushions at the top KUBLAI sits dressed in his heavy gold robes of state. He is a man of sixty but still in the full prime of his powers, his face proud and noble, his expression tinged with an ironic humor and bitterness yet full of a sympathetic humanity. In his person are combined the conquering indomitable force of a descendant of Chinghiz with the humanizing culture of the conquered Chinese who have already begun to absorb their conquerors.[17]

Kublai, in his wary wisdom, can see that the brash young Marco has something "warped, deformed" about his character, but nevertheless decides to make him a commission agent in China, and bids him report on his travels each time he returns to court.[18]

In Act Two, set fifteen years later, it is revealed that Marco has been serving as mayor of Yang-chou, where his financial ruthlessness has dramatically increased revenues but brought his subjects to the edge of revolt. (The ruthless tax-gathering practices of Kublai's agents had also caught the attention of Ezra Pound, as we saw in Canto LVI.) Hearing that Marco is returning to report to Kublai, the Khan's senior minister Chu-Yin comments ironically:

> No doubt he comes to refresh your humor with new copious notes on his exploits. Our Marco has made an active mayor. Yang-Chau, according to the petition for mercy you have received from its inhabitants, is the most governed of all your cities. I talked recently with a poet who had fled from there in horror. Yang-Chau used to have a soul, he said. Now it has a brand new Court House. And another, a man of wide culture, told me, our Christian mayor is exterminating our pleasures and our rats as if they were twin breeds of vermin![19]

The Khan replies:

> He is beginning to weary me with his grotesque antics. A jester inspires mirth only so long as his deformity does not revolt one. Marco's spiritual hump begins to disgust me. He has not even a mortal soul, he has only an acquisitive instinct. We have given him every opportunity to learn. He has memorized everything and learned nothing. He has looked at everything and seen nothing. He has lusted for everything and loved nothing. He is only a shrewd and crafty greed. I shall send him home to his native wallow.[20]

Kublai's granddaughter Kukachin, however, protests vigorously, thus revealing to the two men that she has come to love Marco.

> Why are you both so unjust? Has he not done well everything he was ever appointed to do? Has he not always succeeded where others failed? Has he not by his will-power and determination risen to the highest rank in your service?
> *[Then her anger dying—more falteringly]*
> He is strange, perhaps, to people who do not understand him, but that is because he is so different from other men, so much stronger! And he has a soul! I know he has![21]

When Kublai angrily dismisses Kukachin from his presence, ordering her to prepare at once for her voyage to Persia to marry the Khan there, he asks Chu-Yin how such love can have grown, since Polo and Kukachin have only talked to each other once every year or two, and then only for a brief time. Chu-Yin's response neatly reverses the stereotypes of exoticism: keeping them separated "was unwise, for thus he has remained a strange, mysterious dream-knight from the exotic West, an enigma with something about him of a likable boy."[22] Polo, the successful entrepreneurial bureaucrat, approaches the palace, and Chu-Yin, watching from a window, gives Kublai a running commentary that summarizes in a Chinese context all the crasser forms of boosterism and casual glad-handing that so repelled O'Neill:

> He wears over his Mayor's uniform, the regalia of Cock of Paradise in his secret fraternal order of the Mystic Knights of Confucius! The band of the Xanadu lodge is with him as well as his own! He is riding on a very fat white horse. He dismounts, aided by the steps of your Imperial Palace! He slaps a policeman on the back and asks his name! He chucks a baby under the chin and asks the mother its name. She lies and says "Marco" although the baby is a girl. He smiles. He is talking loudly so everyone can overhear. He gives the baby one yen to start a savings account and encourage its thrift. The mother looks savagely disappointed. The crowd cheers. He keeps his smile frozen as he notices an artist sketching him. He shakes hands with a one-legged veteran of the Manzi campaign and asks his name. The veteran is touched. Tears come to his eyes. He tells him—but the Polo forgets his name even as he turns to address the crowd. He waves one hand for silence. The band stops. It is the hand on which he wears five large jade rings. The other hand rests upon—and pats—the head of a bronze dragon, our ancient symbol of Yang, the celestial, male principle of the Cosmos.[23]

In a strange swerve from history, Marco Polo is presented as the inventor of paper money, his uncle as the developer of the gunpowder-powered cannon, and the family as the introducers of an assembly-line system of cargo transport and loading. And on the long journey to Persia, on the ship that Marco commands, Kukachin's love for him deepens into passion while he, oblivious, concentrates solely on his work and his money.

The denouement is a mixture of tragedy and absurdity. Kukachin pines away for love of him, while Marco returns to Venice, vulgar and mercenary as ever, to marry his childhood sweetheart left behind twenty years before, the now stout and middle-aged Donata. Amid crowds of grasping and envious relatives and hangers-on, the couple are married, unwittingly echoing the bitter farewell cry of Kukachin to Polo, "Guzzle! Grunt! Wallow for our amusement!" When Kublai's courtiers suggest that he send his armies to conquer Europe and incorporate it in his colossal empire, he answers wearily: "It is much too large already. Why do you want to conquer the West? It must be a pitiful land, poor in spirit and material wealth. We have everything to lose by contact with its greedy hypocrisy. The conqueror acquires first of all the vices of the conquered. Let the West devour itself."[24]

In a curious final twist to O'Neill's play, just as the lights come on after the curtain falls, his stage directions read that a man rises from the front row of the stalls, yawns and stretches, puts on his hat, and makes his way toward the exit. His clothes, thirteenth-century Venetian, reveal him to be Marco Polo, "looking a bit sleepy," and as O'Neill's stage direction has it,

> . . . a trifle puzzled, and not a little irritated as his thoughts, in spite of himself, cling for a passing moment to the play just ended. He appears quite unaware of being unusual and walks in the crowd without self-consciousness, very much as one of them. Arrived in the lobby his face begins to clear of all disturbing memories of what had happened on the stage. The noise, the lights of the streets, recall him at once to himself. Impatiently he waits for his car, casting a glance here and there at faces in the groups around him, his eyes impersonally speculative, his bearing stolid with the dignity of one who is sure of his place in the world. His car, a luxurious limousine, draws up at the curb. He

gets in briskly, the door is slammed, the car edges away into the traffic and MARCO POLO, with a satisfied sigh at the sheer comfort of it all, resumes his life.[25]

Griffith, Pound, and O'Neill each found an American way to adapt their vision of Chinese culture to contemporary political and economic preoccupations, by emphasizing selective elements of the Chinese exotic. It was the central originality of Pearl Buck to see that perhaps the greatest exoticism to the West lay in the most mundane and yet the least observed of its China's inhabitants, the countless farmers and their families. Pearl Buck, born in 1892, had lived longer in China, knew more about its land and rhythms of work, than almost any previous American observer, for she was born into a missionary family that lived and worked in the central Yangzi province of Anhui. She grew up attended by Chinese nursemaids, with Chinese school-friends and playmates, and knew the language well. The most popular of her novels, *The Good Earth,* published in 1931, was written while she was living in China; as well as drawing on her youthful memories, the book incorporated her experiences during the Nationalist-led upheavals of the later 1920s, her own unhappy marriage, and her sorrows over the realization that her only child—she could have no more for medical reasons—was severely and incurably retarded.[26]

The Good Earth was a strong story and profoundly self-explanatory, which helps account for its sales of over a million copies in the early thirties (and its subsequent movie audience of more than 20 million). Despite a self-congratulatory and lengthy epigraph from Proust, with whom the casual reader might be excused for believing that she is not unfavorably comparing herself, Pearl Buck's opening paragraphs plunged straight into a powerful tale with direct and unpretentious economy:

> It was Wang Lung's marriage day. At first, opening his eyes in the blackness of the curtains about his bed, he could not think why the dawn seemed different from any other. The house was

still except for the faint, gasping cough of his old father, whose
room was opposite to his own across the middle room. Every
morning the old man's cough was the first sound to be heard.
Wang Lung usually lay listening to it and moved only when he
heard it approaching nearer and when he heard the door of his
father's room squeak upon its wooden hinges.

But this morning he did not wait. He sprang up and pushed
aside the curtains of his bed. It was a dark, ruddy dawn, and
through a small square hole of a window, where the tattered
paper fluttered, a glimpse of bronze sky gleamed.[27]

Wang Lung has to go and collect his new wife from the "Big
House" in the nearby town, where she has been working as an
indentured domestic slave. On this foray into a—to him—alien
world, he is humiliated and cheated, as one would expect, but he
gets his woman, takes her home, and possesses her:

> "There is this woman of mine. The thing is to be done."
> And he began to undress himself doggedly. As for the woman,
> she crept around the corner of the curtain and began without a
> sound to prepare for the bed. Wang Lung said gruffly,
> "When you lie down, put the light out first."
> Then he lay down and drew the thick quilt about his shoulders
> and pretended to sleep. But he was not sleeping. He lay quivering,
> every nerve of his flesh awake. And when, after a long time, the
> room went dark, and there was the slow, silent, creeping move-
> ment of the woman beside him, an exultation filled him fit to
> break his body. He gave a hoarse laugh into the darkness and
> seized her.[28]

After their marriage, Wang Lung and his wife O-lan work and
raise their family, and it is in describing this phase of their life,
with the rhythms of farm labor, harvest, and childbearing, that
Pearl Buck is most moving and convincing. But if the story was
not to get bogged down, Buck had to sunder the routinized sat-
isfactions of this life. She did this by reducing Wang Lung and
his family to beggary after a terrible drought hits their farm,
and having them flee to a nearby city in search of work. Wang

Lung finally becomes a rickshaw puller, until a period of civil commotion is orchestrated by Buck into double, and equally unlikely, coincidences: the exploitation by Wang Lung and O-lan of this chance moment to make two separate but parallel seizures of other people's property hidden in the walls of a looted building—a cache of gold for him, a stash of jewels for her. With his gold, Wang Lung is able to buy back his land and expand his holdings, and eventually to buy the big house where once O-lan was enslaved.

But O-lan's cache of jewels turns out to be the family's undoing. This extra wealth allows Wang Lung to slide into a life of self-conscious sexual indulgence with a paid paramour who brings him unguessed-at levels of pleasure. This allows Buck to plunge into the imagined realms of Oriental sensuality and excess that many readers were waiting for:

> Then she lifted that small curling hand and put it upon his shoulder and she passed it slowly down the length of his arm, very slowly. And although he had never felt anything so light, so soft as that touch, although if he had not seen it, he would not have known that it passed, he looked and saw the small hand moving down his arm, and it was as though fire followed it and burned under through his sleeve and into the flesh of his arm, and he watched the hand until it reached the end of his sleeve and then it fell with an instant's practiced hesitation upon his bare wrist and then into the loose hollow of his hard dark hand. And he began to tremble, not knowing how to receive it.
>
> Then he heard laughter, light, quick, tinkling as the silver bell upon a pagoda shaking in the winds, and a little voice like laughter said,
>
> "Oh, and how ignorant you are, you great fellow? Shall we sit here the night through while you stare?"
>
> And at that he seized her hand between both of his, but carefully, because it was like a fragile dry leaf, hot and dry, and he said to her imploringly and not knowing what he said,
>
> "I do not know anything—teach me!"
>
> And she taught him.[29]

At the novel's end, Wang Lung—his wife O-lan long dead, and the paramour's passion a vanished memory—lives in the drifting mental state of the opium smoker, warmed by the presence of a little serving maid. His sons plan, without their old father's knowledge, to sell off the land that he has so patiently and painfully acquired:

> And the old man let his scanty tears dry upon his cheeks and they made salty stains there. And he stooped and took up a handful of the soil and he held it and he muttered,
>
> "If you sell the land, it is the end."
>
> And his two sons held him, one on either side, each holding his arm, and he held tight in his hand the warm loose earth. And they soothed him and they said over and over, the elder son and the second son,
>
> "Rest assured, our father, rest assured. The land is not to be sold."
>
> But over the old man's head they looked at each other and smiled.[30]

The huge success of *The Good Earth* did not prevent other American searches for the true Chinese exotic from continuing. In his surreal tale *The Circus of Dr. Lao,* of 1935, Charles Finney played with the ideas of timeless Oriental wisdom from an untried vantage point. For what Dr. Lao's circus brings to America is the world of classical mythology brought back to life under Chinese supervision. The newspaper advertisement for the circus that alerts the reader to this is commercial, in just the way O'Neill's Polo might have designed it, "eight columns wide and twenty-one inches long," and its complex promises push to the edges of the imagination and beyond. But the "little old Chinaman" who brings in the advertisement to the office of the "Abalone (Arizona) Morning Tribune for August third," and pays in cash, leaves no name or other sign of who he is or what his show is called. Only the self-selected few, like Mr. Etaoin, the proofreader, or Miss Agnes Birdsong, the high school English teacher, who actually brave the trip to "that dusty field under

the red-hot sun," are privileged to see the huge banner in black
and red, proclaiming this to be THE CIRCUS OF DR. LAO.[31]

Finney's introduction of his Chinese circus philosopher-
huckster is one of the strangest and richest of all passages in the
Western history of Chinese images: though pastiching its own
rhyme scheme, it cumulatively gives a comprehensive portrait of
many centuries of Chinoiserie yearnings and stereotypes:

> Heat waves scorched the skin. Dust waves seared the eyes.
> Sound waves blasted the ears. The gong clanged and banged and
> rang; and one of the tents opened and a platform was thrust out
> and a Chinaman hopped on the platform and the gong's noise
> stopped and the man started to harangue the people; and the cir-
> cus of Doctor Lao was on:

> > "This is the circus of Doctor Lao.
> > We show you things that you don't know.
> > We tell you of places you'll never go.
> > We've searched the world both high and low
> > To capture the beasts for this marvelous show
> > From mountains where maddened winds did blow
> > To islands where zephyrs breathed sweet and slow.
> > Oh, we've spared no pains and we've spared no dough;
> > And we've dug at the secrets of long ago;
> > And we've risen to Heaven and plunged Below,
> > For we wanted to make it one hell of a show.
> > And the things you'll see in your brains will glow
> > Long past the time when the winter snow
> > Has frozen the summer's furbelow.
> > For this is the circus of Doctor Lao.
> >   And youth may come and age may go;
> >   But no more circuses like this show!"

> The little yellow wrinkled dancing man hopped about on the
> platform sing-songing his slipshod dactyls and iambics; and the
> crowd of black, red, and white men stared up at him and mar-
> veled at his ecstasy.[32]

The ecstasy has its reasons, as the visitors at last discover. For true to the promises of the prepaid advertisement, the creatures from the world's mythology are alive and fairly well, if erratic, and the world is about to end.

Finney's Chinese extravaganza tugged one back from Depression America to a dangerous fantasy that few others had tried to explore, except in some apocalyptic late nineteenth-century "yellow peril" books, that made their readers shiver with the thought that American civilization might be swamped by Chinese hordes or wiped out by Chinese disease. This orchestration of destruction was itself a variant in new literary dress of the sagas of Mongol wastage and death. That harsh historical memory had lived on in Western consciousness, as the inevitable obverse image of the strength and power that had briefly enabled the Mongols to forge a unified central Asian empire linking the Black Sea to the Pacific. In yet another variation of this negative vision, John Steinbeck published in the story "Johnny Bear" of 1939 his rendering of the destruction that the Chinese could bring to Western civilization.[33]

In Steinbeck's telling, though at first glance the scale appears intensely intimate—one woman dies, one man is hurt, in the small California town of Loma—the moral dimension turns out to be even wider than Finney's or Buck's. For what a single Chinese man—who remains offstage throughout the story—accomplishes is the destruction of all the moral values by which the community of Loma has structured itself. The story artfully waits until the closing lines to show how the gift of love and language, when conveyed from China to the West, can seduce and destroy. For it is only at the story's end that we are led to understand how the most beloved woman in the community, Miss Amy, has had a love affair that cannot be named with a Chinese field hand who can never be seen. The Chinese lover is glimpsed, if at all, only as a faint shape in the mist, and heard only by the shuffle of his sandals, a soft moaning that may or may not be his, and the sound of a coil of singsong words, softly and lovingly repeated.

Steinbeck's extraordinary achievement was to place Chinatown in the heart of the American countryside, and to create a world where love—struggling to maintain itself across the racial and economic divide—can no more be spoken aloud by anyone, except by the village idiot Johnny Bear, a subhuman force endowed with a single gift, that of mimicry. Mimicry, of course, itself offers nothing, creates nothing. The cycle of experiments in bringing China home to Americans that had started in the mining camps of the Far West in the days of the Gold Rush ended with this bleak vision put forward by the austerest chronicler of the Great Depression.

CHAPTER 10

Radical Visions

IN THE LATER TWENTIES, A DECISIVE CHANGE OCCURRED in the way many observers viewed China. Before then, the China refracted in Western minds had been, in most cases, only loosely bonded in time. The spaciousness of the land was echoed by the endless recesses of its past, and even specific historical personages and events were set in the vaguest of chronological frames. Voltaire and O'Neill had needed merely a broadly conceived "Mongol" period as their backdrop. Pinto's Ming dynasty was always a vague chimera, but Pereira, da Cruz, and Ricci were just as free from concern over current politics. Navarrete and Defoe referred in general terms to the Manchu conquest, as did Anson and Macartney, but the details did not matter to them. Nineteenth-century visitors and missionaries saw the Taiping insurgents and the Boxers as harbingers of menace and death, but rarely paused to inquire into the root causes of their rage. Pearl Buck had characters in Wang Lung's family refer vaguely to the "war to the north of us" or "to the south of us now and nearer every day," but the precise components or causes of war were unimportant to her story. Even when Wang Lung at last cuts off his long queue of braided hair, which to many revolutionaries had become a symbol of degraded servitude to Manchu rule, he does it to please the singing girl with whom he is infatuated, not out of political commitment or coercion. And though Segalen's *René Leys* was structured loosely around the outbreak of the Chinese anti-Manchu revolution of 1911, it did not illuminate the causes of that revolution save in the most idiosyncratic ways that would deepen the sensual components of his plot.

Starting in the late twenties, observers fascinated by the Bolshevik Revolution in Russia began to place China itself within a world revolutionary context, and to trace radical impulses inside China with a new kind of precision. The founding of the Chinese Communist Party in 1921, the massive purging of their ranks in 1927 by the Nationalist forces of Chiang Kai-shek, and the Communists' subsequent near-miraculous survival in the remotest areas of the Chinese countryside, all drew these watchers into a new appreciation of China's left-wing forces.

André Malraux was probably the first to bring these stirring events to the attention of a large, popular readership, with his book *Man's Fate (La condition humaine),* published in 1933. Malraux, at first glance, would have seemed an unlikely purveyor of this new harsh political realism, since in his earliest work on China he appeared to be completely immersed in the worlds of Chinese exoticism as presented by Loti, Claudel, and Segalen. In *The Temptation of the West (La tentation de l'occident),* for instance, published in 1926, the twenty-five-year-old Malraux presented China in these terms:

> Each spring the Tartar roses, white with purple hearts, cover the Mongolian steppes. There caravans pass; dirty merchants lead tall, shaggy camels, loaded down with round packages which burst open like pomegranates when the caravan halts. Then all the enchantment of this snowy kingdom—stones the color of clear sky or frozen stream, stones that glitter like ice, the pale plumage of gray birds, frost-colored furs, and silver-stamped turquoises—pours out into the merchants' agile fingers. . . .[1]

Other images of China that came to him, in the early pages of his book, were those of a land of "opium and dreams," of "older ghosts," and "queens fastened to walls by rough arrows," and one might have thought those would have been enough for him. But though *The Temptation of the West* is full of such elements, it also shows Malraux's emerging views of China's intellectual and social dissonances. In structure, *The Temptation of the West* is an epistolary novel, built around an exchange of letters between a young Frenchman traveling to China, referred to only as "A.D.," and Ling, a young Chinese making his first trip to France. Yet though it is essentially plotless, even more so than Goldsmith's epistolary *Citizen of the World*, it soon becomes clear that what drives the story forward are the criticisms that A.D. and Ling have for their own and each other's societies.

As the novel advances, the political references become more pointed. The crux comes when A.D., having arrived in China, is drawn into a conversation with an old Chinese scholar and former political leader named Wang-Loh. Their meeting, appropriately enough for the new age that is dawning, is in the Astor Hotel in Shanghai, and Wang-Loh soon shows A.D. the contempt he feels both for China's modern youth—"idiots intoxicated on university nonsense"—and for "the bloody comedians" who run the government. But Wang-Loh's deepest sorrow and anger is for a world in which "with Confucianism in ruins . . . our spirit is gradually becoming *empty*." Europe's only contribution to China had been "in making them realize the senselessness of all thought."[2]

Pondering sadly on the letter in which A.D. records this conversation, Ling responds from Paris that he is forced to agree with A.D.'s analysis. But Wang-Loh's remarks provoke Ling into thinking more carefully about the revolutionary government of Sun Yat-sen in Canton, and the effects on China of the encroaching global culture. Ling writes to his friend:

> The South and Central provinces are completely dependent on that strange government at Canton, which holds England in check and venerates the Sages while organizing its propaganda through the cinema; for what we have taken over from the West most rapidly are the forms of its existence. The cinema, electricity, mirrors, phonographs, all have seduced us like new breeds of domestic animals. For the people of the cities, Europe will forever be only a mechanized fairyland.[3]

And this thought leads Ling to reflections on the possible apocalypse to come:

Our miserable millions are conscious of injustice, not of justice; of suffering, not of happiness. Their disgust with their leaders only helps them understand what they have in common. I
await with some curiosity the one who will come and cry to them
that he demands vengeance, not justice. The power of a nation is
greatly increased once it is based on the ethic of force. What then
will be the acts of those who will accept the risk of death in the
name of hate alone? A new China is being created which even we
cannot understand. Will she be shaken by one of those great collective emotions which several times have convulsed her? More
powerful than the chant of prophets, the deep voice of destruction is already heard in the most distant echoes of Asia. . . .[4]

In 1926 and 1927, the implications of Ling's projections
began to be worked out in real life. Sun Yat-sen, who had forged
a united front between the young Chinese Communist Party and
his own Nationalists, had died in 1925. His leadership role was
taken over—not without bitter dissent—by his protégé Chiang
Kai-shek, who in late 1926 led combined revolutionary forces
north to reunify the country and purge it of warlords. While the
Communist-dominated wing of his forces and their Comintern
advisers from the Soviet Union established a governmental base
in Hankou on the Yangzi River, Chiang Kai-shek concentrated
his attentions on Shanghai. And there, in a murderous but
coolly executed coup on April 12, 1927, Chiang's troops in
alliance with local secret society and criminal organizations—
and with the acquiescence of the foreign powers who controlled
the huge city's prosperous international settlements—smashed
the forces of the Communists and the labor unions.

In his novel *Man's Fate,* published in 1933, Malraux set out to
explore the emotional significance and moral impact of these
events in detail. Though Malraux had never been to China, he
had lived for some time in Southeast Asia—he had even been
arrested by the French authorities earlier in the twenties for
stealing and trying to sell Cambodian antiquities—and he had
worked with Vietnamese nationalist and radical groups. So it
was easy for him to foster the impression that he had personally

been involved in the great revolutionary upheavals of China as well, an impression that he conveyed so skillfully that it took decades for readers to realize he had not been in China at all during that momentous time. In *Man's Fate*, which concentrates on Chiang Kai-shek's 1927 purge of the Shanghai Communist organization—a brief, earlier novel had dealt with the previous stage of the revolution in Canton—Malraux built up a meticulous documentation and chronology of this formative moment of China's revolutionary struggle, and offered a narrative interpretation in terms of human integrity and commitment that endured until the Communist takeover of 1949, and even after.

The action of Malraux's entire novel is focused on just six days in the spring of 1927—five of them in Shanghai, and one in Hankou. Each section of the novel is defined by the exact day and hour on which the events unfold, so that the ticking of the clock can always be heard amid the broader din of history. And each character in the novel is introduced at the beginning as if in the cast list of a play, the capsulized descriptions being almost all one needs to anticipate the structure of the plot:

CH'EN TA ERH, Chinese terrorist.
KYO GISORS, half French and half Japanese, one of the organizers of the Shanghai insurrection.
OLD GISORS, Kyo's father, one-time professor of Sociology at the University of Peking.
MAY GISORS, Kyo's wife.
BARON DE CLAPPIQUE, a Frenchman, a dealer in antiques, opium and smuggled wares.
KATOV, a Russian, one of the organizers of the insurrection.
FERRAL, President of the French Chamber of Commerce and head of the Franco-Asiatic Consortium.
VALÉRIE, Ferral's mistress.
MARTIAL, Chief of the Shanghai Police.
KÖNIG, Chief of Chiang Kai-shek's Police.[5]

From this list, one important point is immediately apparent: the only major Chinese character in the entire long novel is

Ch'en, the Chinese terrorist. The others are all European, except for the half-Japanese Kyo. The revolution, in Malraux's hands, is thus presented as the manipulation or suppression by Western- ers of the raw materials of revolutionary potential. The police forces and the business elite are arrayed against the dedicated revolutionaries and their Comintern advisers, while Ch'en the terrorist exults in his newfound power and loss as a killer, even though it has ended by further removing him from his own peo- ple: "Ch'en no longer belonged to China . . . a complete liberty gave him over completely to his mind." True to this change within him, it is with "an ecstatic joy" that Ch'en runs toward the advancing car and certain death in his attempt to assassi- nate Chiang Kai-shek.[6]

Ch'en has moved beyond the ordinary human world, but at least he has been given an identity. The other Chinese who fuel the revolution, by contrast, like those who try to barricade their headquarters against Chiang's marauding forces, are described by Malraux with similes that place them more in the non- human world of impersonal motion, "formless in the fog, like fish in stirred water," or "like a nest of insects . . . alive with an activity whose meaning was obscure but whose movement was clear."[7]

Even Kyo, the totally committed revolutionary, as he prowled the streets of Shanghai seeking to organize the insurrection,

> no longer walked in mud but on a map. The scratching of mil- lions of small daily lives disappeared, crushed by another life. The concessions, the rich quarters, with their rain-washed gratings at the ends of the streets, existed now only as menaces, barriers, long prison walls without windows; these atrocious quarters, on the contrary—the ones in which the shock troops were the most numerous, were alive with the quivering of a multitude lying in wait.[8]

Ferral, the president of the French Chamber of Commerce, who has decided to throw in his lot with Chiang Kai-shek against the Communists, draws his images of the Chinese from the racing world that he knows so well:

> As one racehorse outdistances another, head, neck, shoulders, the crowd was "closing in" on the car, slowly, steadily. Wheelbarrows with babies' heads sticking out between bowls, Peking carts, rickshaws, small hairy horses, hand-carts, trucks loaded with sixty-odd people, monstrous mattresses piled with a whole household of furniture, bristling with table-legs, giants with cages of blackbirds dangling from the end of their arms which were stretched out to protect tiny women with a litter of children on their backs.[9]

The character in *Man's Fate* who faces death with the greatest courage is Katov, the hardened Comintern revolutionary agent. Instead of racing toward his doom with a wild ecstasy, like Ch'en the terrorist, Katov goes methodically and sadly. His final and overwhelming act of grace has been to give up his own cyanide pills so that the two wounded Chinese comrades lying beside him—fellow members of his "pitiful fraternity"—can die in peace by their own hand and avoid the horrifying torture and execution that otherwise awaits them. This Western sacrifice for China was seen by Malraux as "the greatest gift" that Katov could make; and as Katov is taken off to his death—to be burned alive in the boiler of the armored train waiting in the sidings—the massed Chinese "followed the rhythm of his walk, with love, with dread, with resignation."[10]

Malraux's depiction of China's anguish and of the Comintern agents' courage seemed a convincing one to contemporary readers, but Bertolt Brecht for one knew that such depictions of revolutionaries were too simple, and that abstract definitions of the meaning of sacrifice were inadequate. Brecht was born in 1898, and thus was three years older than Malraux. These short three years made a major difference, for Brecht, a native of Bavaria, was just old enough to serve in World War I—on the German side—and though as a student of medicine he

was assigned to a military hospital, he saw enough of the war
and its consequences to be permanently marked by what he perceived as the follies and hypocrisies of bourgeois societies. His
socialism was a curious mixture of the didactic and the personal, not surprising in a man whose own beliefs were influenced not only by Marxism but also by the French poet François
Villon of the fifteenth century, and by the Dadaists of his own
day. Having completed *The Threepenny Opera* in 1928, and *The
Rise and Fall of the City of Mahagony* in 1930, that same year Brecht
completed a dramatic reflection he had been writing on the
impact of the Comintern on the Chinese Revolution. The result
was the experimental didactic play *The Measures Taken (Die Mass-
nahme)*, first performed in Berlin on December 13, 1930.

Brecht centered his play not on Canton or Shanghai—the
focus of Malraux's Chinese novels, and indeed to most Westerners the focal points of the Chinese Revolution—but on the
northern Chinese city of Mukden. He depicted the city as ripe
for revolution: even though the reactionaries' gunboats were
patrolling the rivers and their "armored trains on the railway
embankments," there was a swelling tide of discontent in the
factories of Mukden. Textile workers went out on strike; the
coolies groaned as they skidded in the riverside mud, hauling
the heavy grain barges to the city; the wealthy merchants were
willing to form a United Front with the workers against the
hated foreign imperialists; there were hunger riots among the
unemployed. Four agitators—three men and one woman—are
dispatched from Moscow to foment revolution in Mukden: to
prevent any chance that the gunboats and armored trains might
be turned against the Soviet Union, they must not reveal that
they have been sent from Moscow. Accordingly, the four are
ordered by their control to don masks that will hide their identity. As they prepare to cross over the border into China, their
control tells them: "From this moment on, and in all probability until your disappearance, you are unknown workers, fight-

ers. Chinamen, born of Chinese mothers, yellow-skinned, who in sleep and in delirium speak only Chinese."[11]

The four are joined by a party member from the frontier station, also masked, who has been chosen as their guide and whom they call "the young comrade." On the stage, the agitators give a summary of their journey with the young comrade:

> We proceeded towards Mukden as Chinamen—four men and a woman—for propaganda purposes and to aid the Chinese Party with the teachings of the Classics and the Propagandists, the ABC of Communism. To bring to the ignorant instruction concerning their condition; to the oppressed, class-consciousness; and to the class-conscious, practical knowledge of the revolution.[12]

And the chorus echoes approvingly:

> He who fights for Communism
> Must be able to fight and not fight
> Must tell the truth and not tell the truth
> Render service and not render service
> Place himself in danger and avoid danger
> Be recognizable and be unrecognizable.
> He who fights for Communism
> has of all virtues only one:
> That he fights for Communism.[13]

The more professional the four Moscow agitators are, the more the young comrade assigned to guide them disobeys their orders and acts on the basis of his own emotions, ravaged by the sufferings he sees. In the eyes of the four agitators he has begun to show a dangerous weakness, he has become "a prey to pity." The four work swiftly in Mukden to set up party schools, found party cells in the factories, train activists in the city to serve as cadres, and instruct them how to make and distribute party literature. They give lessons to the workers on street combat, conceal typesetting machines in secret rooms, and even woo a wealthy merchant who has "a large following among youth assemblies" and thus could help greatly in "uniting the Party network in the face of capitalist guns."[14]

But because of his emotional responses, the young comrade constantly undercuts the four agitators' work: instead of working methodically and secretly to build a strong revolutionary base, he urges assaults on the local army barracks, the seizing of factories, and an uprising of the unemployed. His precipitate actions split the workers into conflicting camps, and draw the attention of the authorities to the agitators. In his mind, the suffering of the poor is so unendurable that urging restraint on them is a monstrous absurdity, and teaching them revolutionary practice is a waste of time. For the workers already know all there is to know, he cries:

> They know: that misfortune doesn't grow on the breast like leprosy; that poverty doesn't fall like tiles from the roof; but that misfortune and poverty are the work of Man. Want is cooked in the pots on their stoves, and misery is their only food.[15]

The four experienced agitators rebuke the young comrade sharply, until finally in rage and frustration he tears to shreds the Communist writings they have given him to distribute. He pulls off the mask that hides his identity, and shouts to the assembled crowds of the miserable that he has come to help them. In somber terms, the four agitators report the sequel to their control:

> We watched him, and in the twilight
> We saw his naked face
> Human, innocent, and without guile. He had
> Torn the mask to bits.
> And from their houses came the
> Cries of the exploited: "who
> Disturbs the sleep of the poor?"
> And from an open window a voice cried:

"There are foreigners out there! Chase the agitators!"
And so we were discovered!
And at that moment we heard of riots
In the lower part of the city, and the ignorant waited in the
Assembly houses and the unarmed thronged the streets.
And we struck him down
Raised him up and left the city in haste.[16]

Once the four agitators have hustled their young comrade out of the city, just ahead of their vengeful pursuers, they shoot him and throw him into a lime pit, so his face will be burned bare of any traces of individuality that might betray them all. "Your work was successful," their control tells them at the end of their report:

You have propagated
The teachings of the classics
The ABC of Communism
Instructions to the ignorant concerning their condition
Class-consciousness to the oppressed
And to the class-conscious, practical knowledge of the revolution.
And the revolution marches on there too
And there, too, the ranks of fighters are well organized.
We agree with you.

And yet your report shows us what is
Needed to change the world:
anger and tenacity, knowledge and indignation
Swift action, utmost deliberation
Cold endurance, unending perseverance
Comprehension of the individual and comprehension of the
        whole:
Taught only by reality can
Reality be changed.[17]

In a bizarre literalizing of Brecht's revolutionary drama, six months after the play opened in Berlin, a group of Japanese Army officers in Mukden fabricated a charge of "aggression" by the Chinese troops, and used this excuse to launch major reprisal raids and finally to extend Japanese control over much of the huge, industrially rich region. The Chinese Communists, in the meantime, had been driven out of Shanghai, Hankou, and their other main urban bases, and forced to take shelter in guerrilla bases scattered in the poor mountainous areas of southern-central China. The growth of Japanese power put immense pressures on Chiang Kai-shek, who responded by deciding to purge his country of the Communists first, and to turn against Japan second. Launching assault after assault against the Red base areas, he finally forced the Communist forces to retreat to the north in the autumn of 1934, on the vast and protracted "Long March" that led them at last, with vastly depleted numbers, to a new base in the area around Yan'an, just south of the great bend of the Yellow River. This region was impoverished but had excellent natural defenses, and here the newly emergent leader of the Chinese Communist Party, the Hunan-born peasant Mao Zedong, was able to consolidate his forces, out of the reach of Chiang's armies, sheltered from the Japanese, and largely incommunicado with the Comintern or the Soviet Union.

The Kansas-born Edgar Snow was a witness to many of these events. Born in 1905 to a family of farmers and printers, Snow had ridden the rails to California, passed through journalism school in Missouri, and lived and worked briefly in New York, before he decided in 1928 to head out to China and try his luck. China had not been a self-conscious choice of destination for him; it was just part of the wild restlessness he felt, "the song of cities" beating in his brain, he told his parents before his departure.[18] Though Snow missed the great anti-Communist purges of 1927, he was in Shanghai in 1928, and interviewed many of the Nationalist leaders responsible, as well as some of the opposition. He saw the famines in China in 1931, the effects of the Japanese fighting on the Chinese-Manchurian border later that year, and the Japanese invasion of Shanghai that took place in 1932, a nightmare of violence followed by an uneasy peace settlement that left little doubt that full-scale war must come before too long.

Drawn steadily to sympathy with the leftists in China, Snow was present at the huge 1935 student demonstration in Beiping (as Peking had been called since 1927 when Chiang made Nanjing his capital), and was to learn later that members of the Chinese Communist Party had even used his house for their secret meetings without his knowledge.[19] In the summer of 1936, when Mao and his troops had completed the Long March but had not yet completed their final move to Yan'an, Snow was invited to pay a visit to the Communist base area. He accepted at once, despite the dangers, and arrived in July.

Everything about Snow's experiences in China, and perhaps in his earlier life as well, predisposed him to be a favorable observer of radical ventures in social organization, and that is almost certainly why the invitation was conveyed to him, and why the Communists guided him so considerately through the invading Nationalist forces. Snow did not have Brecht's knowledge of the Communist Party and its tactics, nor did he have Brecht's clearheaded political realism. At one stage in *The Measures Taken,* the young comrade had cried out in frustration, "who is the Party?" and the professional agitators reply:

> We are the Party.
> you and I and he—all of us.
> It is hidden in your clothes, it thinks in your head
> Where I live is its home, and where you are attacked it fights.

The Control Chorus added an additional gloss: "It is the vanguard of the masses \ And it lays out its battles \ According to the methods of our classics, which are derived from \ The recognition of reality."[20]

Though Snow would not have shared such a view, the Communist leader Mao Zedong was outstandingly shrewd in just this pragmatic "recognition of reality," and his rise to power had come from his constant adaption of tactics and ideology to circumstances. Mao was especially skilled at drawing on peasant forces to supplement or even replace the urban workers when it was obvious that the major cities were to be denied as bases for the Communists, perhaps for decades. Snow's portrayal of Mao and his supporters, published in 1937 as *Red Star Over China*, became a bestseller in both England and the United States, where it sold more than any previous non-fiction book on China, missing selection as the Book-of-the-Month Club main choice by a single vote.[21]

As Pearl Buck's book awakened a generation of American readers to the tribulations of Chinese peasant life, so did Snow's account introduce them to the new forces of Chinese radicalism. Snow—oblivious to any coercive or manipulative sides to party mobilization—was particularly drawn to the manifestations of what he saw as Chinese revolutionary spontaneity. As he wrote of the first Red Army troops with whom he traveled:

> Though tragedy had touched the lives of nearly all of them, they were perhaps too young for it to have depressed them much. They seemed to me fairly happy, and perhaps the first consciously happy group of Chinese proletarians I had seen. Passive contentment is the common phenomenon in China, but the higher emotion of happiness, which implies a feeling of positiveness about existence, is rare indeed.
>
> They sang nearly all day on the road, and their supply of songs was endless. Their singing was not done at a command, but was spontaneous, and they sang well. Whenever the spirit moved him, or he thought of an appropriate song, one of them would suddenly burst forth, and commanders and men joined in. They sang at night, too, and learned new fold-tunes from the peasants, who brought out their Shensi guitars.[22]

The troops not only sang with joyful abandon; they seemed to Snow to have an intuitive respect for property and an inherent code of discipline:

What discipline they had seemed almost entirely self-imposed. When we passed wild apricot trees on the hills there was an abrupt dispersal until everyone had filled his pockets, and somebody always brought me back a handful. Then, leaving the trees looking as if a great wind had struck through them, they moved back into order and quick-timed to make up for the loss. But, when we passed private orchards, nobody touched the fruit in them, and the grain and vegetables we consumed in the villages were paid for in full.[23]

Snow's book became the first source in the world to give a detailed appraisal of Mao, and the nature of that appraisal was to have great influence in shaping the image of the Communist leader in the West:

> I met Mao soon after my arrival: a gaunt, rather Lincolnesque figure, above average height for a Chinese, somewhat stooped, with a head of thick black hair grown very long, and with large, searching eyes, a high-bridged nose and prominent cheekbones. My fleeting impression was of an intellectual face of great shrewdness, but I had no opportunity to verify this for several days. Next time I saw him, Mao was walking hatless along the street at dusk, talking with two young peasants, and gesticulating earnestly. I did not recognize him until he was pointed out to me—moving along unconcernedly with the rest of the strollers, despite the $250,000 which Nanking had hung over his head.[24]

Even when Snow appeared to be modifying his own praise, the general effect was often to strengthen it:

> Do not suppose, first of all, that Mao Tse-tung could be the "saviour" of China. Nonsense. There will never be any one "saviour" of China. Yet undeniably you feel a certain force of destiny in him. It is nothing quick or flashy, but a kind of solid elemental vitality. You feel that whatever there is extraordinary in this man grows out of the uncanny degree to which he synthesizes and expresses the urgent demands of millions of Chinese, and especially the peasantry—those impoverished, underfed, exploited, illiterate, but kind, generous, courageous and just now rather

rebellious human beings who are the vast majority of the Chinese people.[25]

Snow was especially effective in presenting Mao as likable and simple, despite his "native shrewdness" and his wide-ranging scholarship. Mao lived in a simple two-room cave dwelling, carved out of the soft loess soil of North China, just as the local villagers did. As to possessions, Mao apparently had only two cotton uniforms, a mosquito net, and a few books to his name. This reinforced Snow's sense of Mao's revolutionary integrity:

> Mao seemed to me a very interesting and complex man. He had the simplicity and naturalness of the Chinese peasant, with a lively sense of humour and a love of rustic laughter. His laughter was even active on the subject of himself and the shortcomings of the Soviets—a boyish sort of laughter which never in the least shook his inner faith in his purpose. He is plain-speaking and plain-living, and some people might think him rather coarse and vulgar. Yet he combines curious qualities of naïveté with the most incisive wit and worldly sophistication.[26]

The long series of interviews that Mao gave to Snow on his upbringing, education, and revolutionary experience remain a staple source on Mao for all scholars and historians since that time, even though their content and twist were fully orchestrated by Mao himself. Snow's conclusion that the Red base area economic structures "might more accurately be called rural equalitarianism than anything Marx would have found acceptable as a model child of his own" perfectly reflected the Communists' current wishes to court liberal allies, who would have been repelled had they known about the more extremist measures taken.[27] As if laying to rest centuries of negative perceptions of China, Snow reported that in the Red areas, beggars were no more, footbinding was banished, infanticide ended, and multiple consorts for men a thing of the past.[28]

At one stage, Snow had a lengthy interview with the Red Army general Peng Dehuai, who reinforced the contrast with the Nationalist Guomindang by recalling the days of 1928 when the Nationalists practiced scorched-earth policies in areas of the countryside where the Communists were entrenched, destroying all the peasants' homes and crops in order to drive the Communists out. Peng reported that the tactic failed because the peasants had buried supplies of grain to hide them from the Nationalist tax collectors, and also shared supplies of potatoes and wild roots with the Red troops.[29] Such a view of the Nationalist Party's clumsy authoritarianism found ready responses among foreign observers, especially those who traveled to Chongqing, deep up the Yangzi River in Sichuan province, which Chiang Kai-shek had named the national capital, after the all-out Japanese assault of summer 1937 had precipitated China into a major war.

One of the most articulate of these observers was the American writer Graham Peck. On an earlier visit to China in the 1930s, wrote Peck, he had "sometimes suspected that everyone I watched was obscurely engaged in an enormous practical joke."[30] Now that he had time to examine the life of Chongqing in the early 1940s, he had grown confirmed in that suspicion. Not only was the city itself "a semi-modern, semi-ruined capital crammed up on cliffs," clearly "a sort of practical joke,"[31] but the city's Chinese residents were obviously in on some secret that eluded the Westerners. For instance, both the rickshaw pullers and their passengers gave a perfect illustration of this as they made their ways through the city's narrow and tortuously winding streets:

> The rickshaws threading through these tangles had been designed for level country. Going uphill on steep grades, the pullers had to bend so far forward that their faces nearly touched the road. They crept upwards at much less than a walking pace but their fares stayed sitting in the carts, lolling contentedly as they smiled that smile. Going downhill, the rickshaw men would balance deep between their shafts, tipping their carts so steeply backward that there was danger of the sitters' landing in the road

on their scalps. Then the pullers would speed alarmingly down the slope, their wide-swinging feet touching the ground only now and then. They smiled at their passengers' screams.[32]

The Nationalist troops may not have sung like Snow's, and their laughter might not be as "boyish" as Mao's, but they too had their place in the same secret world:

> After a while a line of shabby soldiers in gray cotton uniforms and straw sandals came slogging up the hill, technically in double-time, but really mocking the quick step. For all their jogging up and down, they moved forward less rapidly than the burdened housewives. Like soldiers all over China, they were chanting numbers to keep in pace: "One, two, three ... (step, step, step) ... FOUR!" When their officer screamed at them to hurry it up, they began chanting faster and faster, out of time, while their feet pounded the road as slowly as ever. They all wore that smile.[33]

Using this and many other examples, Peck suggested his own version for interpreting China's predicaments: "The Chinese laughed so much in their touching and annoying way because they sensed they were always victims of forces they could not control."[34] Peck used his metaphor to chip away at the admiring portrayals of Chiang Kai-shek that often circulated in the West, and at the "New Life Movement" which Chiang presented as the heart of his moral reforms—and his ideological alternative to the Communists. This New Life Movement, to Peck, taught the Chinese to have a childlike pattern of dependency on Chiang Kai-shek as the ruler-father, and it was always Chiang's wealthiest supporters who spoke up most strongly for the reinstitution of Confucian values. "Thus, Chiang's subjects were children whose parent was always lecturing them on how to improve their lot by being moral and refined, while he indulged in questionable, perhaps criminal, and certainly self-destructive behavior. Many Chinese acted as if they understood this. They naturally wore secret smiles."[35]

In Graham Peck's view, such secret smiles had become the only viable responses to the incessant suffering of the times. In a world in which the revolutionary heroics depicted by Malraux, the revolutionary discipline projected by Brecht, and the revolutionary purity offered by Snow, all seemed to be wearing thin, perhaps the only way back to sanity was by induction into a world of cosmic hilarity.

CHAPTER 11

Mystiques of Power

WHEN *THE MEASURES TAKEN* HAD ITS FIRST PERFOR-
mance at the Berlin Philharmonic Hall on December 13, 1930,
Karl Wittfogel sat next to Bertolt Brecht. Eight days later there
was a public discussion meeting on the play in a local school
hall, with Wittfogel in the chair and Brecht sharing the plat-
form. Those present were naturally familiar with Marxism and
with current Comintern policies, and the discussion was strident. Much of the argument focused on whether the Communist Party did or did not kill erring comrades, whether they were
right to do so or not, and what the alternatives to death might
be. Some present, including Wittfogel, argued that to a committed Communist, physical death was less tragic than expul-
sion from the party; most agreed that it was not actual party
practice to kill erring party members, and Brecht was criticized
by the group for the way he depicted the young comrade's death.

The group also reiterated the concept of party omnipotence—
which Brecht had included in his play—stating that whereas the
individual only has two eyes, the party has a thousand. Brecht
told the group that he had already decided the young comrade
in his play, just before his death, should ask *himself* whether
there was any alternative to his death, and should answer himself in the negative.[1] The final amended scene now was to run as
follows:

> *The Agitators*: . . . We must be the ones to shoot you and cast you
> into the lime-pit, so that the lime will burn away all traces of
> you. And yet we ask you: Do you know any way out?
> *The Young Comrade*: No.

206

The Agitators: And we ask you: Do you agree with us
Pause
The Young Comrade: Yes.[2]

Much of the essence of party discipline and attitude to the Comintern lay behind that "Pause," as both Wittfogel and Brecht would have known full well. They knew the rules of the political world they had chosen to join, though later they were to travel utterly different routes: Brecht, after a long period of disillusion in wartime Hollywood, returned to direct his celebrated Berliner Ensemble in Communist-controlled East Germany; while Wittfogel, after living in China for some years, became bitterly anti-Communist and went on to write his major theoretical work, *Oriental Despotism*, after settling in the United States. But for many years they continued to stay in touch, and as late as 1943, when both were in America, Brecht sent to Wittfogel the typescript of his new play, *The Good Woman of Setzuan*. That play, however, was not about China; it was an exploration of the theme of human goodness and cruelty with China as the backdrop. The gap thereafter widened, and the two men reached a breaking point in an argument in New York, when Wittfogel accused Brecht of denying that the Soviet Union was an exploitative society. Brecht countered that the workers would eventually control the state; when one saw a donkey being whipped by its owner, one should not forget that the whipping was a superficial aspect, for the donkey in fact was using the owner for its own purposes. Wittfogel maintained that it was just such arguments by Stalin in 1931 and 1932 that had helped Hitler come to power.[3]

The initial friendship and later alienation from Brecht were but two of the many stages Karl Wittfogel passed through on his way to becoming the latest in the long series of those who tried to make China the center of a massive system, a system that would contain within itself the explanation for the formations and development of world societies. Born in Germany in 1896, he was the only child of his father's second marriage. His father was an elderly Evangelical Lutheran schoolteacher. By an odd coincidence, André Malraux had made an elderly Lutheran schoolteacher the formative influence on the young orphaned terrorist Ch'en, a teacher who had left his young charge "insolent and taciturn," subject to "limitless love or terror, according to the strength or weakness of hope."[4] But Wittfogel's father, a beekeeper and fanatical hiker, gave his son Karl an idealized rural upbringing, and trained him to be an eclectic and questioning reader.[5]

Over the ensuing years Wittfogel received an excellent education, developed an intellectual infatuation with Nietzsche, discovered Marxism, Buddhism, Max Weber, and Gestalt psychology, grew fascinated by the challenge and the promise of Chinese studies, and drifted via the German youth movement, workers' education societies, and Socialist discussion groups into the revolutionary Spartacist movement of Rosa Luxemburg and Karl Liebknecht. After their deaths in 1919, he joined the Communist Party. He worked as a teacher, playwright, and party activist while pursuing his studies in European economic history and in Chinese historical sources and language at the University of Frankfurt; gradually the two later areas began to converge, as Wittfogel grew absorbed by the complex academic arguments over the exact nature of the early Chinese economic system.

His first book on China, written in 1925 and published in 1926, was contemporary and political rather than historical. Entitled *Awakening China,* it was a Marxist analysis of the early phases of the Chinese Revolution through the United Front of 1925; its basic purpose was to vindicate Lenin's prescience in seeing that the nations of Asia were indeed awakening from their "historic sleep" and were destined to play a major role in the coming world revolutionary movement. The book also praised the various agencies of the Comintern for having "given themselves, with all their power," to the cause of China.[6] *Awakening China* was well received by many members of the Comintern (not by all, for the organization was already sundered by the battle between Stalin and the Trotskyists) and in the fall of 1927 brought Wittfogel a Comintern commission to write a detailed introduction to a major Soviet collection of Sun Yat-sen's speeches: in this long essay, Wittfogel presented the theoretical arguments for concluding that Sun Yat-sen, despite his public expressions of interest in Marxism, was not himself a Marxist, but was rather a "bourgeois revolutionary," whose main role was in developing the forces of anti-imperialism within China.[7]

Only in 1928 did Wittfogel have time to complete his dissertation on early Chinese agriculture, and almost immediately after receiving his degree he made his own long-desired pilgrimage to the Soviet Union. Once there, he plunged into excited and protracted debates with Soviet academicians over what exactly Marx had meant by his term the "Asiatic mode of production," and the pertinence of these theories to the current Chinese Revolution. Wittfogel was also able to discuss these problems with Michael Borodin, the Comintern agent formerly most active in China, whose own literal relayings of Stalin's orders to Chinese revolutionaries had done much to trigger the grim events of 1927 in Shanghai, later so convincingly chronicled by Malraux in *Man's Fate*.[8]

Returning to Germany, Wittfogel began the task of forging from his years of study a master synthesis that would explain the past and present of China, to be titled *Economy and Society in China*. His premise was that the old China, with its ingrained structural elements that resisted all change, was now being swept away. In a powerful metaphor, Wittfogel carried Macartney's vision of China as an old sailing vessel being dashed to pieces on the rocks in an even bleaker direction: "The structure is rotten through and through. The remnant of old 'Asiatic' China is like a blockhouse eaten away by termites. The next greater storm will cause everything to collapse."[9]

The roots of the attempt to create a global intellectual system that would fully incorporate China were laid, as we have seen, by Leibniz in the late seventeenth century, and developed further by Montesquieu and Voltaire in the mid-eighteenth century. At the end of the eighteenth century, Herder had given the systemic study of China a harshly negative twist. Thereafter, a number of other thinkers had grappled with the problems posed by China and sought their own solutions to its enigmas. Adam Smith tried to make economic and political sense of the relationship between China's enormous population and its apparent economic stagnation. Hegel reflected on the place of China in the march toward freedom in the world, which he considered the central premise of historical development. He felt that though Chinese culture appeared early in the chronological span of human history, China had placed itself outside the main developmental lines of human progress, and thus outside the true march of history. This was due to the extraordinary powers arrogated by the Chinese emperors and their powerful yet subservient bureaucracies, who had created a society in which "only one was free" and all the others forced to bow under the tyranny of their yoke. China would only become a part of world history when it was forced into the living present by the dynamic forces emanating from the West.

Marx had echoed Hegel in seeing China as "without movement," and as having a "capacity for resistance" to all social change. Marx conceived of four main stages in the economic formation of society, each linked to the nature of the control over the means of production: these were "progressively" (that is, sequentially) the Asiatic, the Ancient, the Feudal, and the Modern Bourgeois. But though the last three were analytically linked, the Asiatic was isolated and had no specific role in the scheme of development. "From immemorial times," Marx wrote, the Asiatic governments such as China's functioned at only three levels: "plunder of the interior" (finance); "plunder of the exterior" (war); and the sphere of public works, designed to control water use and distribution through irrigation. In the West, private industry seeking equitable water use led to "voluntary association." But in the Asiatic societies, the control by the state was so strong that private industry did not emerge and foster such associations; instead, their place was taken by isolated and dispersed village communities. As part of his inquiry, Marx analysed the Taiping Rebellion carefully, but estimated that British capitalism would have a greater revolutionary effect on China's overall development than would domestic rebels, for the British would end by splitting apart agriculture and industry there, and forcing new patterns to emerge.[10]

At the end of the nineteenth century, and into the early twentieth, Max Weber devoted much of his intellectual labor to China, seeking to explain why China did not develop aspects of capitalist society despite its enormous resources, and what the comparative role of Confucian thought, traditional imperial and bureaucratic structures, and the nature of Chinese cities might be in this case of arrested development. During and after World War I, Oswald Spengler in *The Decline of the West* reflected on Chinese language, government, art, and landscape, as he tried to gauge the earlier impact China had had on world history, the reasons for its decline, and the possibilities of its resumption of a formative role, through its "mystic universalism," in the regeneration of world energies as the West lost its dominating force.[11]

A perpetually voracious reader, Wittfogel knew the works of all these theorists in great detail, and discussed them in his own writings. But one of his central ambitions was to create a synthesis of the views of Marx and Weber on China that would link the profound economic originality of the first to the detailed study of the Chinese bureaucracy made by the second. In addition, Wittfogel felt that he was in a position to develop the theories of Marx—tied so tightly to evidence drawn from a few Western European societies—to additional theoretical insights of his own drawn from his wide reading in Chinese sources; he continued to wonder, for instance, whether feudalism might prove to have been a transitional stage from both the Asiatic and the Ancient phases of human history.[12]

Wittfogel was indeed the only one of this long line of systems builders who knew enough Chinese language to read the historical texts in the original, and hence his views commanded real respect among many readers. But they were already, by 1931, too idiosyncratic to be accepted in Moscow. Wittfogel's lengthy work on the Chinese economy was banned from translation into Russian, and Wittfogel himself was not invited to a key series of Soviet conferences on the meaning of the Asiatic mode of production, even though he was widely known to be the greatest authority on the topic. Still loyal to the principles of Marxism, Wittfogel grew deeply uneasy over the Stalinist directives to the German Communists that they should apply their political energies to overthrowing the Social Democrats rather than opposing the rising power of the Nazi party. By 1933 his hostile writings about Hitler were well known to the Nazis, and after Hitler came to power in March, Wittfogel was arrested, and passed the rest of the year in a grim succession of SS-run concentration camps in Germany. He was finally released thanks to concerted pressure from scholars at home and abroad. Traveling to England and the United States in search of a new base in which to pursue his researches, he decided to go to China, where he arrived in the summer of 1935.

One of his early friends there was Pearl Buck's former husband John Lossing Buck, who shared with Wittfogel his findings from the vastly ambitious survey he had undertaken of conditions in rural China. Later in the year, Wittfogel had extensive talks with Edgar Snow, though he declined the offer to follow Snow in a visit to the Yan'an Chinese Communist base area.[13] Wittfogel stayed in China, working on numerous research projects, and trying to prove to devout leftists the seriousness and horror of the Stalinist purge trials. He left China in July 1937, just after the full-scale Japanese invasion began, and returned to the United States, which thereafter became his home. He broke finally with the Communists in 1939, after receiving news of the Hitler-Stalin Pact.

Wittfogel was thus not only the sole system-building theorist of China to know Chinese language, he was the only one to have lived in the country and to have studied it at first hand. His own synthesis of his manifold experiences emerged at last, in 1957, as *Oriental Despotism*. The subtitle Wittfogel chose for his book, "A Comparative Study of Total Power," accurately reflects the fact that among the many intellectually formidable precursors in system building, the one to whom he felt closest, as far as China was concerned, was not Hegel or Marx but Montesquieu. It was Montesquieu who had first pointed to the essential aloneness of the Chinese emperor, in a world where only one man could be free; it was Montesquieu who pointed also to the abuses of physical punishment, the fragility of personal property for the emperor's subjects, the blurring of the lines between *mores,* manners, and laws, the absence of independent religions or judicial structures, and the fact that the despotism of China was separated out from the monarchies dominant elsewhere because it lacked the guiding concept of honor, replacing it with fear.

But though Montesquieu clearly influenced him, Wittfogel's final synthesis was probably more shaped by the extraordinary pattern of his own intellectual and political journeyings: the Hitler-Stalin Pact of 1939 had confirmed his worst fears about both systems, and the course of World War II did nothing to change that opinion. During the McCarthy period of the early 1950s, Wittfogel became an outspoken critic of American leftists and liberals, an outspokenness for which he was ostracized by many academics and former political friends. The China that he had been studying for so long now became fused in his mind with the workings of modern totalitarianism, whether Stalinist or Nazi, but also with the disquieting gullibility of democracies. In an interesting aside late in his life, Wittfogel referred to

"Tocqueville's *furtive* treatment of Montesquieu's concept of the unchangeability of Oriental despotism."[14] The use of the word "furtive" is curious here, and showed Wittfogel's contempt for so many bourgeois-liberal critics. What Tocqueville failed to show, Wittfogel explained, was that Montesquieu had seen, with sociopolitical precision, the reasons for the "self-perpetuation of Oriental Despotism." It was this self-perpetuation of totalitarian tyranny that was so terrifying, and that separated out such despotisms from the more temporary "tyrannies."[15]

On the very first page of *Oriental Despotism,* Wittfogel noted that Montesquieu's primary focus had been on the "distressing personal effects" that flowed from such harsh regimes. Subsequent thinkers had examined the managerial powers of such states, as well as the hydraulic complexity of the enormous waterworks that were needed to keep open communications and maintain irrigation systems. Such states inevitably developed huge bureaucracies to handle the hydraulic problems, and were also the largest landowners within their own domains. After three decades of study of this phenomenon in many different societies, and across several millennia, Wittfogel wrote, he had come to see that these were systems of "total power," or what he now chose to call "hydraulic" rather than "Oriental" societies. The total power of some of these societies, far from withering away, was "spreading like a virulent and aggressive disease."[16] Such a phrase, correctly to Wittfogel, "stresses human action rather than geography," and made it easier to compare such hydraulic societies with feudal or industrial societies elsewhere. It would also help explain the pervasiveness in hydraulic societies of "bureaucratic landlordism" and "bureaucratic capitalism."[17]

The founding emperor of the harshly authoritarian Qin dynasty in 221 B.C.—Qin Shihuangdi—was to Wittfogel a key figure in the formative stages of the hydraulic society. It was this Qin emperor who linked together the many stretches of wall that existed in China in the third century B.C. "to form the longest unbroken defense installation ever made by man, an act which—like the subsequent reconstructions, expressed so well the continued effectiveness of hydraulic economy and government-directed mass labor." And it was the Qin emperor who undertook other "monster projects" such as palace and underground tomb complexes for which he mustered work teams of over seven hundred thousand men.[18]

The immense erudition on which Wittfogel drew in composing *Oriental Despotism* is constantly apparent, and his was a truly comparative study, of which China was one component, along with Inca, Mayan, Hindu, Babylonian, Byzantine, Egyptian, and Russian elements. Yet at many pivotal moments in the book, especially the passionately written fifth chapter entitled "Total Terror—Total Submission—Total Loneliness," images from China, drawn from Wittfogel's lifetime of study and experience, seem to play the central role. The reader's mind is drawn again and again to parallels between the history Wittfogel is presenting and the worst excesses of Stalinism, Nazism, and the post-Korean War Maoist China of the anti-Rightist campaign and the burgeoning Great Leap Forward. On the terror of hydraulic despotisms, Wittfogel commented in general terms:

> Like the tiger, the engineer of power must have the physical means with which to crush his victims. And the agromanagerial despot does indeed possess such means. He exercises unchecked control over the army, the police, the intelligence service; and he has at his disposal jailers, torturers, executioners, and all the tools that are necessary to catch, incapacitate, and destroy a suspect.
>
> Furthermore, he can employ these devices with maximum psychological effect. Everywhere persons wielding great governmental or proprietary power like to shroud certain of their acts in secrecy; but the procedures of a despotic government are enigmatic because of the very nature of the regime. Accountable only

to themselves, the men of the apparatus tend to handle even insignificant matters with secretiveness; and they raise mystification to an art when they want to intimidate and surprise. Unpredictability is an essential weapon of absolute terror.[19]

Wittfogel singled out Chinese "judicial torture" and "judicial terror" as special aspects of Chinese society, and noted that even Confucius believed that "the good subject is the obedient subject," just as Confucian education "that demands absolute obedience to parent and teacher forms the ideal foundation on which to build absolute obedience to the masters of society." Prostrating oneself on the ground in the presence of authority— as in the case of the Chinese kowtow—was a logical extension of such beliefs. Such behavior was essential training for a society in which "the threat of total terror" leads to the wisdom that if people "want to survive, they must not provoke the uncontrollable monster."[20]

The "total loneliness" created by such a situation spreads from the emperor himself—suspicious of all—to each individual, suspicious of neighbors and even family. As Wittfogel adds:

> There were many lonely people among the free men of classical Greece; and there are many lonely people in the democratic countries of today. But these free individuals are lonely in the main because they are neglected and not because they are threatened by a power that, whenever it wants to, can reduce human dignity to nothingness. A neglected person can maintain associations of some kind with a few relatives or friends; and he may overcome his passive and partial alienation by widening his associations or by establishing new ways of belonging.
>
> The person who lives under conditions of total power is not so privileged. Unable to counteract these conditions, he can take refuge only in alert resignation. Eager to avoid the worst, he must always be prepared to face it.[21]

As an example of what he called "total loneliness in the hour of our doom," Wittfogel gave the case of China's greatest historian, Sima Qian, who angered his emperor in the Han dynasty by defending a defeated general. Unable to commute the assigned punishment since none of his friends dared to aid him, he was castrated—"led into the dark room and mutilated as if he had been an animal," in Wittfogel's bleak comment. Wittfogel adds, tellingly, "measured by the standards of an open society, the Chinese historian suffered appallingly. Measured by the standards of his own world, he was not without luck. Although he was emasculated he remained alive; and being of no political significance, he could continue to work on his history." Modern "total managerial states," to Wittfogel, have added a refinement to such "trials," the false public confession. The older hydraulic despotism could of course have tortured anyone into confessing had they chosen to, but they "saw no reason to publicize their conflicts in the villages or guild quarters." They felt "no need to promote the spectacular and articulate self-alienation in which the totalitarian 'People's' Courts now specialize."[22] This important shift could be succinctly stated: the agrarian despotism of the old society had combined total political power with limited social and intellectual control. The industrial despotism of the "fully developed and totally managerial apparatus society" combined total political power with "total social and intellectual control."[23]

In the concluding chapter of *Oriental Despotism,* Wittfogel moved to a tighter analysis of Chinese Communist society, pointing out to his readers that the Chinese had learned well from the Soviet Union, and had no intention of merely restoring an agrarian despotism of the traditional kind. Mao's retreat into the countryside had never been more than temporary necessity; he knew full well that rapid, state-directed industrialization was the best route to the powerful "total managerial order" that they sought:

> The relation of these ideas to the long-range perspective of the Chinese Communists is evident. A Mao Tse-tung who viewed entrenchment in the countryside as a permanent principle and not as a temporary strategic device would be no deviant Com-

munist, but merely a fool. He would be like the man who always prefers a stick to a gun, because once in the woods he had only a stick to fight with.

But Mao is no fool. He and his followers never considered themselves leaders of a peasant party, whose actions were motivated, and limited, by the interests of the villages. When the conditions of the civil war forced the Chinese Communists to operate in the countryside, they always expected to return to the cities. And when they seized the cities, they did exactly what the Bolsheviks had done after the October revolution. They restored, consolidated, and developed whatever industries there were; and they were noticeably eager to control modern industry and mechanized communication. Thus they were as little interested in an Asiatic restoration as were the bureaucratic masters of the Soviet apparatus.[24]

In asserting boldly that Mao was "no fool," Wittfogel sought to implant him more firmly as the latest manifestation of the trend of self-perpetuation (rather than just the unchangeability) of this new type of hydraulic despotism. To the wielders of power in the United States, this ascription of enormous calculation and cunning to China's leaders came as naturally as it had to Wittfogel; no better witnesses can be found to this tendency than President Richard Nixon and his national security adviser Henry Kissinger in the months of late 1971 and early 1972, when they were planning in secret the trips that were to take the president to China and end the two decades of almost total separation that had affected every aspect of economic and political contact.

In a curious reprise to the past, Nixon used André Malraux to set the scene for the encounter, apparently content to let Malraux's mystique-filled rhetoric—the two men had an Oval Office meeting and dinner together before the president's departure— set the path for the future. Malraux had been granted an interview by Mao on a recent visit to Peking, and the memories were still sharp in his mind. "You will be dealing with a colossus,"

Malraux told Nixon, "but a colossus facing death," and obsessed with the fact that he had no successor.[25] Malraux had already observed that "one does not ask Mao questions," and so one had just to accept Mao's remarks, however oracular they might sound. But a little later, Malraux added some further thoughts on how Nixon might feel in Mao's presence:

> "Mr. President, you will meet a man who has had a fantastic destiny and who believes that he is acting out the last act of his lifetime. You may think he is talking to you, but he will in truth be addressing Death. . . . It's worth the trip!"
>
> I asked him again what came after Mao. Malraux replied, "It is exactly as Mao said, he has no successor. What did he mean by it? He meant that in his view the great leaders—Churchill, Gandhi, de Gaulle—were created by the kind of traumatic historical events that will not occur in the world anymore. In that sense he feels that he has no successors. I once asked him if he did not think of himself as the heir of the last great Chinese emperors of the sixteenth century. Mao said, 'But of course I am their heir.' Mr. President, you operate within a rational framework, but Mao does not. There is something of the sorcerer in him. He is a man inhabited by a vision, possessed by it."[26]

Nixon, already so absorbed in the significance of his trip that he and Kissinger had named the planning for it "Polo II," drew from Malraux reassuring solace of his own importance: "We were embarking upon a voyage of philosophical discovery as uncertain, and in some respects as perilous, as the voyages of geographical discovery of a much earlier time," he later recalled. According to Nixon's memoirs, Mao had indeed proved to be the "colossus" that Malraux promised. Nixon wrote that at their February 1972 meeting, Mao not only showed his "characteristic self-deprecation," but that "his mind was moving like lightning," and enabled the elderly chairman to make repartee "without dropping a beat." Not only that, Mao was "animated and following every nuance of the conversation," so that when

Nixon quoted a well-known line of Mao's poetry to the chairman, Mao capped the quote with a twinkle, adding "generally speaking, people like me sound like a lot of big cannons. . . . For example, things like 'The whole world should unite and defeat imperialism, revisionism, and all reactionaries, and establish socialism.'"[27] The president ended that first visit to Mao's residence by drawing direct parallels between himself and his host:

> "Mr. Chairman," I said, "your life is well known to all of us. You came from a very poor family to the top of the most populous nation in the world, a great nation.
>
> "My background is not so well known. I also came from a very poor family, and to the top of a very great nation. History has brought us together. The question is whether we, with different philosophies, but both with feet on the ground, and having come from the people, can make a breakthrough that will serve not just China and America, but the whole world in the years ahead. And that is why we are here. . . ."
>
> Mao walked us to the door. His walk was a slow shuffle, and he said that he had not been feeling well.
>
> "But you look very good," I replied.
>
> "Appearances are deceiving," he said with a slight shrug.[28]

Despite Kissinger's desire to be known as a hardheaded political realist, his admiration for Mao was as great or greater than Nixon's. Kissinger referred to the Chinese leader as "one of the colossal figures of modern history," and wrote that Mao lived a life as "withdrawn and mysterious even as the emperors he disdained."[29] Like Edgar Snow in Yan'an thirty-five years before, Kissinger was struck by the apparent simplicity of Mao's lifestyle, despite the enormous resources of luxury on which Mao might have called:

> The interior appointments were as modest as the exterior. Mao just stood there, surrounded by books, tall and powerfully built for a Chinese. He fixed the visitor with a smile both penetrating and slightly mocking, warning by his bearing that there was no point in seeking to deceive this specialist in the foibles and duplic-

ity of man. I have met no one, with the possible exception of Charles de Gaulle, who so distilled raw, concentrated willpower. He was planted there with a female attendant close by to help steady him (and on my last visits to hold him up); he dominated the room—not by the pomp that in most states confers a degree of majesty on the leaders, but by exuding in almost tangible form the overwhelming drive to prevail. . . .

There were no trappings that could account for the sense of power Mao conveyed. My children speak of the "vibes" of popular recording artists to which, I must confess, I am totally immune. But Mao emanated vibrations of strength and power and will.[30]

Neither John Bell in the company of Emperor Kangxi nor Lord Macartney facing Emperor Qianlong had been quite so overwhelmed: struck by those mighty rulers' wits and years, they kept their sense of proportion, and even a sense of fun. For closer parallels, we should perhaps return to the beginnings, to the moment when Marco Polo and Rusticello recalled the first impact of Kublai Khan, truly the lord of all he surveyed.

Let me tell you next of the personal appearance of the Great Lord of Lords whose name is Kublai Khan. He is a man of good stature, neither short nor tall but of moderate height. His limbs are well fleshed out and modelled in due proportion. His complexion is fair and ruddy like a rose, the eyes black and handsome, the nose shapely and set squarely in place. . . .

What more shall I say? When Messer Niccolò and Messer Maffeo and Marco arrived at this great city, they went to the chief palace, where they found the Great Khan and a very great company of barons. They knelt before him and made obeisance with the utmost humility. The Great Khan bade them rise and received them honourably and entertained them with good cheer. He asked many questions about their condition and how they had fared after their departure. The brothers assured him that they had indeed fared well, since they found him well and flourishing. . . . When the Great Khan saw Marco, who was a young stripling, he asked who he was. "Sire," said Messer Niccolò, "he is my son, and your liege man." "He is heartily welcome," said the Khan. What need to make a long story of it?[31]

At some other moments, Kissinger's language turns our minds back to Victor Segalen's narrator in *René Leys,* at the moment he reins in his horse in the center of Peking. As Kissinger put it,

> . . . as I comprehended better the many-layered design of Mao's conversation, I understood that it was like the courtyards in the Forbidden City, each leading to a deeper recess distinguished from the others only by slight changes of proportion, with ultimate meaning residing in a totality that only long reflection could grasp.[32]

But then again, Kissinger was nearer to Wittfogel than to either Polo or Segalen when he wrote of Mao's rule that "the suffering inseparable from an enterprise so far beyond the human scale was vast. And the primeval resistance of a society grown great by the smothering of shocks evoked ever-greater spasms from that colossal figure, who challenged the gods in the scope of his aspirations."[33] Kissinger even concluded the account with an image dear to Wittfogel's heart. Looking ahead to the months before death in 1976, when Mao still spent his last scraps of energy in overthrowing his own closest rivals, Kissinger wrote that at last "that great, demonic, prescient, overwhelming personality disappeared like the great Emperor Ch'in Shih Huang-ti [Qin Shi huangdi] with whom he often compared himself while dreading the oblivion which was his fate."[34]

That formidable Qin founding emperor, whose actions had so impressed Wittfogel and Kissinger, found a new kind of chronicler in the work of the young French scholar and novelist Jean Lévi. Lévi, born in 1948, traveled to China in 1973, as a student, the year after Nixon and Kissinger's visit, and stayed there several years. His experiences of life in the Chinese Cultural Revolution affected Lévi deeply, and led him to attempt to recapture the essence of Chinese power by creating a novel out of the life of the Qin dynasty founder. Near the end of this novel, *The Chinese Emperor,* published in France in 1985, Lévi gives a description of the Qin emperor's thoughts on his own transience that are uncannily like Kissinger's and Nixon's recordings of Mao:

> Confused and terrifying images were coming back to him, reawakening the old dread—that the round of the seasons, the alternation of day and night, the joys and sorrows of men—even the poorest and lowliest subjects—would go on without him, as if he had never been. A slight tremor of the earth, the collapse of a mountain, and the world, after a faint quiver at its disappearance, would continue on its way like a cart that has dropped a bit of dung.
>
> He who molded his people as he willed would be swallowed up in the great universal mold—to be ground up, kneaded, and shaped in accordance with a will that was blind, impartial.[35]

In building up his portrait of the young man who was to become one of the most effective and the most tyrannical rulers in China's history—in the early parts of the novel Lévi styles the future ruler "Ordinance," because of his administrative skills—Lévi unabashedly returned to some of the devices of the French exotic to underlie his narrative, as in the depiction of Ordinance's sexual apathy even in the presence of the country's most beautiful young women:

> He preferred the loud voices of generals and the barking of military commands to the sensual songs and provocative laughter of dancing girls. He developed a passion for the writings of the philosophers from the school of law and administration. He longed to take over the reins of government, and silently champed at the bit. But they kept a tight rein on him. They used him like a dummy, a piece of wood painted to look like a king, an effigy in a tomb. . . . He liked hunting, which made him think of the excitement of military campaigns. The splendid horses and chariots, the streamers and banners flapping in the wind, the long pursuit across country, the arrows raining down on the victim, the danger from an angry tiger, the smell of blood, and the

dying snarls of wounded beasts—all this he found intoxicating. Other pleasures left him weary and unsatisfied.[36]

In later life, the round of sexual quests grew stronger and more devious, as Ordinance—now the emperor—driven onward by his competing advisers, sought for mastery over his own body and his own inner forces. One method he tried to follow, recommended in the earliest medical texts, was to withhold his semen even at the height of his desire, so that he could absorb all the woman's inner force without losing his own. Another was purification through fasting, and "the careful placing of his partners at the eight points of the rose of the winds." But even though the son of heaven "circulated among them in a complicated pattern based on the motions of the stars and the symbols of his reign," "scrupulously observed the right rhythms," and "breathed deeply, eyes half closed, mind concentrated, tongue tight against the roof of his mouth," the result was only shortness of breath, dizzy spells, and absence of all desire.[37]

Lévi drew on the great historian Sima Qian—whose fate had been so vividly evoked by Wittfogel—in tracing the details of the Qin emperor's quests for sexual and political power, and his ever harsher actions: the rounding up of scholars, the burning of the books, the deportation of whole populations to build roads and walls, palaces, and tombs. As human servants became wearying to him, their actions unpredictable, their rhythms always changing, the emperor fell back on his most skilled artisans, who created for him sets of puppets, starting with an orchestra:

> The Emperor was soothed by the mechanical repetitions of his bronze dolls, that invariably produced their inexorable notes. He ceased to be offended by the involuntary twitchings of flesh or the imperfections of human breathing and circulation. . . .
>
> Soon servants made of lacquered wood were offering the August Emperor wine and dishes of food. The Emperor had the controls within easy reach and could regulate the speed of his

manikins' movements, making each one do his bidding. He was as happy as a little boy. They were his creatures, and they obeyed him. They had no desires, no thought, no movements other than those dictated by the master of machines. . . .

The concubines languished in the harems, the singing girls lost their voices, and the Emperor's acrobats grew fat. Some of his dancing girls tried to pass for puppets, imitating their jerky movements, parading themselves thus in front of the master of men in the hope of winning back his favor. But they were immediately unmasked and decapitated.[38]

When at last the emperor dies, as Sima Qian recorded and Jean Lévi retells, the news is kept from his own heir-apparent, his courtiers, and his people. To cover the smell of the emperor's decomposing flesh, and thus to maintain the fiction of the emperor's unassailable physical powers, his minions surround the imperial carriage with others filled with rotting fish.[39]

Thus did Lévi draw on the texts from China's past to create an involved yet documented allegory for the travails of China's people and the excesses of the country's rulers. Like other system builders before him, and like Wittfogel himself, Lévi attempted to track the layers of Chinese imperial power down to their roots. But even more skillfully than his precursors in this quest for the mystiques of power, he turned the argument in on itself, and showed the ruler of the universe shivering and impotent in the midst of the terror he had sought to render absolute.

CHAPTER 12

Genius at Play

THE THREE AESTHETICALLY MOST PERFECT FICTIONS about China—Kafka's "The Great Wall of China," Borges's "The Garden of Forking Paths," and Calvino's *Invisible Cities*—were all written in the twentieth century. But they were scattered across its surface chronologically, at intervals of around twenty-five years, one being written in the period of World War I, one in World War II, and one in the early 1970s. Each of the authors emerged from a tangled background in terms of his upbringing and intellectual roots. Franz Kafka, born 1883, was from a Czech-Jewish family, and wrote in German; Jorge Luis Borges, born 1899, was brought up speaking English in Argentina, and studied French and German in Switzerland, before returning to Argentina and writing in Spanish; and Italo Calvino was born in Cuba in 1923, before moving to Italy and receiving a degree at Turin in literature. Each was a prolific, hardworking, and supremely gifted writer, who played with China briefly in his works, though knowing little about the country or its people. Each of the three chose an aspect of China that was of genuine importance in Chinese history: Kafka the question of authority, Borges the question of origins, and Calvino the question of the observed observer. Each wrote of China without pretension, yet with precision and economy, eschewing the erotic and the sensationalist, creating a purely fabricated whole of astonishing verisimilitude that can sustain endless rereadings.

Kafka wrote his short story "The Great Wall of China" in the spring of 1917, when he was working a six-hour-a-day shift in the Workers Accident Insurance Group in Prague . (The German title for the story, *"Beim Bau der Chinesischen Mauer,"* translates more literally as "At the Building of the Chinese Wall.") As a potent symbol for China's archaic greatness, for its enclosure, the Great Wall had stood for centuries, and was perhaps the best known single item about the country; Kafka had also been reading steadily on Chinese themes—both Confucian works and those of the Taoist tradition—through the German translations of Richard Wilhelm, which Karl Wittfogel was also deeply influenced by at just the same time. Kafka kept at least one copy of the translated Taoist classical texts in his office drawer, and had marked up the margins of passages that appealed to him.[1]

But Kafka's Great Wall was supremely his own creation, as were his interpretations of the manner of its building, and the reasons for it. The Great Wall of China, in Kafka's vision, was both deliberate and piecemeal, built in a series of apparently unrelated sections, each some five hundred yards in length, worked on by a team of around twenty workers. Though their stretch might be joined at one end to another stretch of the same length being built at exactly the same time, that was as far as their own knowledge of the whole could ever go. For at that point the workers were transferred elsewhere, to begin afresh. With totally convincing precision, Kafka places himself as narrator in this flow of the Chinese past, recalling how he was raised as a boy "almost on the borders of the Tibetan Highlands," and thus far to the south of the wall's shifting sites, and yet felt inexorably drawn to the stories he heard of the wall's possibilities. The education he received as a youth also prepared him for his future life of wall building:

> I can still remember quite well us standing as small children, scarcely sure on our feet, in our teacher's garden, and being ordered to build a sort of wall out of pebbles; and then the teacher, girding up his robe, ran full tilt against the wall, of course knocking it down, and scolded us so terribly for the shod-

diness of our work that we ran weeping in all directions to our parents. A trivial incident, but significant of the spirit of the time.[2]

With equal precision, the narrator states his good fortune in having been just twenty at the time the construction of the wall began, so that he was not like those who came before him, trained to build but with no opportunities to use their skills. Such people, mused the narrator, "drifted uselessly about with the most splendid architectural plans in their heads, and sank by thousands into hopelessness." Whereas he was able both to work physically at the wall and to serve as its historian, to be the wall's "incorruptible observer": "My inquiry is purely historical; no lightning flashes any longer from the long since vanished thunderclouds, and so I may venture to seek for an explanation of the system of piecemeal construction which goes farther than the one that contented people then."[3]

The province of such an inquiry is, however, "infinite." Each question that the narrator poses has its answer, but each answer is at once subsumed in a deeper question. Why was the wall built, one may ask? To defend against the people of the north. But why should people from the far southeast, like the narrator and his family, give their entire lives for something so far removed? Because the high command decreed it. Yet the high command is no "gathering of mandarins summoned hastily to discuss somebody's fine dream in a conference as hastily terminated"—it has "existed from all eternity, and the decision to build the wall likewise."[4] So if the idea of the wall had always existed, the people of the north could not be the reason for its construction, for there were no such northerners then, nor any emperor to have decreed its building.

To complicate the inquiry, a certain scholar has been circulating another theory, that the wall as we know it is only the foundation for something else—a new Tower of Babel. "First the wall, therefore, and then the tower." But how can such a thing be? Perhaps the answer lies somehow in the heart of the Chinese race itself. As the narrator muses:

> During the building of the wall and ever since to this very day I have occupied myself almost exclusively with the comparative history of races—there are certain questions that one can probe to the marrow, as it were, only by this method—and I have discovered that we Chinese possess certain folk and political institutions that are unique in their clarity, others again unique in their obscurity. The desire to trace the cause of these phenomena, especially the latter, has always intrigued me and intrigues me still, and the building of the wall is itself essentially involved with these problems.[5]

One can see, from the meticulous structuring of the argument, how carefully Kafka worked to open up a route to pierce through the obscurity of the country and its high command. A surviving fragment of a rejected version of the same story lets us see how Kafka initially thought of using conventional images of China rendered familiar by the exoticism still much in vogue at the time he was writing. This abandoned fragment set the scene as follows:

> The news of the building of the wall now penetrated into this world—late, too, some thirty years after its announcement. It was on a summer evening. I, ten years old, was standing with my father on the riverbank. In keeping with the importance of this much-discussed hour, I can recall the smallest details. My father was holding me by the hand, something he was fond of doing to the end of his days, and running his other hand up and down his long, very thin pipe, as though it were a flute. With his sparse, rigid beard raised in the air, he was enjoying his pipe while gazing upwards across the river. As a result his pigtail, object of the children's veneration, sank lower, rustling faintly on the gold-embroidered silk of his holiday gown.[6]

Pipe, pigtail, embroidered silk, those stock items of an earlier Chinoiserie, were all to be rejected by Kafka the artist. Instead, he turned the quest of the historian-narrator to the heart of the society itself. In one extraordinary passage, Kafka tied his vision of the Chinese emperor to the Chinese people's ignorance of their emperor's very existence—though characteristically he added his own disclaimer to the story he was about to tell:

> So vast is our land that no fable could do justice to its vastness, the heavens can scarcely span it—and Peking is only a dot in it, and the imperial palace less than a dot. The Emperor as such, on the other hand, is mighty throughout all the hierarchies of the world: admitted. But . . . the Emperor is always surrounded by a brilliant and yet ambiguous throng of nobles and courtiers—malice and enmity in the guise of servants and friends—who form a counterweight to the imperial power and perpetually labor to unseat the ruler from his place with poisoned arrows. The Empire is immortal, but the Emperor himself totters and falls from his throne, yes, whole dynasties sink in the end and breathe their last in one death rattle. Of these struggles and sufferings the people will never know; like tardy arrivals, like strangers in a city, they stand at the end of some densely thronged side street peacefully munching the food they have brought with them, while far away in front, in the Market Square at the heart of the city, the execution of their ruler is proceeding.[7]

Kafka did not publish "The Great Wall of China" during his lifetime—he died in 1924, of the tuberculosis that had ravaged him since the autumn of 1917—but he did take one fragment from it and publish it separately in 1919, in a Prague Jewish weekly. He titled the fragment "An Imperial Message" ("*Eine kaiserliche Botschaft*").[8] One may surmise therefore that he felt this paragraph could stand alone, although he also left it in the full manuscript version of the story, and thus it was published there, again, after Kafka's death. Read in the context of "The Great Wall" as a whole, the episode seems but a part of Kafka's ruminations on the vastness and evasiveness of the Chinese empire and its meanings. Read in isolation, the passage becomes starker, a hymn to the impossibility of knowing:

The Emperor, so a parable runs, has sent a message to you, the humble subject, the insignificant shadow cowering in the remotest distance before the imperial sun; the Emperor from his deathbed has sent a message to you alone. . . .

The messenger immediately sets out on his journey; a powerful, an indefatigable man; now pushing with his right arm, now with his left, he cleaves a way for himself through the throng; if he encounters resistance he points to his breast, where the symbol of the sun glitters; the way is made easier for him than it would be for any other man. But the multitudes are so vast; their numbers have no end. If he could reach the open fields how fast he would fly, and soon doubtless you would hear the welcome hammering of his fists on your door. But instead how vainly does he wear out his strength; still he is only making his way through the chamber of the innermost palace; never will he get to the end of them; and if he succeeded in that nothing would be gained; he must next fight his way down the stair; and if he succeeded in that nothing would be gained; the courts would still have to be crossed; and after the courts the second outer palace; and once more stairs and courts; and once more another palace; and so on for thousands of years; and if at last he should burst through the outermost gate—but never, never can that happen—the imperial capital would lie before him, the center of the world, crammed to bursting with its own sediment. Nobody could fight his way through here even with a message from a dead man. But you sit at your window when evening falls and dream it to yourself.[9]

Kafka's chosen narrative voice in "The Great Wall of China" (as in many of his stories and fables) is that of the well-informed yet bemused observer, struggling to come to grips with things he witnesses that remain on the edge of his understanding, but which he believes can—with determination—be fathomed, or at least placed in perspective. Almost at the end of his story, however, there is an oddly discordant note of criticism in which he mentions that among the Chinese wall builders he has been describing, there was "a certain feebleness of faith and imaginative power" that prevented them from "raising the empire out of its stagnation in Peking, and clasping it in all its palpable living reality to their own breasts." Yet "this very weakness," Kafka adds, is "one of the greatest unifying influences among our people; indeed, if one may dare to use the expression, the very ground on which we live."[10]

Borges's short story "The Garden of Forking Paths" seems like a deliberate struggle to reaffirm those values of "faith and imaginative power" that Kafka's narrator found lacking in the wall's builders. In Borges's matching metaphor of the labyrinth and garden of the polymathic Ts'ui Pên, he declines to follow Kafka in allowing his Chinese narrator to be a merely anonymous voice—however intimate. Instead, like Goldsmith and others in the past, Borges gives a name and sketches in the life history of his protagonist, Yu Tsun. This man, we learn almost at once, is Dr. Yu Tsun, "former professor of English at the Hochschule at Tsingtao." Those familiar with Chinese history would know that Tsingtao had been the center of the German-controlled areas of Shandong province for decades, and thus a Chinese professor, even one teaching English, in a German school there could be presumed to have knowledge of German and perhaps even pro-German sympathies. Within a few lines, we learn that this is so. Indeed, Yu Tsun is an "agent of the German Reich" in a setting—it has already been established—of World War I during its most murderous hour for both sides in the fray, the Battle of the Somme in 1916. Yet perhaps Yu Tsun is a spy only by compulsion, for, as he tells us, "I care nothing for a barbarous country which imposed upon me the abjection of being a spy."[11]

Yu Tsun has known happiness, it seems—at least "he has been a child in a symmetrical garden of Hai Feng"—and perhaps that is why he acted as he did, out of a sense of pride. "I did it because I sensed that the chief somehow feared people of my race—for the innumerable ancestors who merge within me. I wanted to prove to him that a yellow man could save his armies"[12] But if he has been raised in a symmetrical garden, suggestive of order and

calm, Yu Tsun knows that there is a different kind of garden—
a labyrinth of a garden, also known as a "garden of forking
paths"—that once pulsed through his own family.

"I have some understanding of labyrinths," Yu Tsun tells the
reader:

> . . . not for nothing am I the great grandson of that Ts'ui Pên who
> was governor of Yunnan and who renounced worldly power in
> order to write a novel that might be even more populous than the
> *Hung Lu Meng* and to construct a labyrinth in which all men
> would become lost. Thirteen years he dedicated to these hetero-
> geneous tasks, but the hand of a stranger murdered him—and his
> novel was incoherent and no one found the labyrinth. Beneath
> English trees I meditated on that lost maze: I imagined it invio-
> late and perfect at the secret crest of a mountain; I imagined it
> erased by rice fields or beneath the water; I imagined it infinite,
> no longer composed of octagonal kiosks and returning paths,
> but of rivers and provinces and kingdoms. . . .
>   I thought of a labyrinth of labyrinths, of one sinuous spread-
> ing labyrinth that would encompass the past and the future and
> in some way involve the stars.[13]

The *Hung L[o]u Meng* to which Borges's narrator refers is the
Chinese title of China's most famous eighteenth-century novel,
The Dream of the Red Chamber, itself a novel about truth and fal-
sity, reality and fabrication, where the action takes place within
an enclosed garden. Thus the references by Yu Tsun to this existing novel give an added dimension not only to the garden of his
ancestor but also to the garden of the scholarly Englishman
Stephen Albert, whom Yu Tsun visits in Borges's story. This
garden contains its own labyrinthine complexities, its forking
paths, along with groves, pavilions, and rusty gates, enlivened by
the glow of distant lanterns and the sound of Chinese music,
"high-pitched, almost syllabic," which "approached and receded
in the shifting of the wind, dimmed by leaves and distance."[14] At
the same time they recall—to those interested in past renderings
of China—the garden from the late 1750s conceived by Oliver

Goldsmith, and presented in chapter XXXI of *Citizen of the World*, under a curious double title, "The perfection of the Chinese in the art of gardening. The description of a Chinese garden." In this chapter, Lien Chi writes to his friend Fum Hoan in Peking that the English are beginning to learn from China how to construct a garden, and are improving, but still have far to go in terms of subtlety:

> ... their designers have not yet attained a power of uniting instruction with beauty. An European will scarcely conceive my meaning, when I say, that there is scarce a garden in China which does not contain some fine moral, couched under the general design, where one is not taught wisdom as he walks, and feels the force of some noble truth, or delicate precept, resulting from the disposition of the groves, streams, or grottos. Permit me to illustrate what I mean by a description of my gardens at Quamsi.[15]

As Lien Chi describes it, his Quamsi garden was composed of two distinct units, one with an entrance of forbidding appearance, that turned out to be beautiful and serene after an initial shock of disappointment, one with a beguiling entrance that lost its charm as the viewer penetrated deeper down its sinuous paths. Immediately upon his entering this second garden, Lien Chi commented, the stroller found:

> ... the trees and flowers were disposed in such a manner as to make the most pleasing impression; but, as he walked farther on, he insensibly found the garden assume the air of a wilderness; the landscapes began to darken, the paths grew more intricate, he appeared to go downwards, frightful rocks seemed to hang over his head, gloomy caverns, unexpected precipices, awful ruins, heaps of unburied bones, and terrifying sounds, caused by unseen waters, began to take place of what at first appeared so lovely: it was in vain to attempt returning; the labyrinth was too much perplexed for any but myself to find the way back. In short, when sufficiently impressed with the horrors of what he saw, and the imprudence of his choice, I brought him by a hidden door, a shorter way back, into the area from whence at first he had strayed.[16]

All this labyrinth, Lien Chi explained, could be enclosed in a tiny space, ten times less than would be required in England for a garden of such complexity.

The Chinese side of Borges's condensed yet intricate plot thus fitted into certain preconceptions of earlier Chinoiserie, but the two other main aspects of his story—its relation to the missionary Stephen Albert, and the history of World War I—were drawn from the imaginative use of quite different sources of history. Stephen Albert, the scholarly English missionary—described as tall, sharp-featured, with gray eyes and a gray beard—who has solved the riddle of Ts'ui Pên's labyrinth by realizing that it and the novel are one, would be, at most levels, completely believable in the context of the late nineteenth-century world: working in Tientsin before abandoning a life of preaching for sinology, acquiring Chinese art and a fine library, retiring at last to a country house at Fenton in Staffordshire, and drawing on the resources of Oxford University for help in translating his rare Chinese texts. There were many men like Stephen Albert in retirement in Britain and America.

It is only the piercing brilliance of Albert's mind—Yu Tsun compares him to Goethe—that separates him out from his missionary contemporaries. As Albert explains to Yu Tsun, his ultimate triumph has been the discovery that "The Garden of Forking Paths" is "an enormous riddle, or parable, whose theme is time." But just because time was the central theme, Ts'ui Pên chose never to mention it. Borges here has hit with remarkable subtlety on the theme of the comparative nature of Chinese and biblical chronologies, one of the central preoccupations of generations of earlier Western scholars and missionaries. As Stephen Albert continues:

> I have corrected the errors that the negligence of the copyists has introduced, I have guessed the plan of this chaos, I have re-established—I believe I have re-established—the primordial organization, I have translated the entire work: it is clear to me that not once does he employ the word "time." The explanation is

obvious: *The Garden of Forking Paths* is an incomplete, but not false, image of the universe as Ts'ui Pên conceived it. In contrast to Newton and Schopenhauer, your ancestor did not believe in a uniform, absolute time. He believed in an infinite series of times, in a growing, dizzying net of divergent, convergent and parallel times. This network of times which approached one another, forked, broke off, or were unaware of one another for centuries, embraces *all* possibilities of time. We do not exist in the majority of these times; in some you exist and not I; in others I, and not you; in others, both of us. In the present one, which a favorable fate has granted me, you have arrived at my house; in another, while crossing the garden, you found me dead; in still another, I utter these same words, but I am a mistake, a ghost.[17]

One can guess that the third main plot line in Borges's story, that of World War I, came in a random flash to Borges, a shard from his earlier reading of B. H. Liddell Hart's history of the war. It is in Liddell Hart that one can find the information that the headquarters and supply depot of the British before the disastrous July 1916 assaults in the Somme fronts, which cost them the worst casualties of the entire war, was a town called Albert. This prosaic name with its deadly implications suggested to Borges the outline for a plot in which the Germans must be informed that Albert should be preemptively bombed.[18] Yu Tsun accordingly murders Albert, aware that the shocking news will be recorded in the English newspapers, and thus will reach his superiors in Germany. It is a wildly improbable idea for a plot, but in Borges's hands it all somehow becomes possible—the intensest possible subtlety of the Chinese blends with their treachery and ruthlessness, for which Stephen Albert unwittingly claims the credit. "To me, a barbarous Englishman," he exclaims to Yu Tsun, "has been entrusted the revelation of this diaphanous mystery." Yet Albert's knowledge of history leads him later to remind Yu Tsun that "Time forks perpetually toward innumerable futures. In one of them I am your enemy."[19]

As Stephen Albert also tells Yu Tsun, "In all fictional works, each time a man is confronted with several alternatives, he chooses one and eliminates the others; in the fiction of Ts'ui Pên, he chooses—simultaneously—all of them. *He creates,* in this way, diverse futures, diverse times which themselves also proliferate and fork."[20] This concept of endlessly intersecting plot lines absorbed Italo Calvino equally, and led him in *If on a Winter's Night a Traveller* of 1979 to experiment with them formally. Already, though, in *Invisible Cities* of 1972, Calvino had begun to focus on the infinite variations that the art of storytelling can take, and he chose as his focus the relationship between Marco Polo and Kublai Khan. The few lines on this relationship, as found in Marco Polo's original *Description of the World,* were tantalizingly brief but full of possibilities:

> And so when [the Khan] discerned Marco to have so much sense, and to conduct himself so well and beseemingly, he sent him on an ambassage of his, to a country which was a good six months' journey distant. The young gallant executed his commission well and with discretion. Now he had taken note on several occasions that when the Prince's ambassadors returned from different parts of the world, they were able to tell him about nothing except the business on which they had gone, and that the Prince in consequence held them for no better than fools and dolts, and would say: "I had far liever hearken about the strange things, and the manners of the different countries you have seen, than merely be told of the business you went upon;"—for he took great delight in hearing of the affairs of strange countries. Marco therefore, as he went and returned, took great pains to learn about all kinds of different matters in the countries which he visited, in order to be able to tell about them to the Great Khan.[21]

In an exquisite re-evocation of this early record of the communication between the Venetian traveler and his temporary master, Calvino discusses the progression of the two men's first discourses, from Polo's initial rendering of his experiences through "gestures, leaps, cries of wonder and of horror," and simple pantomimes—"A fish escaping the cormorant's beak," "a

naked man running through fire"—and thence to their use of
words substantiated by gestures, as "the Great Khan's white
hands, heavy with rings, answered with stately movements the
sinewy, agile hands of the merchant."[22]

But at this stage of mutual understanding the Khan, wearied
by the repetitive information he is getting from Polo, begins to
create his own cities and to ask Polo if they exist as he has conceived them. Finally he orders Polo to track down the cities
that have appeared to the Khan in dreams. On melancholy days,
Kublai is sure Polo's cities cannot exist; they are nothing but
"consolatory fables" of an empire that "is rotting like a corpse
in a swamp." At other times, in euphoria, the Khan sees his
empire as "the stuff of crystals, its molecules arranged in a perfect pattern."[23]

Moving ever further into his own mind, Kublai begins to
construct cities "from which all possible cities can be deduced"
since they "contain everything corresponding to the norm."
Marco counters with his own model city, "made only of excep-
tions, exclusions, incongruities, contradictions."[24] As the tales
flow and the visions deepen, Kublai's empire grows ever richer
and becomes burdened with its own weight, "swollen, tense,
ponderous." To edge this heaviness aside, the Khan conjures up
in his own dreams "cities light as kites . . . pierced cities like lace,
cities transparent as mosquito netting, cities like leaves' veins."[25]

When all avenues of inquiry seem to have been exhausted,
when the Khan has exhausted his dreams and Polo claims to
have described every city he has ever visited, the Khan confronts
his foreign visitor with a challenge:

> "There is still one of which you never speak."
> Marco Polo bowed his head.
> "Venice," the Khan said.
> Marco smiled. "What else do you believe I have been talking to
> you about?"
> The emperor did not turn a hair. "And yet I have never heard
> you mention that name."

And Polo said: "Every time I describe a city I am saying something about Venice. . . ."

The lake's surface was barely wrinkled; the copper reflection of the ancient palace of the Sung was shattered into sparkling glints like floating leaves.

"Memory's images, once they are fixed in words, are erased," Polo said. "Perhaps I am afraid of losing Venice all at once, if I speak of it. Or perhaps, speaking of other cities, I have already lost it, little by little."[26]

Accused now by the Khan his ruler of conducting merely "a journey through memory,"

Marco thought of the mists that cloud the expanse of the sea and the mountain ranges and, when dispelled, leave the air dry and diaphanous, revealing distant cities. It was beyond that screen of fickle humors that his gaze wished to arrive: the form of things can be discerned better at a distance.[27]

Finally the two men begin to question whether their conversation can be taking place at all: Are they sitting in this particular garden, at this particular time, talking together, or is Kublai perhaps fighting on some distant campaign while Polo is far away "bargaining for sacks of pepper in distant bazaars."[28]

Perhaps, [suggests Kublai] this dialogue of ours is taking place between two beggars nicknamed Kublai Khan and Marco Polo; as they sift through a rubbish heap, piling up rusted flotsam, scraps of cloth, wastepaper, while drunk on the few sips of bad wine, they see all the treasure of the East shine around them.

And Polo replies:

Perhaps all that is left of the world is a wasteland covered with rubbish heaps, and the hanging garden of the Great Khan's palace. It is our eyelids that separate them, but we cannot know which is inside and which outside.[29]

To try to attain a final clarity, Kublai limits Marco Polo's descriptions to the silent play of moves upon a giant chessboard at the foot of the palace steps, in search of "a coherent, harmonious system underlying the infinite deformities and discords," and he keeps Polo always at his side, hoping that the rulebound movements of the game would bring him knowledge of his empire. In return, Polo teaches him to read the meaning of nature's specific past in the shape of every wooden piece from which the board itself is made—the ring of trunks that tried to grow in drought; "a barely hinted knot," or a bud that "tried to burgeon on a premature spring day."[30]

Finally the two men, ruler and traveler, huddle together around the atlases that the Khan has found. They see the cities like Kambalu, in which the Khan has lived; they see those that Polo remembers, like Jerusalem and Samarkand; they see the cities they know exist but cannot visit: Granada, Paris, Timbuktu; heads almost touching, they muse on cities no one from the West has found as yet, Cuzco and Novgorod; they see the cities that are vanquished and have disappeared beneath the sand or soil, Troy, and Ur, and Carthage. New cities, waiting to be born, stretch out their strange new shapeless networks, Los Angeles, Osaka.[31] They visit, in name, the promised lands as yet unwritten, Utopia, New Lanark, and the City of the Sun.[32] And they see the cities that menace them in nightmares, Enoch, Yahooland, and Brave New World.

> "It is all useless," says the Khan, "if the last landing place can only be the infernal city, and it is there that, in ever-narrowing circles, the current is drawing us."
>
> And Polo said: "The inferno of the living is not something that will be; if there is one, it is what is already here, the inferno where we live every day, that we form by being together."[33]

In a quiet moment of mutual reconciliation, when the two men are briefly rooted in a shared reality, Calvino has the Khan turn affectionately to Marco Polo:

"When you return to the West," Kublai asks the Venetian merchant, "will you repeat to your people the same tales you tell me?"

Marco Polo will not respond directly to the question: "I speak and speak," he tells Kublai,

> ... but the listener retains only the words he is expecting. The description of the world to which you lend a benevolent ear is one thing; the description that will go the rounds of the groups of stevedores and gondoliers on the street outside my house the day of my return is another; and yet another, that which I might dictate late in life, if I were taken prisoner by Genoese pirates and put in irons in the same cell with a writer of adventure stories. It is not the voice that commands the story: it is the ear.[34]

The premise behind Polo's circular response is deliberately absurd: there is no conceivable reason why, even if he can rouse himself to leave his piles of silken cushions and his adopted Chinese home, he should ever end up in Genoa, incarcerated with a professional romancer. And even if something so improbable happened, why should anyone who lived after him ever heed his words?

The answer provided by Calvino is as good a one as we will get, and applies to all our story. The secret lies in the ear, the ear that hears both what it wants and what it is expecting. In the case of China across the centuries, the listeners have been constantly bold, and constantly eager to move "beyond that screen of fickle humors" to the "dry and diaphanous" air. The curious readiness of Westerners for things Chinese was there from the beginning, and it has remained primed, over the centuries, by an unending stream of offerings. Precisely why this should be so remains, to me, a mystery. But the story we have traced seems to prove that China needs no reason to fasten itself into Western minds.

Notes

INTRODUCTION

1. I am particularly indebted to John Hollander for his discussion of these and other references.
2. The finest brief analysis of this topic that I know is that by T. H. Barrett, *Singular Listlessness: A Short History of Chinese Books and British Scholars* (London, 1989). Among other overviews, with their often very different goals or points of view, see Harold Isaacs, *Scratches on Our Minds: Images of China and India, 1600–1950* (New York, 1962); Raymond Dawson, *The Chinese Chameleon* (Oxford, 1967); Donald Lach, *Asia in the Making of Europe*, multiple volumes, ongoing (University of Chicago Press); Colin Mackerras, *Western Images of China* (Hong Kong, 1989); Edward Said, *Orientalism* (New York, 1978); René Étiemble, *L'Europe chinoise*, vol. 1 (Paris, 1988), *De l'empire romain a Leibniz*, vol. 2 (Paris, 1989), *De la sinophilie à la sinophobie*; Robin Winks and James Rush, eds., *Asia in Western Fiction* (Manchester, U.K., 1990); Lewis Maverick, *China, A Model for Europe* (San Antonio, Texas, 1946); Federico Masini ed., *Western Humanistic Culture Presented to China by Jesuit Missionaries* (Rome, 1996); and Thomas H.C. Lee ed, *China and Europe, Images and Influences in Sixteenth to Eighteenth Centuries* (Hong Kong, 1991).

CHAPTER 1

1. Peter Jackson with David Morgan, *The Mission of Friar William of Rubruck: His Journey to the Court of the Great Khan Mongke, 1253–1255*, Hakluyt Society, second series, no. 173 (London, 1990), 161–62.
2. Ibid., 203.
3. Ibid., 202, and 52 for MSS and dates.
4. The arguments for and against Polo's residence in China are concisely and wittily summarized in Frances Wood, *Did Marco Polo Go to China?* (London, 1995). Parallel arguments are also cogently pre-

sented by Herbert Franke, "Sino-Western Contacts Under the Mongol Empire," *Journal of the Hong Kong Branch of the Royal Asiatic Society,* 6 (1966), 49–72, especially pp. 53–56. A good general edition of Polo is that by Ronald Latham, *The Travels of Marco Polo* (Harmondsworth, UK, 1988), drawing on all variant MSS.

5. Henry Yule and Henri Cordier, *The Book of Ser Marco Polo the Venetian Concerning the Kingdoms and Marvels of the East,* revised edition in 3 vols. (London, 1920 and 1926), I: 72.

6. Ibid., I: 64–65, 70; II: 505–20.

7. Ibid., I: 1. John Critchley, *Marco Polo's Book* (Aldershot, UK, 1992), 3–8, 27–28.

8. Cited in Yule and Cordier, I: 113.

9. Ibid., II: 158–60.

10. Ibid., II: 167, n. 5; see also A. C. Moule and Paul Pelliot, ed. and trans., *Marco Polo, the Description of the World,* 2 vols. (London, 1938), I, chap. 146, 318–19.

11. Moule and Pelliot, II: 22; M. G. Pauthier, *Le livre de Marco Polo, citoyen de Venise* (Paris, 1865), chap. CXLV, 472–76.

12. Yule and Cordier, II: 168, n. 5.

13. Ibid., I: 27–30, converting Mark to Marco. The variant manuscripts are traced in Moule and Pelliot, I: 85–87, and Pauthier, 23–24.

14. Yule and Cordier, II: 154; Pauthier, 468; Moule and Pelliot, I: 316.

15. Francis A. Rouleau, SJ, "The Yangchow Latin Tombstone as a Landmark of Medieval Christianity in China," *Harvard Journal of Asiatic Studies,* 17:3 and 17:4, (December 1954), 346–65, 349, 353; Robert Lopez, "Nouveaux documents sur les marchands italiens en Chine à l'époque mongole," *Académie des inscriptions et belles lettres* (comptes rendus, 1977), 445–58, 456.

16. Lopez, "Marchands," 457 (which misprints 1344 as 1324). Unfortunately, as the editors note, Lopez's reference notes did not arrive in time to be printed.

17. Manuel Komroff, ed., *Contemporaries of Marco Polo* (New York, 1928), 235.

18. Critchley, 78.

19. Ibid., 80, 85, 111.

20. Yule and Cordier, I: introduction, 117; Herbert Franke, "Some Sinological Remarks on Rasid ad-Din's History of China," *Oriens,* 4 (1951), 21–26, 22; C. W. R. D. Moseley, ed., *The Travels of Sir John Mandeville* (Harmondsworth, UK, 1983), 9–10. Stephen Green-

blatt, *Marvelous Possessions, The Wonder of the New World* (Chicago, 1991), chap.2, gives an ingenious reading of Mandeville in the context of Western expansion.

21. Yule and Cordier, I: introduction, 140.

22. Morris Rossabi, *Voyager from Xanadu: Rabban Sauma and the First Journey from China to the West* (Tokyo and New York, 1992), 1–2, 41, 46, 147.

23. Critchley, 52, suggests the elder uncle Marco did just that.

24. Ibid., 130.

25. Ibid., 173–75. See the Latin transcription of "Z" in Moule and Pelliot, II: xlii–iii.

26. Critchley, 38–39, 40–41.

27. Moule and Pelliot, I: 304. Cited also, with minor variants, in Critchley, 176, and Latham, 196.

28. Critchley, 177.

29. Yule and Cordier, I: introduction, 121–27, and text, 140, 142.

30. Ibid., I: introduction 124, text 356–58; and Moule and Pelliot, I: 206.

31. Felipe Fernandez-Armesto, *Columbus* (Oxford, 1991), 23, 36–37; Yule and Cordier, II: 553 and 558; Juan Gil, ed., *El libro de Marco Polo anotado por Cristobal Colon* (Madrid, 1987), ix and lxviii, discusses the handwriting variants of the various editions, ascribing some to Columbus and some to his son or a third, unknown hand.

32. Luigi Giovannini, *Il Milione, con le postille di Cristoforo Colombo* (Rome, 1989), 256, 183, 186.

33. Ibid., 84, 72 and 246, 110.

34. Ibid., 189, 178, 78, 227, 252, 78, 96, 254.

35. Ibid., 242, 268, 224.

36. Ibid., 217.

37 Ibid., 154 and n. 1; photograph p. 137; 253 and n. 3; Gil, 77.

CHAPTER 2

1. Charles Boxer, ed., *South China in the Sixteenth Century: Being the Narratives of Galeote Pereira, Fr. Gaspar da Cruz, O.P., Fr. Martin de Rada, O.E.S.A.,* The Hakluyt Society, second series, CVI (London, 1953), introduction.

2. Ibid., 18–19; 22–24 for prison conditions.

3. Ibid., 9 and 28, 7–8, 9, 32, 42.

4. Ibid., 30–31, 37–38.

5. Ibid., 20.

6. Ibid., 20–21.

7. Ibid., 8, 14, 42, 7.

8. Ibid., 33 and 37.

9. Ibid., 16–17.

10. Ibid., 25, 41.

11. Ibid., 109–110.

12. Ibid., lxii.

13. Ibid., 55.

14. Ibid., 56-57.

15. Ibid., 121, 122, 150–51.

16. Ibid., 136, 141–42.

17. Ibid., 114, 115, 122, 132, 148.

18. Ibid., 143, 145, 144.

19. Ibid., 149.

20. Ibid., 162.

21. Ibid., 140.

22. Ibid., 178–79.

23. Ibid., 223.

24. Fernao Mendes Pinto, ed. and trans. Rebecca D. Catz, *The Travels of Mendes Pinto* (Chicago, 1989), xv and xxiv.

25. Boxer, li and lvii; Pinto, chaps. 21–32, 203–17.

26. Pinto, 163, 192–94; Boxer, 115, 121.

27. Pinto, 199, and Boxer, 16–17.

28. Pinto, 192, and near repetition, 220.

29. Pinto, 195.

30. Ibid., xv, xxv, xxxix–xl, xlii. Also Pinto on Chinese religion, 234–35.

31. Ibid., 230–32.

32. Ibid., 240–41, and 576, n. 4.

33. Jonathan Spence, *The Memory Palace of Matteo Ricci* (New York, 1984), and Jacques Gernet, *China and the Christian Impact: A Conflict of Cultures* (Cambridge, 1985).

34. Matteo Ricci, ed. and trans. Louis Gallagher, *China in the Sixteenth Century: The Journals of Matteo Ricci, 1583–1610* (New York, 1953), 30.

35. Ibid., 77, 29, 58, 68.

36. Paul Rule, *K'ung-tzu or Confucius? The Jesuit Interpretation of Confucianism* (Sydney, 1986).

37. Ricci, 30.

38. Spence, *Memory Palace,* 219–21; Polo, ed. Moule and Pelliot, I: 236; Polo, ed. Latham, 129.

39. George Dunne, *Generation of Giants: The Story of the Jesuits in China in the Last Decade of the Ming Dynasty* (London, 1962); Jonathan Spence, *Emperor of China, Self-Portrait of K'ang-hsi* (New York, 1974).

40. Friar Domingo Navarrete, ed. and trans. J. S. Cummins, *The Travels and Controversies of Friar Domingo Navarrete,* 2 vols., Hakluyt Society, second series, no.118 (London, 1960), I: xx–xxvi, and II: 365, for landing.

41. Ibid., I: lxxxiv–cx.

42. Ibid., I: 136, 138, 145.

43. Ibid., I: 147–48.

44. Ibid., I: 137.

45. Ibid., I: 151, 160.

46. Ibid., II: 173, 196, 200, 216, 217, and I: 162.

47. Ibid., II: 193.

48. Ibid., II: 194, 180.

49. Ibid., II: 176.

50. Ibid., I: 154.

51. Ibid., I: 154.

CHAPTER 3

1. Navarrete, ed. Cummins, II: 218.

2. John E. Wills, Jr., *Embassies and Illusions: Dutch and Portuguese Envoys to K'ang-hsi, 1666–1687* (Cambridge, Mass., 1984), chap.6.

3. Ibid., 78–80.

4. Ibid., 203.

5. Ibid., 203.

6. Ibid., 208–09.

7. Ibid., 212–13.

8. John Bell, ed. J. L. Stevenson, *A Journey from St. Petersburg to Pekin, 1719–1722* (Edinburgh, 1965), 12–20.

9. Ibid., 1–6.

10. Ibid., 115.

11. Ibid., 116–17.

12. Ibid., 125–26.

13. Ibid., 135.

14. Ibid., 134.

15. Ibid., 155.

16. Ibid., 143–44.
17. Ibid., 146.
18. Ibid., 126–27.
19. Ibid., 152.
20. Ibid., 167–68.
21. Ibid., 183.
22. Ibid., 184.
23. Ibid., 183.
24. Ibid., 183.
25. Ibid., 169.
26. Ibid., 181–86; Oriental robes, 6; subscribers' list, 225–31.
27. George Anson, ed. Glyndwr Williams, *A Voyage Around the World in the Years 1740–1744* (London, 1974), 347–49, 352–54.
28. Ibid., 351–52.
29. Ibid., 355–56, 361.
30. Ibid., 366, 369.
31. Ibid., 366–67.
32. Ibid., 367.
33. Ibid., 367–68.
34. Lord George Macartney, ed. J. L. Cranmer-Byng, *An Embassy to China, Being the Journal Kept by Lord Macartney During his Embassy to the Emperor Ch'ien-lung, 1793–1794* (London, 1962), 42; Barbara Widenor Maggs, *Russia and "le rêve chinois": China in Eighteenth Century Russian Literature*. Voltaire Foundation (Oxford, 1984), 133.
35. Macartney, *Journal*, 2, 72, 74.
36. For the presents, ibid., 79, 96, 99, 123.
37. Ibid., 84–85.
38. Macartney, *Journal*, 90.
39. Ibid., 119. For a full discussion of this compromise and the other ritual dimensions, see Joseph Esherick, "Cherishing Sources from Afar," *Modern China*, 24:2 (1998), 135–61.
40. Macartney, *Journal*, 123.
41. Ibid., 113.
42. Ibid., 87–88.
43. Ibid., 127.
44. Ibid., 212–13.
45. Ibid., 210.
46. Ibid., 124.
47. Ibid., 114.

CHAPTER 4

1. Macartney, *Journal*, 116–17.
2. John Evelyn, ed. E. S. de Beer, *The Diary of John Evelyn* (Oxford, 1959), 460–61.
3. Ibid., 689, 728.
4. In *Merry Wives of Windsor* and *Twelfth Night*.
5. John Milton, *Paradise Lost*, XI, lines 387–90.
6. On Shen, see Theodore Foss, "The European Sojourn of Philippe Couplet and Michael Shen Fuzong, 1683–1692," in Jerome Heyndrickx, ed., *Philippe Couplet, S.J. (1623–1693), the Man who Brought China to Europe* (Nettetal, Germany, 1990).
7. Cited in Hugh Honour, *Chinoiserie: The Vision of Cathay* (New York, 1961), 78. Also discussed in B. Sprague Allen, *Tides in English Taste (1619–1800): A Background for the Study of Literature*, 2 vols.(Cambridge, Mass., 1937), II: 20.
8. Allen, *Tides*, II: 34; see also Ch'en Shou-yi, "Daniel Defoe, China's Severe Critic," in *Nankai Social and Economic Quarterly*, 8:3 (October 1935).
9. Daniel Defoe, *Robinson Crusoe, Part II* (Boston, 1903), 256.
10. Ibid., 256–58.
11. Ibid., 260–61.
12. Ibid., 261.
13. Ibid., 262.
14. John Mandeville, ed. Moseley, *Travels*, 187.
15. Defoe, *Crusoe*, 263.
16. Ibid., 271.
17. Mandeville, 107–08.
18. Montesquieu, ed. and trans. J. Robert Loy, *The Persian Letters* (Cleveland, 1969), 15–16 for his sources.
19. John Forster, *The Life and Times of Oliver Goldsmith*, 2 vols. (London, 1877), chap. 1–4.
20. Cited ibid., I: 139–40, letter of August 14, 1758.
21. Cited Allen, *Tides*, II: 25.
22. Ibid., II: 26; and Forster, *Goldsmith*, I: 173.
23. The full title of Walpole's pamphlet was "A Letter from Xu Ho, a Chinese Philosopher at London, to his friend Lien Chi at Peking." The French popular writer Gueulette had used "Fum Hoam" as the name of the mandarin in his *Chinese Tales*.
24. Forster, *Goldsmith*, passim for these works. For further background

see Ch'en Shou-yi, "Oliver Goldsmith and his Chinese Letters," in *T'ien-hsia Monthly*, 8:1 (January 1939).

25. Oliver Goldsmith, *The Citizen of the World, or Letters from a Chinese Philosopher Residing in London to his Friends in the East*, 2 vols. (London, 1800), I: ii.

26. Ibid., I: iii.

27. Ibid., I: 34-35.

28. Ibid., I: 36.

29. Ibid., I: 133.

30. Ibid., I: 134-35.

31. Ibid., II: 239.

32. John Bell's *Journey*, 229, includes Walpole among the subscribers under his title, Earl of Orford.

33. Horace Walpole, "Mi Lai, A Chinese Fairy Tale," in *Hieroglyphic Tales* (London, 1785), 342.

34. Ibid., 347.

CHAPTER 5

1. Pinto, *Travels*, ed. Catz, 164, 166; Defoe, *Crusoe*, II: 264.

2. A fine survey of these developments is Knud Lundbaek, *T. S. Bayer (1694–1738): Pioneer Sinologist* (London and Malmo, 1986).

3. Gottfried Wilhelm Leibniz, ed. and trans. Daniel J. Cook and Henry Rosemont, Jr., *Writings on China* (Chicago and La Salle, 1994), 133–38.

4. Leibniz, 56, on the key; on figurism, see David Mungello, *Curious Land: Jesuit Accommodation and the Origins of Sinology* (Stuttgart, 1985). On science and China, see especially Catherine Jami and Hubert Delahaye, *L'Europe en Chine: Interactions scientifiques, religieuses et culturelles aux XVIIe et XVIIIe siècles* (Paris, 1994).

5. Leibniz, 88.

6. Ibid., 10, comment by the editors; also David Mungello, *Leibniz and Confucianism: The Search for Accord* (Honolulu, 1977).

7. Ibid., 45–46.

8. Ibid., 46; Donald Lach, ed., *The Preface to Leibniz' Novissima Sinica* (Honolulu, 1957).

9. Ibid., 46–47.

10. Ibid., 48, 51, 57. Some of Emperor Kangxi's sons may indeed have learned some words of European languages from the polyglot Jesuit misssionaries employed at court.

11. Ibid., 51.

12. See Heyndrickx, ed. *Philippe Couplet, S.J. (1623–1693);* Jonathan Spence, *The Question of Hu* (New York, 1988), and "The Paris Years of Arcadio Huang," in *Chinese Roundabout* (New York, 1992).

13. Leibniz, 63.

14. Ibid., 64.

15. Ibid., 71.

16. Ibid., 78.

17. Ibid., 105.

18. Ibid., 47.

19. Montesquieu (Baron Charles de Secondat), "Geographica," in André Masson, ed., *Montesquieu, oeuvres completes* (Paris, 1955), II: 927; Danielle Elisseeff, *Moi Arcade, interprète chinois du roi-soleil* (Paris, 1985); and *Nicholas Freret (1688–1749): Reflexions d'un human- iste du XVIIIe siècle sur la China* (Paris, 1978); Spence, "Paris Years." The "Geographica" notes were discovered in the library of Mon- tesquieu's former chateau after World War II by the British scholar Robert Shackelton.

20. Montesquieu, "Geographica," 927–30.

21. Ibid., 930–33.

22. Ibid., 934–37.

23. Ibid., 940–41.

24. Montesquieu, *The Spirit of the Laws,* ed. and trans. Anne M. Cohler, Basia Carolyn Miller, and Harold Samuel Stone (Cambridge, 1994), especially 314, 317.

25. Ibid., 126–27.

26. Ibid., 127–28.

27. Ibid., 128.

28. Ibid., 280.

29. Ibid., 318–19.

30. François Arouet Voltaire, ed. John Morley, *Collected Works,* 42 vols. (Paris and London, 1901); vol. XXIV, "Ancient and Modern His- tory" (Essais sur les moeurs); vol. XV, "Orphan of China." Quoted XV: 217.

31. Ibid., XV: 236.

32. Ibid., XV: 179.

33. Voltaire, XXIV: 11.

34. Ibid., XXIV: 25.

35. Ibid., XXIV: 28–29.

36. Ibid., XXIV: 29.

37. Ibid., XXIV: 30.

38. Ibid., XXIV: 33–34.

39. Montesquieu, *Spirit of the Laws*, 243; Johann Gottfried Herder, *Outlines of a Philosophy of the History of Man* (London, 1800), 296.

40. Herder, 296.

41. Ibid., 293, 295.

42. Ibid., 293.

43. Ibid., 297–98.

CHAPTER 6

1. Jane Austen, *Mansfield Park* (New York, 1964), 121, 124. The China theme is present throughout much of chapter 16 of the novel. See also Peter Knox-Shaw, "Fanny Price Refuses to Kowtow," in *Review of English Studies*, new series, XLVII, no. 186 (1996), 212–17. (My special thanks to Julia Kang for this reference.)

2. J. H. Hubback and Edith C. Hubback, *Jane Austen's Sailor Brothers* (London, 1906, 1976 reprint), 219–23.

3. Macartney, *Journal*, 223.

4. Goldsmith, *Citizen of the World*, I: 131 (Letter XXXIII).

5. Jonathan Spence, *God's Chinese Son: The Taiping Heavenly Kingdom of Hong Xiuquan* (New York, 1994).

6. *Memorials of Protestant Missionaries to the Chinese*, comp. Alexander Wylie (Shanghae [sic], 1867), 40.

7. Ibid., 65–69, 72.

8. Eliza J. Gillett Bridgman, *Daughters of China: or, Sketches of Domestic Life in the Celestial Empire* (New York, 1853), 29–30.

9. Ibid., 30.

10. Carlo Gozzi, *La Princesse Turandot*, trans. Jean-Jacques Olivier (Paris, 1923), 28, 38, 51.

11. Bridgman, *Daughters*, 29, 56.

12. Ibid., 31–34.

13. Ibid., 34–35.

14. Ibid., 59–60.

15. Ibid., 60–61.

16. Ibid., 62–65.

17. Jane R. Edkins, *Chinese Scenes and People* (London, 1863), 44–45.

18. Ibid., 53–54.

19. Ibid., 56, 60.

20. Ibid, 57–58.

21. Ibid., 64, 76.

22. Ibid., 154–56.

23. Ibid., 71.

24. Ibid., 95, 98, 100–01, 126–27.

25. Ibid., 138–39.

26. Ibid., 142–43.

27. Ibid., 156–57.

28. Ibid., 231–32, 235, 237. The details on her death are in *A Memoir* by Jane's father, Rev. William Stobbs (printed in ibid.), 29–31.

29. Mary Crawford Fraser, *A Diplomat's Wife in Many Lands* (New York, 1910), 106.

30. Ibid., 107.

31. Ibid., 115.

32. Ibid., 115.

33. Ibid., 119.

34. Sarah Pike Conger, *Letters from China* (Chicago, 1909), 68.

35. Ibid., 68–69.

36. Ibid., 69–70.

37. Ibid., 116.

38. Eva Jane Price, ed. Robert H. Felsing, *China Journal 1889–1900: An American Missionary Family During the Boxer Rebellion* (New York, 1989), 14.

39. Ibid., 16, 21.

40. Ibid., 26.

41. Ibid., 27.

42. Ibid., 27, 31.

43. Ibid., 34–35.

44. Ibid., 71–72, 144.

45. Ibid., 194.

46. Ibid., 169.

47. Ibid., 215.

48. Ibid., 239, Chinese convert's testimony.

CHAPTER 7

1. Eva Price, *Journal*, 19.

2. Yung Wing, *My Life in China and America* (New York, 1909).

3. H. G. Jones, *North Carolina Illustrated, 1524–1984* (Chapel Hill, 1983), 214–15. (My special thanks to Gary Reeder for this reference.)

4. Mark Twain, *Roughing It*, 2 vols. (New York, 1913), 2: 106.

5. Cited by Twain himself from the "Enterprise" in *Roughing It*, 2:

109-10. For this period in Twain's life, see Henry Nash Smith, *Mark Twain of the Enterprise: Newspaper Articles and Other Documents, 1862–1864* (Berkeley, 1957).

6. Twain, *Roughing It*, 2: 110.
7. Ibid., 2: 111.
8. Ibid.
9. Ibid.
10. Ibid., 2: 105–06.
11. Ibid., 2: 105, 107, 109.
12. Cited in William Purviance Fenn, *Ah Sin and His Brethren in American Literature* (Peiping, 1933), 47.
13. Ibid., xiv, n. 15.
14. Bret Harte, *The Complete Poetical Works of Bret Harte* (Boston, 1910), 129–31.
15. Fenn, *Ah Sin*, 45–46, n. xi and xii.
16. Harte, *Poetical Works*, 143–45.
17. Mark Twain, "Goldsmith's Friend Abroad Again," in Frederick Anderson, ed., *A Pen Warmed Up in Hell* (New York, 1972), 110.
18. Ibid., 111–13.
19. Ibid., 114.
20. Ibid., 115–16, 125.
21. Ibid., 123.
22. Spence, *The Question of Hu*.
23. In vol. 55: 300–303, cited in Fenn, *Ah Sin*, 93, and xxv, n. 93.
24. *Harper's*, 39 (1869), 783, "Excelsior in Pigeon English"; discussed in Fenn, 93–94, xxv, n. 93.
25. Longfellow, "Excelsior," stanza 1, and *Harper's*, 39 (1869), 783.
26. Harte, *Poetical Works*, 143.
27. Ibid., 143–44.
28. Bret Harte, "Wan Lee, the Pagan," in *Tales of the Argonauts* (Boston, 1896), 262.
29. Ibid., 264.
30. Ibid., 279.
31. Bret Harte, *Two Men of Sandy Bar, A Drama* (Boston, 1876), 59.
32. Mark Twain and Bret Harte, *Ah Sin, A Dramatic Work* (Fairfax, Calif., 1961), introduction, p. xi, and playbill frontispiece.
33. Fenn, *Ah Sin*, 104.
34. Harte, *Argonauts*, introduction, xxxii.

35. Ibid., xxxii–xiii.
36. As well as Fenn, *Ah Sin*, see William F. Wu, *The Yellow Peril, Chinese Americans in American Fiction, 1850–1940* (Hamden, Conn., 1982).
37. Twain and Harte, *Ah Sin*, 10, 11, 52, 65.
38. C. W. Doyle, *The Shadow of Quong Lung* (Philadelphia and London, 1900), 251, 255.
39. Sax Rohmer [Arthur S. Ward], *The Return of Fu-Manchu* (New York, 1916), 279.
40. Ibid., 284.
41. Ibid., 286.
42. See the case *Rice* v. *Gong Lum*, 139 Miss., March 1925.
43. Jack London, "Tales of the Fish Patrol," in Lawrence Teacher and Richard Nicholls, eds., *The Unabridged Jack London* (Philadelphia, 1981).
44. Jack London, *Short Stories*, eds. Earle Labor, Robert C. Leitz III, and I. Milo Shepard (New York, 1990), 729.
45. Jack London, "The Chinago," in *Selected Stories* (New York, 1909), 155.
46. Ibid., 159.
47. Ibid., 164.
48. Ibid., 168.
49. Ibid., 185.

CHAPTER 8

1. Prosper Giquel, ed. Steven A. Leibo, *A Journal of the Chinese Civil War, 1864* (Honolulu, 1985).
2. Gustave Flaubert, trans. Robert Baldick, *Sentimental Education* (Harmondsworth, UK, 1987), 56, 80, 205.
3. Ibid., 37, 97.
4. Ibid., 190, 406, 283.
5. Ibid., 80, 97, 205.
6. Lesley Blanch, *Pierre Loti, The Legendary Romantic* (New York, 1983).
7. Cited in ibid., 169.
8. Ibid., 169.
9. Pierre Loti [Julien Viaud], *Figures et choses qui passent* (Paris, 1898), 265–69, 270–71, 280.
10. Cited in Funaoka Suetoshi, *Pierre Loti et l'extrème-orient: du journal à l'oeuvre* (Tokyo, 1988), 33. Translation by JS.

11. Pierre Loti, *Les derniers jours de Pekin* (Paris, 1914), 44, 91 on the walls, "couleur de deuil."

12. Ibid., 81–82, translation by JS; Funaoka, 139.

13. Loti, *Derniers jours*, 406.

14. Funaoka, 143 n. and 147.

15. Cited in Funaoka, 147–48.

16. Blanch, *Loti*, 173.

17. Ibid., 256–57.

18. Ibid., 290–91.

19. Bernard Hue, *Litteratures et arts de l'orient dans l'oeuvre de Claudel* (Librairie C. Klincksieck, 1978), 56; Eugene Roberto, "Le theatre chinois de New York en 1893," in *Cahiers Canadien Claudel*, no. 5, *Formes et Figures* (Ottawa, 1967), 109–33, esp. 109–13. For comprehensive discussion and bibliography of Claudel's Chinese works, see Gilbert Gadoffre, "Claudel et l'univers chinois," *Cahiers Paul Claudel*, no.8 (Paris, 1968).

20. Hue, 73; Roberto, 120–29, 133.

21. Cited in Hue, 54, translation by JS.

22. Paul Claudel, ed. Gilbert Gadoffre, *Connaissance de l'est* (Paris, 1973), 118–22, translation by JS.

23. Paul Claudel, "Ville la nuit," in Gadoffre, ed., *Connaissance*, 91; Paul Claudel, trans. Teresa Frances and W. R. Benét, *The East I Know* (New Haven, 1914), 13. On the dates of the MS, see Gadoffre, ed., *Connaissance*, 95–97.

24. Claudel, *Connaissance*, 93; *East I Know*, 14.

25. Claudel, *Connaissance*, 93–94; *East I Know*, 15–16.

26. Claudel, *Connaissance*, 64.

27. Victor Segalen, trans. Eleanor Levieux, *The Great Statuary of China* (Chicago, 1978), 186–87.

28. Victor Segalen, *Steles* (Paris, 1973), 25.

29. As translated in Michael Taylor, *Steles* (Santa Monica, Calif., 1987), np.

30. Ibid., np.

31. Ibid., np.

32. Yvonne Hsieh, *Victor Segalen's Literary Encounter with China: Chinese Moulds, Western Thoughts* (Toronto, 1988); Marc Gontard, *Victor Segalen, une esthetique de la différence* (Paris, 1990).

33. Hsieh, 157–58; Pierre-Jean Remy, preface, in Segalen, *Steles*, 9.

34. Victor Segalen, trans. J. A. Underwood, *René Leys* (Chicago, 1974), 171–72, ellipses in the original.

35. Ibid., 121.

36. Ibid., 121–22.

37. Ibid., 210–11.

38. Segalen, *Statuary*, 13.

39. Ibid., 20.

CHAPTER 9

1. Marilyn A. Levine, *The Found Generation: Chinese Communists in Europe During the Twenties* (Seattle, 1993).

2. Gina Marchetti, *Romance and the "Yellow Peril": Race, Sex, and Discursive Strategies in Hollywood Fiction* (Berkeley, 1993), chap.2; Vance Kepley, Jr., "Griffith's 'Broken Blossoms' and the Problem of Historical Specificity," *Quarterly Review of Film Studies*, 3:1 (1978), 37–47.

3. Thomas Burke, "The Chink and the Child," in *Limehouse Nights* (New York, 1973).

4. Kepley, "Broken Blossoms," 42–43.

5. Hugh Kenner, *The Pound Era* (Berkeley, 1971), 192–222; Humphrey Carpenter, *A Serious Character: The Life of Ezra Pound* (London, 1988), 270–71, 570–71; John J. Nolde, *Blossoms from the East: The China Cantos of Ezra Pound* (Orono, Maine, 1983), 14–17.

6. Ezra Pound, *Cathay* (London, 1915), 5–6; Wai-lim Yip, *Ezra Pound's Cathay* (Princeton, 1969), 107–21. In ibid., 182–85, Yip also gives a literal translation of the original Chinese for the purposes of comparison.

7. Pound, *Cathay*, 7; Yip, 128–138, 187.

8. Ezra Pound, *The Cantos* (New York, 1995), XIII, 58; the passage combines *Analects*, IX: 2 and XI: 26.

9. *Analects,* XI: 25.

10. Pound, *Cantos,* XIII: 60. *Analects*, XV: 26 on the blanks, III: 3 on the music, IX: 1 on the blossoms.

11. *Analects,* IX: 30.

12. Pound, *Cantos,* LVI: 304.

13. Ibid., LX: 329–30.

14. Ezra Pound, trans., *The Confucian Odes* (New York, 1954), xiii, introduction by Achilles Fang.

15. Marco Polo, *Travels*, ed. Latham, 42 and 45.

16. Eugene O'Neill, *Marco Millions, a Play* (New York, 1927), 16.

17. Ibid., 70.

18. Ibid., 79.

19. Ibid., 89.

20. Ibid., 90.

21. Ibid., 90–91.

22. Ibid., 92.

23. Ibid., 92–93.

24. Ibid., 111, 145, 152.

25. Ibid., 182.

26. Peter Conn, *Pearl Buck, A Cultural Biography* (Cambridge, 1996).

27. Pearl S. Buck, *The Good Earth* (New York, 1994), 1–2.

28. Ibid., 24.

29. Ibid., 182.

30. Ibid., 360.

31. Charles G. Finney, *The Circus of Dr. Lao* (New York, 1935), 13, 39.

32. Ibid., 40–41.

33. John Steinbeck, "Johnny Bear," in *The Long Valley* (New York, 1938).

CHAPTER 10

1. André Malraux, trans. Robert Hollander, *The Temptation of the West* (Chicago, 1992), 4–6.

2. Ibid., 101–04.

3. Ibid., 109–10.

4. Ibid., 112–13.

5. André Malraux, trans. Haakon M. Chevalier, *Man's Fate* (New York, 1990), title page. A powerful analysis of the novel, especially the character of Kyo, is in Claude Tannery, trans. Teresa Lavender Fagan, *Malraux, the Absolute Agnostic* (Chicago, 1991). On Malraux's life, see Jean Lacouture, trans. Alan Sheridan, *André Malraux* (New York, 1975).

6. Malraux, *Man's Fate*, 58 and 243.

7. Ibid., 268, 270.

8. Ibid., 18.

9. Ibid., 79–80.

10. Ibid., 325.

11. Bertolt Brecht, trans. Carl R. Mueller, *The Measures Taken*, in *The Measures Taken and Other Lehrstucke* (London, 1977), 12–13.

12. Ibid., 13.
13. Ibid., 13.
14. Ibid., 14, 25.
15. Ibid., 26.
16, Ibid., 30.
17. Ibid., 34.
18. S. Bernard Thomas, *Season of High Adventure: Edgar Snow in China* (Berkeley, 1996), 33.
19. Ibid., 123-24.
20. Brecht, *Measures Taken*, 28-29.
21. Thomas, *Snow*, 168-70.
22. Edgar Snow, *Red Star Over China* (New York, 1944), 66-67.
23. Ibid., 67.
24. Ibid., 70.
25. Ibid., 71.
26. Ibid., 74.
27. Ibid., 232.
28. Ibid., 241.
29. Ibid., 304.
30. Graham Peck, *Two Kinds of Time* (Boston, 1967), 85.
31. Ibid., 86.
32. Ibid., 87.
33. Ibid., 93.
34. Ibid., 98.
35. Ibid., 98-101.

CHAPTER 11

1. G. L. Ulmen, *The Science of Society: Toward an Understanding of the Life and Work of Karl August Wittfogel* (The Hague, 1978), 123. Several analytical essays on Wittfogel are included in Ulmen, ed., *Society and History: Essays in Honor of Karl August Wittfogel* (The Hague, 1978).
2. Brecht, *Measures Taken*, 33.
3. Ulmen, *Life of Wittfogel*, 238-40.
4. Malraux, *Man's Fate*, 62.
5. Ulmen, *Life of Wittfogel*, 7-9.
6. Ibid., 59-60, 84, and bibliographic list, 509-13.
7. Ibid., 84-86.
8. Ibid., 88, on the Moscow visit and meeting with Borodin.
9. Cited in ibid., 111.

10. On Marx, see ibid., 44, 66–68.

11. Oswald Spengler, *The Decline of the West*, trans. Charles Francis Atkinson, 2 vols. in 1 (London, 1932), 2: 373.

12. For Weber and Marx, see Ulmen, *Life of Wittfogel*, 36–39, 44–45.

13. Ibid., 190, for Buck, 202–05 on Snow. Wittfogel's influence on Snow is not recorded in Thomas, *Snow*.

14. Ulmen, *Life of Wittfogel*, 504, speech of Nov. 2, 1973, italics added.

15. Ibid., 505, suggests Wittfogel was following Aristotle here.

16. Karl A. Wittfogel, *Oriental Despotism, A Comparative Study of Total Power* (New Haven, 1963), 2.

17. Ibid., 3–4.

18. Ibid., 37 and 40.

19. Ibid., 141.

20. Ibid., 144, 149, 151.

21. Ibid., 157.

22. Ibid., 159–60.

23. Ibid., 400

24. Ibid., 442–43.

25. Richard Nixon, *RN, Memoirs* (New York, 1978), 558.

26. Ibid., 558.

27. Ibid., 559–63.

28. Ibid., 564.

29. Henry Kissinger, *White House Years* (Boston, 1979), 1057.

30. Ibid., 1058–59.

31. Marco Polo, *Travels*, ed. Latham, 40, 121–22.

32. Kissinger, 1061.

33. Ibid., 1064.

34. Ibid., 1065-66.

35. Jean Lévi, trans. Barbara Bray, *The Chinese Emperor* (New York, 1989), 243–44.

36. Ibid., 99–100.

37. Ibid., 286–87.

38. Ibid., 302–03.

39. Ibid., 324.

CHAPTER 12

1. Gustav Janouch, *Conversations with Kafka* (New York, 1985); for Wittfogel and Richard Wilhelm, see Ulmen, *Life of Wittfogel*, 16.

2. Franz Kafka, *The Complete Stories*, ed. Nahum N. Glatzer (New York, 1983), 236.
3. Ibid., 236–37, 240–41.
4. Ibid., 241.
5. Ibid., 242.
6. Ibid., 248.
7. Ibid., 243.
8. On these editions, see the bibliography in ibid., 467, 471.
9. Ibid., 4–5, 244.
10. Ibid., 247.
11. Jorge Luis Borges, "The Garden of Forking Paths," in *Labyrinths: Selected Stories and Other Writings* (New York, 1964), 21.
12. Ibid., 20–21.
13. Ibid., 22–23.
14. Ibid., 23.
15. Goldsmith, *Citizen of the World*, I: 123, Letter XXXI. The full title is given thus by Goldsmith in the table of contents. In the novel itself it is merely headed "From the same," in consonance with the novel's epistolary form.
16. Ibid., I: 125.
17. Borges, "Garden," 27–28.
18. The relevant passages in Liddell Hart, *A History of the World War, 1914–1918* (London, 1934), are on pp. 306–18, not p. 22 as Borges states. He also slightly mistakes the date, writing June instead of July 1916. But the rest is remarkably accurate.
19. Borges, "Garden," 25, 28.
20. Ibid., 26; italics in the original.
21. Marco Polo, ed. Yule and Cordier, I: 27–30.
22. Italo Calvino, trans. William Weaver, *Invisible Cities* (New York, 1972), 21, 30.
23. Ibid., 59, 60.
24. Ibid., 69, 73.
25. Ibid., 73, changing "laces" to "lace."
26. Ibid., 86–87.
27. Ibid., 98.
28. Ibid., 103.
29. Ibid., 104.

30. Ibid., 122, 131.
31. Ibid., 135, 136, 138, 139.
32. Ibid., 164.
33. Ibid., 165.
34. Ibid., 135.

Credits

p. v: Excerpt from "The Bridge," by Hart Crane, from *Complete Poems of Hart Crane*, edited by Marc Simon. Copyright 1933, ©1958, 1966 by Liveright Publishing Corporation. Copyright ©1986 by Marc Simon. Reprinted with the permission of Liveright Publishing Corporation.

p. 2: *The Mission of Friar William of Rubruck: His Journey to the Court of the Great Khan Mongke, 1253–1255,* 2nd series, no. 173. Peter Jackson with David Morgan. The Hakluyt Society. Reprinted with permission.

pp. 21, 22, 23, 25, 26, 27: *South China in the Sixteenth Century: Being the Narratives of Galeote Pereris, Fr. Gaspar da Cruz, O.P., Fr. Martin de Rada, O.E.S.A.,* 2nd series, CVI. Charles Boxer, ed. The Hakluyt Society. Reprinted with permission.

pp. 37, 38, 39, 40: *The Travels and Controversies of Friar Domingo Navarrete,* 2 vols., 2nd series. Ed. and trans. J. S. Cummins, The Hakluyt Society. Reprinted with permission.

pp. 43, 44: From John E. Wills, Jr., *Embassies and Illusions: Dutch and Portuguese Envoys to K'ang-hsi, 1666–1687.* Excerpted with permission from Council on East Asian Studies.

pp. 53, 54, 55, 56: From George Anson, *A Voyage Around the World in the Years 1740–1744,* edited by Glyndwr Williams. Copyright © 1974. Reprinted by permission of Oxford University Press.

pp. 63, 64: From John Evelyn, *The Diary of John Evelyn,* edited by E. S. de Beer. Copyright © 1998. Reprinted by permission of Oxford University Press.

pp. 70, 71, 72: From *The Travels of Sir John Mandeville,* translated by C. W. R. D. Moseley (Penguin Classics, 1983). Copyright © C. W. R. D. Moseley, 1983. Reprinted by permission.

pp. 92, 93, 94, 95: From Charles de Montesquieu, *The Spirit of the Laws.* Anne M. Cohler, Basia Carolyn Miller, and Harold Samuel Stone,

263

Index